INSTANT PET

READY-TO-USE TASKS AND ACTIVITIES

MARTYN FORD

CAMBRIDGE
UNIVERSITY PRESS

CAMBRIDGE UNIVERSITY PRESS

Cambridge, New York, Melbourne, Madrid, Cape Town, Singapore, São Paulo

CAMBRIDGE UNIVERSITY PRESS

The Edinburgh Building, Cambridge CB2 8RU, UK

www.cambridge.org
Information on this title: www.cambridge.org/9780521611237

First published 2007

Printed in the United Kingdom at the University Press, Cambridge

A catalogue record for this publication is available from the British Library

ISBN 978-0-521-61123-7   Resource Book

ISBN 978-0-521-61125-1   Audio Cassette Set

ISBN 978-0-521-61126-8   Audio CD Set

ISBN 978-0-521-61124-4   Resource Book and Audio CD Pack

Contents

Thanks and acknowledgements

The author would like to thank Niki Donnelly and Alison Silver for their hard work and patience during the preparation of this book.

The author and publishers would like to thank the following teachers and consultants who commented on the material:
France: Robert Wright; Germany: Rachel Connabeer, Nicole Gaudet, Thea Ferrari; Greece: Marina Vlachou; Italy: Monica Flood, Tim Julian; Mexico: Rosalia Valero Elizondo; Spain: Henry Burke, Chris Turner; Switzerland: Julia Muller; United Arab Emirates: Philip Lodge; UK: Sally Bowen, Clare West; Pam Lewis and Penny Moon (both from the English Language Centre, Hove).

Picture research by Hilary Fletcher.
Proof reading by Ruth Carim.
Recordings produced by John Green, TEFL Tapes, recorded at The Audio Workshop, London.
Cover design by Tim Elcock.
Designed and produced by HL Studios, Oxford.

The author and publishers are grateful to the following for permission to reproduce copyright material.

Texts
p. 33: *The Guardian* for the adapted text 'Into the deep' by Libby Brooks, 23 July 2003, © Guardian Newspapers Limited; p. 38: *The Independent* for the adapted text 'The curious incident of the hungry dog in the night time' by Matthew Beard, 5 October 2004 and p. 41: for the adapted text 'A summer holiday with the family (all 109 of them)' by Terry Kirby, 29 July 2004, © Independent News and Media Limited.

Photos
Key: l = left, r = right, c = centre, u = upper, w = lower

The publishers would like to thank the following people for permission to reproduce copyright photographs:

Alamy/Ethno Images/Eric Fowke p 21 (1r), /©David Gregs p 21 (3t); Apex News and Pictures p 41; Corbis/©Leland Bobbé p 122 (b), /©Rolf Bruderer p 21 (3b), /©George Disario p 117 (b), /©Robert Essel NY p 119 (t), /©Jon Feingersh p 117 (t), /©Owen Franken p 121 (b), /©Mitchell Gerber p 121 (t), /©Michael Prince p 119 (bc), /©Ariel Skelley p 122 (t), /Zefa/©Benelux p 119 (cl), /Zefa/©A. Inden/ p 17 (t), /Zefa/©Joson p 119 (bl), /Zefa/©Newmann p 23, /Zefa/©Michelle Pedone p 22 (t), 94 (tr), /Zefa/©M.Thomsen p 22 (wc), Zefa/©Turbo p 21 (5b), /Zefa/©Larry Williams p 22 (uc); ©EMPICS/Ian Nicholson/PA p 38; Getty Images/DK Stock/Christina Kennedy p 17 (c), /©Tim Graham p 46, /Robert Harding World Imagery/Gavin Hellier p 87 (l), /The Image Bank/Hans Neleman p 21 (4), /The Image Bank/stevenvotedot.com p 94 (br), /Photodisc/Kevin Peterson p 17 (b), /Photonica/Leland Bobbé p 22 (b), /Photonica/Ranald Mackechnie p 21 (2), /Photographer's Choice/Daniel Arsenault p 119 (cr), /Stockdisc Classic p 21 (5t), /Taxi/Dirk Anschutz p 119 (br), /Taxi/Greg Betz p 119 (c), /Taxi/Chabruken p 94 (tl), /Taxi/David Lees p 94 (bl), /Taxi/Harvey Lloyd p 87 (r), /Taxi/Anne-Marie Weber p 21 (1l); Rex Features p 33, /©Dan Charity p 96.

Illustrations
p. 35: Dover Publications for the dog (left) from *Animals: A Pictorial Archive from Nineteenth Century Sources*; p. 35: Martyn Ford for the dog (centre) from *The How To Be British Collection* by Martyn Ford and Peter Legon, LGP 2003; p. 35: Charles Barsotti for the dog (right) from *The Best of Barsotti*, by Charles Barsotti.

Artists
Phillip Burrows, Jim Eldridge, Tony Forbes, Martyn Ford, Phil Garner, HL Studios, Gordon Lawson, Paul McCaffrey, Mark McLaughlin, Chris Pavely

Introduction

Who is *Instant PET* for?

Instant PET is a resource book containing photocopiable materials covering all the parts of the Cambridge Preliminary English Test (PET). It provides candidates with useful and enjoyable preparation and practice for the exam, and it can also be used as supplementary material with other young and young adult learners studying at early intermediate level. There are 64 activities, providing self-contained lessons for the busy teacher. Each activity consists of a page of clear step-by-step instructions, plus answers to the tasks, for the teacher and a photocopiable page for the students.

How will *Instant PET* help my students?

The activities in *Instant PET* are carefully designed to provide lively and interesting lesson material with an emphasis on communicative language learning. Thus, for example, an activity devoted to reading will nevertheless provide opportunities to practise speaking, through games, role-play or discussion. The first three practice activities in each part will help students acquire the language and the skills necessary for PET, but with the emphasis on fun and interaction, exploring topics of general interest. The fourth, which is always the exam-style task (see below), is there for those who wish to focus more on exam technique.

How is *Instant PET* organised?

The book is organised into four sections: Reading, Writing, Listening and Speaking, which reflect the order of the exam. (In the PET exam Reading and Writing together make up Paper 1, the longest paper in the exam; in this book they are given separate sections.) In each section there are four activities to practise each part of the exam; the fourth of these is always an **exam-style task**, which follows very closely the format of the exam and can be done as timed examination practice.

The student's page of the exam-style task includes a section called **Hints and tips** which offers advice to candidates on how to tackle that part of the exam, and how to prepare for it through additional practice and by developing independent learning strategies.

Reading

There are five parts in the Reading section; there are 20 activities in all.

Writing

There are three parts in the Writing section; there are 14 activities in all (two extra activities are included in the section).

Listening

There are four parts in the Listening section; there are 17 activities in all (an extra activity is included in the section). The tapescripts, which you may want to photocopy and use for follow-up work, start on page 124. Recorded material is indicated by this symbol ▶▶|.

Note: the exam-style tasks recorded on the accompanying CDs / cassettes have repeats and pauses in line with the actual exam. The other recordings do not.

Speaking

There are three parts in the Speaking section; there are 13 activities in all (an extra activity is included in the section).

Parts 3 & 4 of the exam, which are based on the same two photographs, are combined in three practice activities and one exam-style task.

The speaking activities include recordings of sample tasks.

How is each activity organised?

Each activity consists of one page of step-by-step teacher's notes, plus answers to the tasks, and a photocopiable page for the students. There is minimal preparation before class. You simply have to photocopy the appropriate number of sheets and sometimes cut up the sheets. The teacher's notes have a key information panel for quick reference. The headings in this are:

Exam part	the part of the exam the activity relates to, e.g. Reading Part 1
Exam skills	the exam skills the activity practises, e.g. Understanding signs, notices and instructions; matching synonymous sentences
Topic	a brief description of the topic, e.g. Signs and notices in public places
Time	the time needed for the whole activity (usually 40 or 50 minutes; this is only a guideline and timings will vary from class to class)
Key language	vocabulary and structures that occur in the activity, e.g. Synonyms and antonyms; concrete nouns and action verbs
Preparation	what needs to be done before the lesson, e.g. photocopying; whether you need to bring anything else to the lesson

The lesson is divided into three main stages:

Warm up	this helps students focus on the topic and prepare them for the main activities; this stage only appears on the teacher's page
Main activities	the number of tasks varies; the teacher's notes provide a step-by-step guide to carrying out the tasks, and full answer keys to all exercises
Follow up	an opportunity to develop the scope of the lesson; many of the suggestions are suitable for homework

How long will the activities take?

Each activity is designed to take a complete lesson of between 40–50 minutes. You will need to tailor the time an activity takes to fit in with your requirements. If an activity takes too long for the length of your lesson, some of the tasks can be given as homework.

What about classroom management?

Most of the tasks can be done collaboratively in pairs or small groups, and this approach is recommended for groups of learners who need variety and lots of interaction. However, many of the exercises can also be done by students working individually.

Are the activities graded?

The activities are not graded to distinguish between confident learners, who are ready to take PET, and those who are at the beginning of this level. Inevitably, some tasks will be more challenging than others.

What about other materials for PET?

In order to develop candidates' skills, you may find the following books useful:

Objective PET by Louise Hashemi & Barbara Thomas (CUP)

Insight Into PET by Helen Naylor & Stuart Hagger (CUP).

For a more detailed explanation of the specifications for PET, see *The Preliminary English Test Handbook: Specifications and Sample Papers* (University of Cambridge ESOL Examinations).

For further exam-style practice, see *Cambridge Preliminary English Test (Books 2–4): Examination Papers from University of Cambridge ESOL Examinations* (CUP).

For online help for teachers, see www.cambridgeesol.org.

PET content: An overview

Paper	Name	Timing	Content	Test focus
Paper 1	Reading / Writing	1 hour 30 minutes	Reading: Five parts which test a range of reading skills with a variety of texts, ranging from very short notices to longer continuous texts. Writing: Three parts which test a range of writing skills.	Assessment of candidates' ability to understand the meaning of written English at word, phrase, sentence, paragraph and whole text level. Assessment of candidates' ability to produce straightforward written English, ranging from producing variations on simple sentences to pieces of continuous text.
Paper 2	Listening	30 minutes (approx.)	Four parts ranging from short exchanges to longer dialogues and monologues.	Assessment of candidates' ability to understand dialogues and monologues in both informal and neutral settings on a range of everyday topics.
Paper 3	Speaking	10–12 minutes per pair of candidates	Four parts: In Part 1, candidates interact with an examiner; In Parts 2 and 4 they interact with another candidate; In Part 3, they have an extended individual long turn.	Assessment of candidates' ability to express themselves in order to carry out functions at *Threshold* level. To ask and to understand questions and make appropriate responses. To talk freely on matters of personal interest.

Reading the signs

Warm up

Ask students to stand up. Tell them that you are going to give them some very short instructions. They must **show** they understand the instruction by miming the action. To help those who don't understand an instruction, point to a student who is doing the correct mime: *Look at what Anna is doing*. Of course, if no one understands the instruction, show by example and test again later. Choose from the following instructions or think of others:

Push. Pull. Press. Lift. Twist. Lock. Unlock. Shake. Pick up. Put down.
Press the button. Turn the handle clockwise. Turn the handle anti-clockwise.
Shake the bottle well before opening. Twist off the cap. Replace the cap firmly after use.
Light the candles. Blow out the candles. Fasten your seatbelt. Check your rear view mirror. Ring the bell for assistance. Insert coins and select option. Sign your name.
Fold the paper in half. Pump up the tyres. Blow up the balloon. Look both ways before crossing the road. Peel the potatoes. Cut the cheese into cubes. Now wash your hands. Shake excess water from hands and rub hands gently in air stream. Bell out of order, please knock. Switch off light before leaving.

Repeat the instructions in a different order. As you do so, discuss where and when you might hear or see such instructions, and why you might follow them.

Main activities

Students can do these activities in pairs or small groups.

1 Ask students what types of signs or notices they might see in a street, a public building and a park.
Give out the activity sheets.
After doing the exercise, discuss with students what the signs and notices mean. For example: FOR SALE and TO LET can both be signs outside a house or flat. The first one indicates that the owner wants to **sell** the property, and the second one that the owner is looking for a tenant to **rent** the property.

Answers

In a street: Closed; No parking; To let; For sale

In a building: Way out; Visitors must report to reception; Fire exit

In a park: No bathing; Keep off the flowerbeds; Dogs must be kept on a lead

2 The symbols are a convenient way of conveying information that can also be expressed verbally.

Suggested answers

A Information: At a station or airport or a public event like an exhibition

B Men's and women's toilets: On the doors of toilets/washrooms

C No entry (one-way street): A traffic sign at the entrance to a road

D No smoking: In public buildings, buses, trains, etc.

E Recycle: On recycling bins and at collection points; on public information leaflets

F Refreshments (food and drink): In a museum; on a motorway

G First aid: In a public building, e.g. a school or college

H Baby care: In a public building, perhaps on the door of the facility

I Children crossing: A traffic sign on a road

3
Answers
1 D Theatre   2 A Hotel   3 H Hospital
4 C Construction site   5 F Supermarket
6 E Station platform   7 B Motorway   8 G Airport

4
Answers
1 7 S   2 8 D   3 4 S   4 1 D   5 3 S
6 5 D   7 6 D   8 2 D

Follow up

- Ask students to look again at the iconic symbols in exercise **2** before they start drawing. (Desk top icons on the computer are also an excellent example of this pictorial shorthand.) Make a class display of the students' work. Students can vote on the best icon.

- Most word-processing software programs include some kind of clip art or image library. You might like to print some of these out for a similar discussion activity.

Reading the signs

1 Where might you see these signs?

• in a street   • in a building   • in a park

What do the signs mean?

 WAY OUT

 No Bathing

CLOSED

Visitors Must report to reception

 FIRE EXIT

 KEEP OFF THE FLOWERBEDS

NO PARKING

DOGS Must be kept on a lead

TO LET

FOR SALE

2 What do these symbols mean? Where might you see them?

A   B   C

D   E   F

G   H BABY CHANGING AREA   I STOP

3 You can see the following notices in different places. Match the notices 1–8 with the places A–H.

1 There will be one interval of 15 minutes.

2 PLEASE LEAVE YOUR ROOM BY 11 AM.

3 *Visiting hours 10.00 am–11.30 am and 5.00 pm–6.30 pm.*

4 HARD HATS MUST BE WORN AT ALL TIMES.

5 Buy two and get the second half price.

6 PLEASE STAND BEHIND THE YELLOW LINE.

7 **Tiredness can kill: take a break**.

8 Flight now boarding at gate 17.

A	Hotel	**E**	Station platform
B	Motorway	**F**	Supermarket
C	Construction site	**G**	Airport
D	Theatre	**H**	Hospital

4 Read the notices in exercise 3 again. Match each of the following sentences with one of the notices. If the sentence means the same as the notice, write S; if it means something different, write D. The first one is done as an example.

1 It's dangerous to drive when you're tired. [7] [S]

2 You've got plenty of time for shopping before your plane leaves. ☐ ☐

3 In this place you could be injured if you don't protect your head. ☐ ☐

4 The play will be performed in one act, without a break. ☐ ☐

5 You can come to visit a patient in the morning or in the evening. ☐ ☐

6 If you buy two bags of oranges you can have the second bag free. ☐ ☐

7 Please let passengers get off the train before you try to get on. ☐ ☐

8 You cannot leave your room before 11 am. ☐ ☐

Follow up

Draw simple icons to represent the following:

No dogs permitted in the shop • Silence in the library, please • No flash photography • Beware of the dog • No fishing • Music room • Film club • Poisonous

Didn't you notice the notice?

EXAM PART
Reading Part 1

EXAM SKILLS
Understanding signs, notices and instructions

TOPIC
Notices and instructions

TIME
30 minutes

KEY LANGUAGE
Antonyms

Word order in instructions and notices

PREPARATION
One photocopy of the activity page for each student

Pieces of paper for display of notices (see exercise **3**)

Warm up

- Point to one or two examples of signs and notices in the classroom. If they are in English, cover them and test students' recall of them. If they are not in English, write on the board a few signs or notices that might be found in public places. Ask students where they might see them and what they mean. For example:

  Please do not touch the exhibits. (A museum or art gallery: don't touch the objects on display, they are valuable!)

  You must be this height to go on this ride. (A fairground or theme park: you have to be a certain age to go on this ride. Rather than ask for ID, your size is taken as the measure of your maturity.)

  All breakages must be paid for. (A shop selling breakable goods such as china or glassware: if you accidentally break something in the shop you'll have to pay for it.)

  Your tray table should be in the upright position for take-off and landing. (An aeroplane: part of the safety instructions/announcement. The little table in front of your seat must be folded away before the plane takes off or lands.)

  This week only: fantastic bargains on sportswear and swimwear. (Shop or store selling clothes: the prices of some types of items are reduced for this period.)
  OR

- Ask students to imagine they are living for a while in an English-speaking country. What signs, notices or instructions might they see in a supermarket, restaurant, museum, or at a swimming pool, railway station, doctor's surgery or internet café?

Main activities

Students can do these activities in pairs or small groups.

1 Give out the activity sheets.

This exercise practises antonyms. It's better not to say too much about the vocabulary before students start to correct the notices/instructions. The meaning of items like *batteries*, *lift* and *feed* should be clear from the pictures. Words like *heat*, *rinse* and *give up* may need explaining afterwards, when checking the answers.

Answers

1 Remove the **old** batteries and then insert the **new** ones.
2 Heat well **before** serving.
3 Safety notice: no **more** than 8 persons in this lift.
4 Rinse well with **clean** water.
5 Special offer: **two** for the price of **one**.
6 Please switch **off** your mobile phone before coming into class.
7 Please do **not** feed the animals at the zoo.
8 It is an offence to travel **without** a ticket.
9 Wanted: waiter/waitress – must be **over** 16.
10 Please give up this seat to **an older** passenger.

2 Introduce a competitive element: the quickest pair or group to sort out the messages correctly is the winner.

Answers

1 Only one piece of hand luggage is allowed in the cabin.
2 Take one or two tablets before meals. (on medication, i.e. a bottle or packet of pills)
3 This machine is temporarily out of order. (on a photocopier or other equipment)
4 No food or drink in the classrooms, please. (in a school)
5 Security cameras in use around this building. (many types of building, business premises, etc.)
6 Please do not leave luggage unattended. (at an airport, station, etc.)

3 Students write signs and notices to put around the classroom. These should obviously be appropriate to their situation, but here are some possible examples:
PUSH (on one side of the door)
PULL (on the other side of the door)
DO NOT LEAN OUT OF THE WINDOW
ONLY EMPTY DRINK CANS IN THE BIN
DO NOT LEAVE VALUABLES UNATTENDED IN THIS ROOM
LAST PERSON TO LEAVE, PLEASE SWITCH OFF THE LIGHT
CAUTION — ELECTRIC CABLES
NO FOOD AND DRINK IN HERE, PLEASE
ENGLISH ONLY, PLEASE
TEACHERS: PLEASE TAKE BOOKS BACK TO THE RESOURCES ROOM

Encourage them to experiment, and don't worry at this stage if the sign or notice is realistic or not. Humour should be allowed, e.g. QUIET PLEASE: STUDENTS ASLEEP.

Students write drafts of their notices.

Check the notices are correct.

Students write their final draft in large bold letters on the pieces of paper provided and then put them around the classroom.

Follow up

- If your students have access to computers and a printer, they could write their notices on the word-processor using a variety of fonts and even clip art images.
- *For learners in an English speaking country*: Ask them to go out and do some field work. For example: 'Write down five short examples of notices you have seen in public places, for example, in a street, park, supermarket, restaurant, museum, swimming pool, railway station, internet café or a doctor's surgery.'

Didn't you notice the notice?

1 **Look at these notices. They all contain mistakes. Find the mistakes and correct them.**

1 Remove the new batteries and then insert the old ones. *Remove the old batteries and then insert the new ones.*

2 Heat well after serving.

3 Safety notice: no fewer than 8 persons in this lift.

4 Rinse well with dirty water.

5 Special offer: one for the price of two!

6 Please switch on your mobile phone before coming into class.

7 Please feed the animals at the zoo.

8 It is an offence to travel with a ticket.

9 Wanted: waiter/waitress – must be under 16.

10 Please give up this seat to a younger passenger.

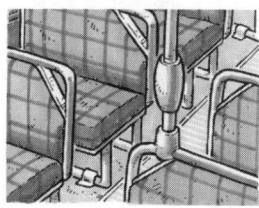

2 **Rearrange the words to make short messages.**

1 LUGGAGE CABIN IS ONLY THE ONE OF PIECE HAND ALLOWED IN.

Only one piece of hand luggage is allowed in the cabin.

2 ONE MEALS TABLETS OR BEFORE TAKE TWO.

3 IS ORDER OF MACHINE THIS OUT TEMPORARILY.

4 FOOD PLEASE IN NO THE DRINK OR CLASSROOMS.

5 AROUND USE CAMERAS IN BUILDING THIS SECURITY.

6 *LUGGAGE NOT PLEASE UNATTENDED DO LEAVE.*

Where would you see these messages?

3 **Write signs and notices to put up in your classroom.**

DO NOT LEAN OUT OF THE WINDOW

Mixed messages

EXAM PART
Reading Part 1

EXAM SKILLS
Understanding
short messages

TOPIC
Notes and
messages

TIME
50 minutes

KEY LANGUAGE
Mixed functions,
e.g. inviting and
responding to
invitations, making
arrangements,
requests

PREPARATION
One photocopy of the
activity page for each
student

Some realia (see
Warm up)

Small strips of paper
(see exercise **3**)

Warm up
- If you have access to realia in English (authentic functional texts), take in some examples for students to look at and discuss. They could include: a form, some packaging, a timetable, a leaflet (e.g. junk mail), a student ID card, a sticker, a supermarket shopping bill.
- Alternatively, ask students to give examples of types of short text they might read, and possibly write, in everyday life for information and communication. This should elicit some of the following: emails, letters, street signs, notices, advertisements, timetables, recipes, instructions (e.g. with product), post-it notes, postcards, birthday cards, menus. Write suggestions on the board until there is a fairly comprehensive list.

Main activities
Students can do some of these activities in pairs or small groups.

1 Give out the activity sheets.

If you have done the **Warm up** activity on different short text types, students should understand the categories listed here and be able to match them to the texts. You may want to explain some of the vocabulary before or after the task, for example: *allergies, nuts, time off, current, Human Resources, to schedule, to 'make' a time or an appointment, to be 'into' different hobbies or interests, jewellery, follow-up, unemployment, the 'gang'.*

Answers
1 E   2 A   3 B   4 F   5 D   6 C

2 Make sure students know they have to find the one correct statement for each message.

Answers
Correct statements: 1 F   2 C   3 E   4 D   10 A   12 B

Incorrect statements: 5   6   7   8   9   11

3 When students have written their messages, ask some of them to read them out to the class.

4 Students choose **one** of the two replies to write. Make sure they understand the scenario.

Model answers

Hello Tommy,

Thanks for your message about the extra practice. Unfortunately, I can't come on Thursday evening because I'm going to watch my brother take part in a swimming competition. But I'd still like to play against Burwater on Saturday. It's true they are good, but I think we can beat them!

Cheers,

Karl

Karen,

Thanks for returning the DVD. I'm glad you liked it. Thanks for the suggestion, but actually I've already seen *Greased Lightning*. It's great, so you should go and see it.

I know you like dance – the National Ballet Company are coming to the Arts Centre on May 17th. Would you like to go? I could book tickets for us both. Let me know.

All the best,

Mike

Follow up
Emailing Dracula

Each student chooses to be a famous historical figure or fictitious character. Students then form pairs. They write messages to each other *in character*. The message can be a request, invitation, apology, etc. They should reply, in character, with another written message. Continue like this, depending on the time available.

In pairs, students read out their 'correspondence'. The class votes on which is the funniest message.

Mixed messages

1 **Read the messages A–F. Match each message with one of the following descriptions.**

1   A request for advice/suggestions   `E`
2   A notice on a restaurant menu   ☐
3   A message about a phone call   ☐
4   A note left with an object which is being returned to someone   ☐
5   An email sent to several different people   ☐
6   An announcement on a staff noticeboard at work   ☐

A   ALLERGIES: Customers who are concerned about nuts in our food are welcome to ask a member of staff for advice when choosing their meal.

B   *Tina,*

Emma phoned. She can't meet you on Tuesday evening. Wednesday would be OK, Thursday too, but only after 9 pm.

                              Sally

C   PLEASE NOTE: AS FROM NEXT JANUARY <u>ALL</u> STAFF WILL BE REQUIRED TO HAVE A CERTIFICATE IN FIRST AID. TIME OFF WILL BE GIVEN TO ATTEND A TWO-DAY TRAINING COURSE. IF YOU DO NOT HAVE A CURRENT FIRST AID CERTIFICATE, PLEASE SEE JAN MARKS IN HUMAN RESOURCES TO ARRANGE TRAINING.

D   Message: To all team members
From: Tommy@training.co.uk

As Saturday's match against Burwater is going to be a difficult one, I think we should schedule an extra practice this week. I suggest Thursday evening at 6.30 at the sports ground. Could you let me know if you can't make this time – otherwise I'll see you there.

E   Hannah,

It's nice of your sister to invite me to her birthday party. I'd like to buy her a present. You're very close to her – what kinds of things is she into? Does she like reading? Or would she prefer a CD, or maybe a T-shirt, or some jewellery? Could you give me some ideas, please, as soon as possible? Thanks.

Rick

F   Mike,

Sorry it's taken me so long to return this DVD. I really enjoyed watching it. Have you seen the follow-up, 'Greased Lightning', which is on at the moment? I've heard it's really good. If you haven't, maybe we could go together?

Karen

2 **Here is a list of statements about the six messages. They are in a different order from the messages. There are two statements for each message, but only one of them is correct for each message. Find the correct statement and write the letter next to the appropriate message.**

1   Karen hasn't seen *Greased Lightning* yet.   `F`
2   Staff can do a training course during work time.   ☐
3   Rick is asking Hannah for advice.   ☐
4   Tommy is sending the same message to all the players.   ☐
5   Mike borrowed a DVD from Karen.   ☐
6   There are no nuts in the food at this restaurant.   ☐
7   Sally can't meet Tina on Tuesday evening.   ☐
8   The players must email Tommy if they intend to come to the extra practice.   ☐
9   All staff have done a First Aid training course.   ☐
10   If you are worried you can ask the waiter's advice.   ☐
11   Hannah's sister prefers music to reading.   ☐
12   Emma is not free early on Thursday evening.   ☐

3 **Work in pairs. Each of you should choose one of the messages A–F in exercise 1. On a small piece of paper, write two sentences about the message you have chosen, one correct and one incorrect. Give the paper to your partner, who must:**

•   find which message it refers to
•   decide which of your sentences is correct.

4 **Write an email message to Tommy (text D) to tell him that you won't be able to come to the extra training. Apologise, and explain that you would still like to play in the match against Burwater.**

OR

You are Mike (text F). Write your reply to Karen. Thank her for returning the DVD. Explain that you have already seen the film *Greased Lightning*, which you enjoyed very much. You know that Karen likes dance, so suggest a trip to see the National Ballet Company on May 17th.

Exam-style task

Hints and tips for Reading Part 1

What you have to do

- Read six short texts (the first one is an example).
- Read the multiple-choice questions that go with each text.
- Choose your answer from the three options, A, B, C.

How to approach it

- First read the text carefully. Where might you see it? Why was it written?
- The style or format of the text (e.g. a postcard) may help you to understand its purpose.
- Read all three options and compare them with the text before choosing your answer.

- Reread your answer and the text again to make sure they express the same idea.

How to prepare yourself

- The texts can be notices, signs, messages, postcards or instructions. Try to look at as many examples as you can of this type of text. (You can find some in *Insight into PET* pages 10–11 and *Objective PET* pages 102–103, both published by Cambridge University Press.)
- If possible, follow your own interests – music, sport, fashion, films, whatever they are – by looking at websites and magazines in English.

PART 1

Questions 1–5

- Look at the text in each question.
- What does it say?
- Mark the letter next to the correct explanation – A, B or C.

Example:

> **Unfortunately, tonight's show has been cancelled owing to illness. Tickets can be exchanged or refunded at the box office.**

A People with tickets for tonight's show can get their money back. ✓

B Tickets for tonight's show can be bought at the box office.

C Tickets for tonight's show can be used for a later performance.

1

> **GUITAR LESSONS**
>
> *Patient and friendly teacher is taking new students of all levels for acoustic and electric guitar lessons. All styles of music can be covered, plus music theory for those who are interested.*
>
> *Call Jeff on 01982 886510.*

Jeff teaches music theory

A if the student has covered all styles of music.

B if the student is new to the class.

C if the student wants to learn it.

2

Thameslink will offer a revised service from Brighton to London. Some early services will be replaced by bus between Brighton and Three Bridges.

A If you travel early you may have to travel part of your journey by bus.

B From Three Bridges station you will be taken by bus to London.

C There will not be any Thameslink trains from Brighton to Three Bridges.

3

Please make sure all your child's school clothes are marked with their name. This helps us to return lost items to the children.

A Children's clothes must have the name of the school on them.

B The school will mark clothes with the children's names.

C School clothes should have the child's name on them.

4

Dear Annette,

You were right — Daleport is lovely. I'm so glad we listened to you and not to John. I wonder why he disliked it so much.

Love, Meg

A Meg is surprised that John liked Daleport.

B Meg thinks John should visit Daleport.

C Meg followed Annette's advice.

5

Children with a bus ID card pay only 25% of the full fare on schooldays up until 6 pm. And if they're travelling with an adult, the same discount applies at weekends too.

A Adults with children pay only 25% fare at the weekends.

B With a bus ID card travel is cheaper for children going to and from school.

C Children cannot use their bus ID cards at the weekend.

Answers

1 C **2** A **3** C **4** C **5** B

Which course?

Warm up

Explain the idea of non-obligatory further and continuing education courses. (In the UK, many institutions of higher and further education offer part-time courses to people interested in learning or improving their skills in a subject for recreation and personal development. Many of these courses are practical, i.e. non-academic in nature.) The examples in this activity are educational/recreational rather than vocational, so you could ask students:

What kind of part-time courses do adults do in their spare time?

What are their motives for doing them? (Older students may have personal experience of these types of part-time courses.)

For school-age students: *What sort of subjects would you like to learn which are not in your present school curriculum?*

Main activities

Students can do exercises **1** and **2** on their own or in pairs. Exercise **3** is a paired interview.

1 Give out the activity sheets.

Having discussed the motives of people who do part-time courses, ask students to look at the first couple of lines of the text and say what **City College** itself says about the value of doing a course. Ask them to suggest examples of 'new skills' and 'new talents'.

Students match the course descriptions A–F with their titles. During this phase they can also underline any words they don't understand.

Elicit students' understanding of key words in the text to do with education and learning, e.g. *coaching, qualified, introductory, basics, tuition,* plus the names of the subjects, e.g. *Squash, IT, Conjuring.* They may also want to ask about: *shy, court, energetic, phobia, vigorous, desserts, magician, hands-on, disappear.*

Answers

A Squash
B IT for the Terrified
C Dance
D Basic Cookery
E Introduction to Conjuring
F Guitar

2 The aim of this exercise is to guide students through the processes of comprehension, comparison and matching that are required in this part of the exam. This is done through a structured writing exercise where they both eliminate unsuitable options, and choose suitable ones, giving reasons drawn from the text.

Suggested answers

1 George shouldn't choose *IT for the Terrified* because he already knows a lot about computers. He should choose Squash because he wants some vigorous physical exercise and he likes tennis.

2 Fiona shouldn't choose *Basic Cookery* because she is already a good cook. She should choose *Dance* because she wants physical exercise (but not a sport) and she wants to have fun. Also, she likes music from different parts of the world and salsa comes from Latin America.

3 Frank shouldn't choose *Guitar* because he already has guitar lessons at his school every week. He should choose *Introduction to Conjuring* because he wants to be an entertainer when he's older.

3 *Variation 1*: If students find it difficult to imagine themselves doing any of these courses, ask them to think of adults they know – for example, family members – and to imagine which courses *they* would do and why.

Variation 2: This develops the topic into a more extended role-play. You will need to explain the roles to students.

Student A is City College's student adviser. He/she suggests possible courses for Student B to do.

Student B is someone who would like to do a course at City College, but can't decide which. He/she should find a good reason for rejecting four or five of Student A's suggestions before agreeing to one. He/she must give a different reason each time. Note that the excuse 'I'm not interested in that subject' can only be used once.

Follow up

Make a classroom display of the finished posters.

EXAM PART
Reading Part 2

EXAM SKILLS
Matching descriptions of people to information-based texts

Finding paraphrases in parallel texts

TOPIC
Further education courses

TIME
50 minutes

KEY LANGUAGE
Names of courses and subjects

Adjectives: *shy, nervous, strong, confident, flexible, energetic,* etc.

Expressions for giving advice and making suggestions

PREPARATION
One photocopy of the activity page for each student

Pieces of paper, coloured pens, etc. for posters (see **Follow up**)

Which course?

1

Look at these titles and descriptions of courses. Find the right title for each course and write it in the space.

> • Squash • Guitar • Introduction to Conjuring
> • IT for the Terrified • Dance • Public Speaking ✓
> • Basic Cookery
>
> ## City College
>
> Join one of our part-time courses: learn new skills, discover new talents in yourself, make new friends and, above all, have fun!
>
> Public Speaking..............
>
> Do you feel shy or nervous about speaking to groups of people? Our practical course will build your confidence step by step. No experience necessary.
>
> **A** ....
>
> You can book an hour on the court weekday evenings between 6 and 9 pm. Coaching available from a qualified teacher. NOTE: this is an energetic sport – you must be fit and active with no serious health problems.
>
> **B** ....
>
> Don't be afraid of computers – they are friendlier than you think! If you are a beginner in Information Technology, or you have a bit of a phobia about computers, this introductory course will teach you the basics. You'll be amazed at your progress!
>
> **C** ....
>
> Prepare to be moved! If you like Latin American music and you are ready for some vigorous exercise in a friendly group setting, then why not try salsa? All ages welcome!
>
> **D** ....
>
> If your idea of cookery is limited to putting a plastic box in the microwave, then this may be the course for you. We take you through the basics, from how to cook simple but interesting meals to baking cakes and creating delicious desserts.
>
> **E** ....
>
> The secrets of the magician's circle revealed in this 'hands-on' class. Learn to do tricks with playing cards and coins, to make objects disappear and reappear, and to be an entertainer!
>
> **F** ....
>
> Group tuition in all styles of music including rock and country. This class has been together for two terms and some of the students have passed grade 3. New students are welcome, but no beginners, please.

2 Now read about these people. They all want to choose a course from the college programme, but they are finding it difficult. Help them to choose by completing the sentences after each description.

1 *George, 19, is a student studying Information and Communications Technology. He spends a lot of time sitting in class or working alone in front of a computer. He wants*  *an evening class which involves vigorous physical exercise, but he's not very keen on team games such as football. When he was younger he used to play tennis, which he enjoyed very much.*

George shouldn't choose *IT for the Terrified* because ....

....

He should choose

....

because ....

....

2 *Fiona, 30, likes listening to music from all over the world, and cooking. She's a really good cook, with lots of experience. She doesn't like sport but she wants to do a*  *class which involves physical exercise and she wants it to be fun.*

Fiona shouldn't choose *Basic Cookery* because ....

She should choose ....

because ....

3 *Frank, 16, is a self-confident boy. He wants to be an actor or entertainer when he's older. He already does guitar club at school on Wednesdays and would like to do something else on another evening.*

Frank shouldn't choose *Guitar* because

....

He should choose ....

because ....

3 Work in pairs. Which of these courses would be the best for your partner and why? Interview each other to find out. If you don't like any of these courses, describe a course you *would* enjoy doing.

Follow up

Choose one of the courses in the programme and design a poster to advertise it. The poster must give some practical details about the course (e.g. dates, times, number of classes), but also use pictures and graphics to try to interest people and capture their attention.

Ready to order?

EXAM PART
Reading Part 2

EXAM SKILLS
Matching descriptions of people to information-based texts

TOPIC
Food; eating habits

TIME
30 minutes

KEY LANGUAGE
Food vocabulary

PREPARATION
One photocopy of the activity page for each student

Warm up

Write this sentence on the board: *King Philip loved food*. Write a list of common quantifiers underneath, for example: *a, an, some, a few, several, lots of*. Revise **ordinal numbers**, i.e. *first, second, third*. Going round the class, each student must say the sentence *On the (first) day King Philip ate …*, add a quantifier and then say the name of a food which begins with the next letter of the alphabet.
For example:
*On the **first** day King Philip ate an **apple**.*
*On the **second** day King Philip ate a few **biscuits**.*
*On the **third** day King Philip ate some **cake**.*
*On the **fourth** day King Philip ate lots of **dates**.*
If a student can't think of a food beginning with that letter in five seconds they say, 'Pass' and the next student tries. If three successive students can't think of a food, the next letter in the alphabet is chosen.

Main activities

Students can do some of these activities in pairs or small groups.

1 Give out the activity sheets.
Students look at the pictures A–H and match them with the descriptions in the menu. Some of the descriptive vocabulary in the menu is redundant as far as the tasks in exercises **1** and **2** are concerned. However, it is important for students to understand key words: *pastry, salmon, steak, prawn, lamb, spicy, vegetarian*, and the idea of a *light* meal and a *filling* meal.
Students may also ask about non-essential items such as *tender, fillet, rump, organic, seeded, dumplings, hearty*, etc. You could suggest they look them up in the dictionary.

Answers
A Healthy choice: prawn salad
B Fillet of salmon
C Mushroom and cashew nut bake
D Chicken pie
E Burger
F Spicy lamb casserole
G Vegetable madras
H Rump steak

2 Before students start, ask them to look at the menu and pictures again. Which are the **filling** meals and which are the **light** meals?

Answers
Steve ('Dad'): Rump steak with vegetables or salad
Susan ('Mum'): Fillet of salmon with vegetables or salad
Mark: Spicy lamb casserole with pepper dumplings
Jasper: Healthy choice, probably ham salad because it's 'lean'
Christine: Vegetable madras
NOTE: These are the most suitable choices. Other options are not impossible, for example, Mark could overcome his dislike of vegetables and have the Vegetable madras because he likes food from other countries!

3 Once students have shown each other their profiles, you could ask them to compare profiles with another pair.

Follow up

For a multilingual or multicultural class
Students work alone to start with. Using a dictionary to help them, they write a menu made up of famous or typical dishes from their country. One starter, one main course and one dessert will be enough. They may find it difficult to translate the name of the dish into English, but they should be prepared to explain to a partner what the dish is made of and how it is cooked. In pairs or small groups they compare menus.

For a monolingual or monocultural class
Students work in small groups. They compile a menu that consists of their favourite foods, for an imaginary restaurant. Each student must suggest one starter, one main course and one dessert. They should think of a name for 'their' restaurant. When complete, they give you the menus. You then read them out anonymously. The class must guess who wrote the menu.

Ready to order?

1 Read the menu and look at the pictures A–H. Which picture goes with which description? Write the name of the dish under the picture.

A

B

C

D

E

F

G

H

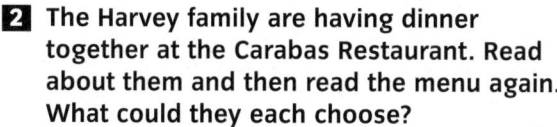

Carabas Restaurant
Menu

Chicken pie Tender pieces of chicken in a rich and creamy sauce with a pastry topping. Served with boiled potatoes and seasonal vegetables. Filling.

~

Fillet of salmon Lightly cooked with lemon and served with vegetables or salad. Light.

~

Rump steak Grilled and seasoned with garlic. Served with vegetables or salad. Light.

~

Burger Made at the restaurant by our own chef, using the finest organic beef. In a plain or seeded bun, served with French fries and salad.

~

Healthy choice A selection of salads available, including cheese, prawn and lean ham. Light.

~

Spicy lamb casserole with pepper dumplings A big hearty meal with an exotic taste that will keep you warm for hours afterwards! Filling.

~

Vegetable madras A hot spicy curry dish from India. Served with rice. Filling.

~

Mushroom and cashew nut bake A tasty vegetarian alternative to roast meat. Served with a jacket potato and vegetables. Very filling.

2 The Harvey family are having dinner together at the Carabas Restaurant. Read about them and then read the menu again. What could they each choose?

Steve ('Dad') His doctor has told him not to eat fattening foods, such as chips, but he is bored with salads and sandwiches and wants a hot meal today. He likes red meat, but is not very keen on fish.

Susan ('Mum') doesn't eat red meat but she likes chicken and fish. She prefers food that is not too rich or spicy. She doesn't have a big appetite.

Mark loves to try food from different countries, and he enjoys hot and spicy flavours. He prefers meat to fish and doesn't eat a lot of vegetables. He's feeling hungry today.

Jasper is on a diet. Usually, he likes things like pasta and pastry but he is avoiding them at the moment because they are fattening. He would prefer to have a cold meal as long as it's low in calories.

Christine is a vegetarian. She has a good appetite, but she is allergic to nuts and has to avoid them. She is feeling quite hungry today and would like a hot meal.

3 Work in pairs. Ask your partner what foods he/she likes and dislikes. Write a profile of your partner like those for the Harvey family in exercise 2. Write *at least three* sentences.

What's on?

Warm up

In the UK films are classified as suitable or unsuitable for audiences according to age using the following categories:

18	No one under the age of 18 is allowed to see this film.
15	No one under the age of 15 is allowed to see this film.
12	No children under the age of 12 can see this film.
12A	Children under the age of 12 can only see this film if accompanied by an adult.
PG	Parental guidance. Some scenes in this film may be unsuitable for children under the age of 12. It is for parents to decide if they want their child to see this film.
U	Universal. Anyone can see this film.

- Write the UK film classifications on the board. Tell students they refer to films and invite them to guess what they mean. Explain the classifications.
- Brainstorm the names of film genres. If students don't know these names (in English), write them on the board and invite them to suggest examples they have seen or heard of, for example: *horror, (romantic) comedy, psychological thriller, science fiction, cartoon, historical, drama, action.*
- If you are working in an English-speaking country, get hold of a current edition of a local newspaper which contains 'what's on' cinema notices. Make copies, or put one copy on the class noticeboard.
- If you are not working in an English-speaking country, you might like to check out what's on in UK cinemas and reviews of current films by looking at suitable websites.

Main activities

Students can do these activities in pairs or small groups; exercise **3** starts as an individual exercise.

1 Give out the activity sheets.

Students read the film reviews only to start with. Ask them which one is a cartoon, which a romantic comedy, and so on. With younger students, ask them which films they would be allowed to see in the UK.

Students then read about each of the people and, as they do so, answer the questions. Remind them that when the choice is for two people, the film must be suitable for *both* of them.

Answers

1 No, because Rita wouldn't like it. Also Paul's parents might disapprove of the violence.
2 Because it's an 18 (she's 15).
3 No, because it's a psychological thriller / classic film, and they like up-to-date action movies with special effects.
4 No, because it's a 'rather silly' physical comedy and she prefers serious films and cinema classics.
5 No, because Nabuko doesn't like action movies and she might not understand it.

2 Students choose the most suitable film for each individual or couple. Ask a few pairs to explain their choices to the class.

Answers

Paul and Rita: *See How They Run.* It's a children's film with a U certificate. They both like cartoons. Rita will be happy with the animal characters.

Natasha: *Heaven Sent.* It has the romantic element which she likes, there are 'some comic moments', and she's old enough to see it.

Thomas and Marek: *Spy Another Day.* It's an action movie, with special effects and an exciting chase.

Zeena: *Shadow on the Curtain* because it's a classic film by a famous director and she's a student of film production. Also it sounds a bit more 'serious' than some of the others on offer.

Nabuko and Ian: *Mrs Parsnip Takes Off.* They both like comedies (but Ian doesn't like cartoons, which rules out *See How They Run*). It's physical comedy with not much dialogue so it won't be difficult for Nabuko to understand.

3 Pre-teach the reporting expression *I thought you would like ... because ...*

Students work on their own and write down the film (from this selection) that they would choose to watch.

When they have written down choices for four or five other members of the class, they stand up and mingle in small groups to talk about the choices they made for others.

Follow up

- Ask students to discuss any films they have seen that resemble the eight films described or which fit one of the genres discussed in the **Warm up** activity. They should describe them and give them a personal star rating of * to *****.
- Ask students to write a short review of a film they have seen recently (75–100 words). To help with this, they should be encouraged to reread the reviews here, and if possible, other examples.

EXAM PART
Reading Part 2

EXAM SKILLS
Matching descriptions of people to information-based texts

TOPIC
Films

TIME
50 minutes

KEY LANGUAGE
Words to describe genres of film

PREPARATION
One photocopy of the activity page for each student

What's on?

1 **Read these reviews of films on DVD. Then read about the people who want to watch a film.**

 Reviews

Mrs Parsnip Takes Off (PG)
Lots of mess and confusion as Mrs Parsnip in her bright red helicopter tries to solve the world's problems. There's not much dialogue and the story is rather silly, but there are plenty of laughs if you like this kind of physical comedy.

Heaven Sent (15)
When Josh dies in a fishing accident, his young wife, Tara, is heartbroken. Then Brad comes along, Josh's best friend from college. Or so he says. A romance develops between them, but Brad is not what he seems to be. A touching love story with some nice comic moments.

Spy Another Day (12)
Special agent, Mike Strong, is on a mission to stop the evil genius Professor Zinc from melting the polar ice caps with a giant laser. The usual exotic locations and fantastic special effects. Worth seeing for the final, exciting chase across Antarctica on dog sleighs. Contains some fantasy violence.

Love? No, thanks! (18)
Music fan Rick Greaves adores singer Lotus O'Connell, and follows her from concert to concert. But when Rick finally gets to meet his idol, he is shocked by the selfish and conceited character behind the glamorous public image. Some funny scenes, and some sad and tender moments too, in this movie about two people looking for love in the wrong places.

Pirates of the Black Star (PG)
Zeke Suntredder and his companion, Narai, are investigating so-called 'time holes' at the edge of the universe when they are taken prisoner by space pirates from the planet Ovona B. Lots of hi-tech spaceships blasting each other, weird and wonderful aliens, and — of course — the robot-with-the-heart-of-gold.

Shadow on the Curtain (B&W 1947) (12A)
A tense psychological thriller from the master of suspense, Wilfred Warlock. Piano teacher, Marcus Peabody, is convinced he has witnessed a murder but the police don't believe him because Marcus is blind. 60 years after it was made, this film is as powerful as ever and shows why Warlock has been such an important influence on younger film directors.

See How They Run (U)
Mr and Mrs Twitcher have lived happily at 21 Hickory Street for as long as they can remember. Which is not very long, since the Twitchers, and their 17 children, are mice! But everything changes with the arrival of Moog — 25 kilos of spitting, scratching, angry CAT! But do they run? Not the Twitchers — they fight back! Great family entertainment from the Dimestar Cartoon Studios.

Rear View Mirror (18)
A good old-fashioned ghost story. Jeff Peach is pleasantly surprised to be offered a second-hand car, in excellent condition, for only 20 dollars. But when he and his family set off on holiday in their new car, strange things start to happen. Nervous viewers, cover your eyes — you're in for a scary ride!

The people

1 **Paul**, 6, likes films with knights and pirates, but his parents won't let him watch anything which is violent or frightening. **Rita**, 8, enjoys films about animals, but doesn't like science fiction. They both like watching cartoons.

Could the children watch *Pirates of the Black Star?*

2 **Natasha** is 15. She sometimes watches action films but she doesn't like science fiction. Her favourite films are romantic comedies. Her parents like old, 'classic' films, but Natasha thinks they are 'boring'.

Why can't Natasha watch *Love? No, thanks!*

3 **Thomas** and **Marek** are both 13. They like up-to-date action movies with lots of special effects, fighting, car chases and so on. They saw *Pirates of the Black Star* last week and really enjoyed it.

Is *Shadow on the Curtain* a suitable choice for Thomas and Marek?

4 **Zeena**, 25, is studying film production at college. She hopes to be a film director herself one day. She likes 'serious' movies that make you think, and at the moment she is very interested in classic films by directors who are important in the history of cinema.

Do you think Zeena would enjoy *Mrs Parsnip Takes Off?*

5 **Nabuko**, 21, is studying English in the UK. Her English is not good enough yet to understand 'difficult' films with a lot of dialogue. She doesn't like action movies or thrillers, but she enjoys films that make her laugh. Her boyfriend, **Ian**, 23, also likes comedies, apart from cartoons. When he's not with Nabuko, he occasionally watches horror movies.

Is *Spy Another Day* a good choice for them?

2 **Choose the most suitable film for each individual or couple.**

3 **Write down the name of the film *you* would choose to watch. Then write down choices for four or five other members of the class.**
Talk about your choices together.

Exam-style task

Hints and tips for Reading Part 2

What you have to do

- Read five short descriptions of people and eight texts on a particular topic.
- Match the people to five of the texts.
- The texts represent possible choices (things to buy, jobs, courses, etc.) for the people.

How to approach it

- First read the descriptions of the five people.
- Next read the eight texts. Underline any matches you find in them.
- Go back and check carefully that the text has **all** the things that the person (or people) wants or needs. There may be one or two details that make the match wrong.

How to prepare yourself

- If you find the same words or phrases in both a description and a text, be careful: there may be one or two details that make the match wrong. Read for similar meaning rather than for identical words.
- Try to read a variety of texts that contain information about goods and services, for example holiday brochures, TV and film reviews, college courses, etc.

PART 2

Questions 1–5

- The young people below are all students who would like to take a break from full-time study by doing a Gap Year Challenge.
- On the opposite page there are descriptions of eight Gap Year Challenges.
- Decide which challenge (**letters A–H**) would be the most suitable for each of the following people (**numbers 1–5**).

If you are a student between 18 and 25 and you would like to take a break from full-time study, why not try a **Gap Year Challenge**? You could be a volunteer on a project to help people in a poor country; you could work and earn money to travel; you could even take another course of study in a different country. Whatever you choose, it's bound to be exciting, challenging and different! And you'll come back to your studies afterwards with new skills, new knowledge and greater self-confidence.

NOTE: It's called a Gap *Year*, but you can find jobs or projects which last for six months or less.

1  **Jez** is planning to train as a secondary school teacher. Now he wants to do voluntary work overseas, preferably with young people. He would like to learn another language, too. He has saved some money and can pay at least some of the costs of his gap year challenge.

2  **Diane** hopes to train as a nurse next year. She has experience of running a playgroup for pre-school children. She is keen to learn about other cultures and she would like to do voluntary work with children.

3  **Anita** is very good at sport and wants to spend her gap year working outdoors, perhaps on a farm or as a group leader of adventure activities for young people. She would prefer to be in an English-speaking country, and she would like to earn a little bit of money, too, if possible.

4 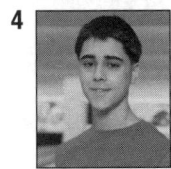 **Rohan** is studying History of Art in London. He wants to get away from England for six months and work to earn a little money. After that he would like to go travelling, somewhere warm and sunny. He has had some work experience helping in his uncle's café.

---

5  **Jasmine** is a student of biology. She loves her subject, but she is fed up with sitting in a class or at a library desk. She would like to get some experience of practical scientific research, working outdoors, perhaps on a conservation project. She doesn't have a lot of money and will need help with the cost of her gap year challenge.

Gap Year Challenges

A   Location: Mumbai (Bombay), India
Young people wanted to help in a home for children and babies without parents. Volunteers will play with the children, help them with schoolwork, including English, and take them on visits outside the school. This work would suit someone who is thinking of taking up a caring profession later on.

B   Location: Queensland, Australia
Opportunities for males and females to work on environmental projects in the fascinating landscape of north-east Australia. If you love nature and being outdoors, and you are willing to work hard as part of an international team, then this could be the gap year challenge for you! Flights and living expenses paid.

C   Location: Canada
Camp Caribou is in a beautiful part of British Columbia near the Rocky Mountains. We need enthusiastic and energetic young people to work at our summer camp, leading a group of children aged 11–16 in outdoor activities like camping, rock climbing and canoeing. You need to be fit and sporty, but friendly and patient too. All travel and other expenses paid, plus generous pocket money (and you won't spend much at camp!).

D   Location: Brazil
Is English your first language? We need Language Assistants to work in small community schools in north-east Brazil. You would help Brazilian teachers to prepare their English lessons, hold discussions in English, and answer questions about the English language. We cannot pay your flights, but in return you would receive free accommodation and meals, plus free lessons in Portuguese.

E   Location: East Africa
We need volunteers to teach English and sport to secondary school students. Our village schools are simple, with few resources, but the local people are friendly and the pupils are very keen to learn. All living expenses paid. Plenty of time off to travel and see the wonderful big game parks of Kenya and Tanzania.

F   Location: Pacific Ocean
If you are interested in sea life and have had at least a little experience of sailing, then you could be one of the volunteer crew of the Starfish Enterprise — a research ship on an exciting voyage along the Great Barrier Reef. You will have to pay your own travel and living expenses, but you will get free training in scuba diving. Some serious science, but lots of fun too!

G   Location: Greece
Do you want to earn some money in order to finance the trip of a lifetime around the beautiful islands of Greece? We have vacancies for waiters and kitchen staff in hotels and restaurants on many different islands between May and October.
Good rates of pay, plus free accommodation.
Useful work experience in a friendly international holiday setting — with lovely weather! A knowledge of Greek helpful but not essential.

H   Location: Italy
Interested in art? Why not spend your gap year in the beautiful historic city of Perugia? Here at the International University we offer a nine-month course in Italian Art and Culture. And you can join in the lively social life of students and local people in this busy, fashionable town. There are also opportunities to study the Italian language (at an extra cost).

A245 Sailing

Answers

1 D   **2** A   **3** C   **4** G   **5** B

A helping hand

Warm up

Dictate these questions to the class or write them on the board. Explain that they come from a poster advertisement on a college noticeboard.

Are you 16 years old or over?
Are you physically fit?
Could you spare a few hours a week of your free time?
Would you like to do some useful voluntary work in your community?

Explain the idea of voluntary work and community service. Ask students to suggest what kind of work this could be: what groups in the community need special help and support?
Why do you think the advertisement asks 'Are you physically fit'?
Write their suggestions on the board.

Main activities

Students can do these activities in pairs or small groups.

1 Give out the activity sheets.

Explain that the phrase *a helping hand* is used to refer to a person giving *help* or as a synonym for the noun *help*, as in 'I need a helping hand.' *A hand* is also commonly used to mean *help*, as in 'Here, let me give you a hand.' The charity has chosen to call itself *Helping Hand*, without the article.

To get a general idea of the text, students read the headings and paragraphs and decide on the correct headings.

Note that some of the questions are easy 'word spot' items, but some are more demanding, requiring the ability to look for paraphrase, for example in F, *companionship* means spending social time with the elderly people, through conversation or playing games with them.

Answers
A What *Helping Hand* does   **B** Shopping   **C** Housework
D Pets   **E** Gardening   **F** Companionship   **G** A valuable experience for you

2 To practise looking for precise information in the text, students identify the parts that confirm the truth of sentences 1–5 and those that contradict the incorrect sentences 6–10.

Answers
1 … by going to the supermarket with them …
2 … they like to be read to. Others just enjoy an opportunity for some friendly conversation or playing a game such as cards or backgammon.
3 Some of the elderly clients we help have failing eyesight and often they like to be read to.
4 What you do for your client is discussed and agreed by you, your Volunteer Support Officer, and the person you are helping.

5 … volunteers learn so much from their clients' experience of life as well as acquiring new skills by taking on the responsibility of a caring role.
6 … volunteers, many of them young people … Many of the volunteers are young, but not *all* of them.
7 … charity that helps such people to live independent lives in their own home environments … *Helping Hand* helps elderly people to live independently in *their own* homes.
8 … playing a game such as cards or backgammon … Volunteers may play games *such as* backgammon.
9 You will not be asked to do anything you are not happy to do … Volunteers *can* refuse to do housework.
10 As Roy (18) said: *I thought voluntary work would be* … Roy was an 18-year-old volunteer.

Follow up

You may want to give students some help before they start writing their paragraph.
Here is a suggested approach:
- Working alone, students think of an elderly person they know. They make notes about that person's life using these headings: *health, financial circumstances, independence and mobility, social life, hobbies and other activities.*
- Working in small groups and referring to their notes, students take it in turns to describe 'their' elderly person. Then they discuss together:
What are the needs of the elderly in society?
What positive contribution do the elderly make to society?

A helping hand

1 Look at these headings and read about the charity called *Helping Hand*. Find the right heading for each paragraph and write it in the space.

Pets
Companionship
Shopping
Gardening
What *Helping Hand* does ✓
Housework
A valuable experience for you

A ‿What ‿Helping‿Hand‿does‿ ‿ ‿ ‿ ‿

There are many elderly people in Erdingford who live alone and find it difficult to go out and to look after themselves. Yet the majority of them love their homes and want to go on living in them as long as possible. *Helping Hand* is a registered charity that helps such people to live independent lives in their own home environments. But our work depends on volunteers, many of them young people, who visit our clients and help them with the activities of daily living, or just provide some friendly company for an hour or so.

B _

Helping Hand volunteers help elderly clients with their shopping trips by going to the supermarket with them and carrying bags back home for them. For those who can't walk very far and who find a trip to the shops is more than they can manage, *Helping Hand* is there to go shopping for them.

C _

Those who find housework difficult appreciate the help of our volunteers with everyday jobs like vacuuming, dusting and cleaning windows, or with practical tasks such as moving furniture or changing a light bulb. (Volunteers are not expected to wash clothes or do heavy or dirty housework.)

D _

Elderly people with pets may appreciate help, for example taking a dog for a walk, or taking a sick animal to the vet.

E _

A garden can be a lovely place to sit on a sunny day, but to keep it looking nice can be hard work. *Helping Hand* volunteers help elderly clients by doing some of the harder physical tasks like digging, weeding and cutting grass.

F _

Some of the elderly clients we help have failing eyesight and often they like to be read to. Others just enjoy an opportunity for some friendly conversation or playing a game such as cards or backgammon.

G _

What you do for your client is discussed and agreed by you, your Volunteer Support Officer, and the person you are helping. You will not be asked to do anything you are not happy to do. A *Helping Hand* volunteer can be a trusted link with the 'outside world', helping to keep our senior citizens independent. But it's not a one-sided benefit: volunteers learn so much from their clients' experience of life as well as acquiring new skills by taking on the responsibility of a caring role. As Roy (18) said:

I thought voluntary work would be a matter of doing little jobs for an old person I didn't know, and then feeling pleased with myself because I'd done something good. But it wasn't really like that. It was more like a friendship: I learnt so much from Margaret about her generation, how things were in the past, and about life itself. And she seemed to take me seriously, and to listen to what I had to say.

2 Sentences 1–5 about the text are all correct. Read the text again and underline the parts of the text that show they are correct.

1 Some of the elderly clients are able to walk to the shops.

2 Volunteers don't always do physical work for clients.

3 Some clients find reading difficult because of their eyesight.

4 A member of staff at *Helping Hand* will talk to you about your work as a volunteer.

5 Many volunteers find the experience important for them too.

Sentences 6–10 are all incorrect. Underline the part of the text that shows they are incorrect and correct the sentence.

6 To be a *Helping Hand* volunteer you must be aged 16–18.

7 *Helping Hand* runs special homes for elderly people who cannot look after themselves.

8 Volunteers need to know how to play backgammon.

9 Volunteers cannot refuse to do housework for clients.

10 Roy was an elderly client of *Helping Hand*.

Follow up

Write a paragraph of about 100 words beginning:
To enjoy a good life, elderly people need ...

Curious exhibits

Warm up

Ask students these questions:

Have you ever visited a museum?

What kind of museum was it and what did you see there?

Have you ever collected things? (Anything from football stickers to Barbie dolls, as long as the object was collected for something other than its use or value.)

Why do some people like collecting things?

Main activities

Students can do these activities in pairs or small groups.

1 Give out the activity sheets.

Ask students to predict which museum they would expect to find each of the objects in. Don't spend time at this stage going through what the objects are called, as students will do this in the next exercise.

2 Students may find that their predictions about the objects weren't completely accurate for all the museums.

Check that they have labelled the illustrations correctly with words from the text.

Answers

The Runciman Toy Museum   c, e

The World of Football   b, f

The Erdingford Museum of Money   a, d

Illustrations:

a coins   **b** shorts   **c** rocking horse

d playing cards   **e** steam locomotive   **f** whistle

3 Tell students to look carefully for the relevant information and to underline the words in the text which give them their answers.

Answers

1 Incorrect   **2** Incorrect   **3** Correct   **4** Incorrect
5 Correct   **6** Correct   **7** Incorrect   **8** Correct
9 Correct   **10** Incorrect   **11** Incorrect   **12** Correct

4 Ask students for the reasons why they would choose to visit one of these museums.

Follow up

Ask students to invent their own 'unusual' museum. Tell students that their invented museum can be one that reflects their own hobbies or interests but it must 'work' as a museum, i.e. it should display things which people will want to come and look at. What would it be called? What would be displayed there? What sort of people would come and visit it? Ask students to write a short description of their museum (they can look at the descriptions in exercise **2** to help them).

Variation: Rather than writing a description of their imaginary museum, students can design a website for it. This would include information under these suggested headings:

The collection (what's in the museum)

Special (temporary) **exhibitions**

Education (meaning educational visits, opportunities for study and research in the museum, teachers' information packs, etc.)

Opening times

Admission charges (if any)

How to find us

Many museums in Britain and elsewhere have excellent websites, which students might like to refer to.

Curious exhibits

1 You are going to read about some unusual museums.

The Runciman Toy Museum &

The World of Football

The Erdingford Museum of Money

Look at the objects in the pictures. In which of the museums would you expect to see them?

a  b 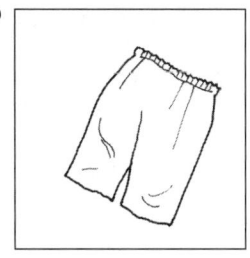 c

2 Now read about the museums and check your answers. As you do so, write the words from the text that describe the object under the picture of it.

d  e  f

e: Steam locomotive

The Runciman Toy Museum

Mon–Sat 9.30–5.00 Sunday 10.00–4.00
Admission: Free

A fascinating collection of dolls, soft toys, rocking horses, model soldiers and specially made musical instruments, including a tiny grand piano (which the guide assured me made 'a very sweet sound'). My daughter was delighted by the doll's house (which has been lent to the museum by Princess Alice) with its beautifully made furniture. But the star exhibit, the thing that everyone wants to see, is the 100-year-old model railway, its painted steam locomotives in good working order. It was given to the museum by the Duke of Corsham (along with a lot of cash!) on condition that the public didn't have to pay to see it. Which was good luck for us!

The World of Football

Mon–Sat 9.30–6.00
Admission: Adults £7.50 Children £5.00

This museum comes right up to date with information on contemporary heroes of 'the beautiful game' plus photos and video replays of them in action. But for visitors who are tired of today's young celebrities, there's tons of information about the football heroes of the past. You can see mementoes such as George Wright's

shorts and Henrique Pessoa's boots, and there's the silver whistle blown by the referee in the final of the first World Cup ever. Oh, and just in case you thought that football is only about world famous teams making lots of money, take a look at the wonderful display of photos of ordinary people playing football in public parks, playing fields and back streets all around the world.

The Erdingford Museum of Money

Tues–Sat 10.00–5.00

Admission: Adults £6.50 Children £3.50

You may not *love* money, but you'll certainly find the history of it fascinating. Three thousand years ago the Chinese used tools as money and then, gradually, they started to exchange little models of those tools instead. In 18th century Canada, soldiers were paid in playing cards, each of which was given a certain value and signed by the governor of the country. The Erdingford Museum is full of curiosities like these. You can see coins and banknotes so rare and valuable they have to be kept behind thick unbreakable glass. And, in contrast, there are famous forgeries – false notes and coins – that are worth nothing at all, except of course for their historical value. What the museum doesn't have, I'm glad to say, is any plastic credit cards!

---

3 Read these sentences about the museums and decide if they are correct or incorrect.

The Runciman Toy Museum

1 The writer played a toy piano at the museum.

2 The doll's house belongs to the museum.

3 The Duke of Corsham didn't want the public to pay to see his model railway.

The World of Football

4 Henrique Pessoa and George Wright are contemporary football heroes.

5 You can see both pictures and objects in the museum.

6 *The World of Football* is about the past as well as the present.

The Erdingford Museum of Money

7 In 18th century Canada, soldiers played cards in order to earn money.

8 The forged money in the museum has only historical value.

9 The writer is not sorry there are no credit cards on display at the museum.

10 All the museums charge for admission.

11 All the museums are open six days a week.

12 All the museums display objects.

4 Which of the three museums would you choose to visit?

Dear parents

Warm up

Write this question on the board:

What do students do at school apart from attend lessons?

Students work in pairs or small groups and make a list of their ideas – as many as possible in, for example, 2 minutes.

The group with the longest list reads it out to the class. Other groups then add any other points not mentioned.

If appropriate, you can then focus on particular activities that are not directly to do with lessons:

At school do you / did you ever ...?
  play in a school sports team against other schools
  have any periods of work experience in local companies or organisations
  have after-school clubs (what kind?)
  take part in musical or theatrical productions (= concerts or plays)
  go on educational trips and excursions
  have fund-raising activities

Confident students can then go on to compare the value of these different activities and even to consider the meaning of the word *education*: does it mean more than going to lessons and doing homework; what does that 'more' consist of?

Main activities

Students can do these activities in pairs or small groups.

1   Give out the activity sheets.

Explain the idea of a school newsletter: it is a letter, addressed mainly to the parents and families of school students, sent out regularly to inform them of what is happening in the school as a whole and sometimes asking them to respond to certain issues, e.g. the use of mobile phones.

After students have read the text, check that they have understood key vocabulary, particularly: *fortunate, carers, queries, requested, waiting list, drop out, disrupted, audition, costumes*.

Students complete the dialogues by writing what B said to contradict A's incorrect statement.

Suggested answers

1 None. We're not allowed to take money on the trip.

2 No, there aren't. I'm afraid all the places are taken. (But you can put your name on the waiting list.)

3 That's not true, actually. If someone wants to call you they have to phone the school office first.

4 But you don't have to have a performing role; you can help with sound, light, costumes or publicity.

5 You're wrong, actually. They've won *five* times in a row.

2

Answers

1 Incorrect They are going to do short work experience placements.

2 Incorrect Paper and pencils will be provided.

3 Incorrect The poster competition is open to the whole school.

4 Incorrect They are allowed but they must be switched off during lessons.

5 Correct

Follow up

Ask the class to produce a newsletter for their own school or college. First, students choose two people to be the editors. In discussion, the items to include are agreed by the class and allocated to pairs of students to write. The results are submitted to the editors who then do the page layout and – where possible – photocopy the finished result so that everyone can have a copy.

EXAM PART
Reading Part 3

EXAM SKILLS
Reading a longer information-based text

Selecting the important (relevant) information

Answering true or false questions

TOPIC
School life

TIME
50 minutes

KEY LANGUAGE
Vocabulary of school subjects and activities

Sentence transformation

PREPARATION
One photocopy of the activity page for each student

Dear parents

1 **Read the newsletter carefully. Then read these conversations between students or teachers at Hunter's Park School. *The first speaker is always wrong* about the news, and the second speaker corrects him/her. Complete what the second speaker says.**

Example:

A: Have you heard the news? Mrs Bolney is going to write to our parents about our work experience placements.

B: No, you're wrong.

She's already written to our parents.

1 **A**: It's our Art Gallery trip on Wednesday, Sally. How much money are you going to bring with you?

B: None! We're

2 **A**: If you hurry up, there are still a few places in the Green Club for this term.

B: No, there aren't. I'm afraid

3 **A**: You shouldn't make phone calls while you're in class, but it's OK to receive a call on your mobile if it's something really important.

B: That's not true, actually. If someone wants to call you

4 **A**: I'd love to get involved in the school drama production next November, but I can't because I'm no good at singing or dancing!

B: But you don't have to

5 **A**: The school basketball team won on Saturday – for the third time in a row this season!

B: You're wrong, actually.

2 **Read these sentences about the Hunter's Park School Newsletter. Are they correct or incorrect? If they are incorrect, correct the sentence.**

1 Year 11 students are leaving school soon to get jobs in local companies. **Incorrect** They are going to do short work experience placements.

2 Year 8 students need to bring paper and pencils with them on their school trip.

3 Only members of the Green Club can take part in the poster competition.

4 It is now forbidden to bring mobile phones to school.

5 If students want to take part in the musical, they should see Mr Marchant.

Hunter's Park School Newsletter

29th March

Dear parents and carers,

Year 11 students have now been told where they are going for their work experience placements in June. We are fortunate that five new local companies and organisations (including a restaurant, a software company and a travel agent) have offered our students places for the two weeks. Parents/carers of Year 11 students should have received a letter giving details about your child's placement. If you have any queries, please contact the head of year, Mrs Bolney.

~

Next Wednesday (5 April), Year 8 students will be going on a visit to the City Art Gallery. Children must bring a packed lunch and water to drink. Paper and pencils for drawing will be provided. The bus leaves at 8.30 am, so they need to be at school half an hour early. Children are requested not to bring money on this trip.

~

GREEN CLUB has proved as popular as ever. Apologies to those who were too late to get a place – don't forget you can still put your name on the waiting list, in case anyone drops out. This month the club members are organising a competition, open to the whole school, to design a poster entitled Save Our Planet – with great prizes for the three best designs.

~

Please remember that mobile phones are only allowed at school on condition they are switched off during lesson times. This is still proving a problem, and lessons are being disrupted by unnecessary calls. In the event of an emergency, where it is necessary to contact a student during lesson time, the school office should always be called first. We ask for parents' support in enforcing this rule.

~

The school drama production next autumn will be a musical, *Rock and Roll Holiday*. As well as actors, we need a lot of energetic singers and dancers. If you would like to audition for a performing role please see Mr Marchant after school this week. If you are interested in helping with sound, light, costumes or publicity, please get in touch with Ms Williams.

~

Congratulations to the school basketball team on their 12–3 win against Margaret Mead School. This means they've had five fantastic victories in succession this season – a record for Hunter's Park.

Deborah McCarthy
Headteacher

Exam-style task

Hints and tips for Reading Part 3

What you have to do

- Read ten statements about a longer factual text.

- Read the text and decide if the statements are correct or incorrect. If they are correct, write A, if they are not correct, write B.

How to approach it

- The ten statements are printed first and it's a good idea to read them first. The questions are in the same order as the information in the text.

- Read the text fairly quickly to get a general idea.

- Read the text again and look for the precise information that will help you decide if the statements are correct or incorrect.

- You may find some vocabulary in the text which you don't know. Don't worry: you won't usually be tested on this more 'difficult' vocabulary.

How to prepare yourself

- The texts are similar to 'real-life' examples of factual reading material, such as brochures, advertisements and website information.

- Try to read some examples of this 'real-life' English. The BBC website is a good source of such material: as well as information about radio and television programmes it has links to sites dealing with education, leisure, travel, the arts, health and hobbies.

PART 3

Questions 1–10

- Look at the sentences below about Zeno's Zoo and Play Park.

- Read the text to decide if each sentence is correct or incorrect.

- If it is correct, write **A**.

- If it is not correct, write **B**.

1. In the Animal families room, there is information about how animals look after their young. ☐

2. The exhibition in the Rainforest room appeals to different senses. ☐

3. Animals at work is a special feature for disabled visitors to the zoo. ☐

4. Lots of visitors want to watch the animals being fed. ☐

5. Children who come on special educational visits can touch some of the animals. ☐

6. A teacher bringing ten children or more doesn't have to pay for them. ☐

7. Teachers can take away materials to use in their lessons. ☐

8. The special educational sessions are free for children under two years old. ☐

9. The ride on the model train lasts for one hour. ☐

10. Visitors to the zoo have to pay extra for the model train. ☐

Zeno's Zoo and Play Park

With lots of fascinating creatures and fun entertainments, places to eat and places to play, Zeno's Zoo and Play Park offers a great day out for all the family.

Animal families room
Learn about the lives of animal babies: how their parents feed and care for their young and the homes they create to protect them.

Rainforest room
Experience the sights and sounds, and even some of the smells, of the Brazilian rainforest in our recreation of this amazing environment. It includes rare species of animals and insects, some in danger of extinction.

Animals at work
A special feature on how animals help us in our daily lives, from guide dogs for the blind to dolphins that can be trained to help disabled swimmers.

Animal feeding time
Come and watch the penguins diving for their dinner (4.30 pm), or the monkeys munching their mid-morning snack (11 am). This is one of our most popular attractions, so get there early if you want to see the action!

Special educational visits
Teachers: why not bring your class to Zeno's? Our guides use creative teaching methods and we offer children an unforgettable hands-on experience of some of our animals.
We offer a special group rate for schools of £1 per child, and with every ten children admitted, one adult goes free. You will also receive a special Teacher's Pack containing background information about the animals and ideas for follow-up activities in the classroom. (Note: this discount does not apply at weekends or in school holidays.)
Children under the age of two are admitted free at all times but please note that only children aged two and above may attend the special educational sessions.

Play Park
Our outdoor play and activity park has been specially designed for children aged 12 and under. As well as swings and rides and climbing frames, children and adults can take a 20 minute ride on our model train, Noah's Express. Starting from the café, the little train travels all round the park, past the lake with its lovely pink flamingos. Journeys start on the hour, every hour.
The price of entry to Zeno's includes admission to the Zoo and the Play Park and unlimited rides on the model train. A small additional charge is made for some other attractions.

Reading Part 3

Answers

1 A   **2** A   **3** B   **4** A   **5** A   **6** B   **7** A   **8** B   **9** B   **10** B

Redefine your limits

Warm up

- One way of introducing some of the key vocabulary would be to draw a simple picture on the board of the upper half of the human body, showing the heart, lungs and rib cage. Ask a volunteer to label the picture.
- You could also introduce some of the key vocabulary 'naturally' through a combination of discussion and 'listen-and-do', as follows.

  Ask students to stand up, breathe in, hold their breath for a count of four, then breathe out slowly. Tell them to repeat the exercise, but this time to notice what happens to their chest and rib cage. Ask them to hold their breath for a count of ten, and then to breathe out with a sigh. Did it feel different this time? Was it less comfortable, or the same? (NB We don't recommend this if any of your students have respiratory or other problems.)

- Discuss with students their experiences of swimming and diving. For example:

  Who can swim the length of a swimming pool underwater?
  Has anyone ever dived using breathing equipment?
  What do you think is the longest time anyone could hold their breath when underwater?

Main activities

Students can do these activities in pairs or small groups.

1 Give out the activity sheets.

Ask students to look at the picture of Tanya Streeter, and talk about these questions.
What kind of person do you think she is?
What do you think she does?

Refer them to the map of the Turks and Caicos Islands.

What do you think this environment is like?
What kind of environment is suitable for diving and other water sports?

Tell students to read the article once fairly quickly in order to understand what free diving involves. They should not worry too much at this stage about the meaning of every word in the article. They answer the multiple-choice question.

Answer
C

2 Students reread the first half of the article.

Suggested answers
1 She broke the world record by diving to 121 metres on one breath, which lasted for 3 minutes 38 seconds.
2 It was difficult because the body needs a constant supply of oxygen and it's very difficult to stop breathing for that long.

3 Check that students understand the key vocabulary: *heart, lungs, blood, oxygen*. Students reread the article in order to answer the multiple-choice questions. Point out to students that in this exercise there are three multiple-choice options, while in the exam itself there are four.

Answers
1 B 2 A 3 A 4 B 5 C 6 C 7 A 8 A

Follow up

Ask students to write 100–150 words about a sportsman or woman they would like to meet.
Describe what they do and their sporting achievements.
What questions would you like to ask them?

EXAM PART
Reading Part 4

EXAM SKILLS
Answering multiple-choice questions

TOPIC
Extreme sports

TIME
50 minutes

KEY LANGUAGE
Vocabulary: organs of the body; how we breathe

PREPARATION
One photocopy of the activity page for each student

Redefine your limits

1 **Read the article quickly and answer this question.**

Free diving is

A diving with special breathing equipment.

B a competition for groups of divers.

C diving as deep as you can on just one breath of air.

2 **Read the first half of the article again.**

1 What did Tanya Streeter do in July 2003?

2 Why was it a difficult thing to do?

3 **Read the article again and choose the correct answer, A, B, or C.**

1 Which heading best summarises the article?

A The dangers of free diving

B Free diving: the power of mind over body

C Water sports in the Turks and Caicos Islands

2 During Tanya Streeter's record dive, her heart beat

A more slowly than usual.

B faster than usual.

C at the normal rate for an adult.

3 What happened to Tanya's lungs?

A They were squeezed smaller.

B They expanded.

C They stopped working.

4 While you are holding your breath,

A your body doesn't use any oxygen.

B your body still uses oxygen.

C your body breathes by itself.

5 What does the writer feel about Tanya's dive?

A She wants to try it herself.

B She couldn't try it because she has a normal heart.

C She thinks it would be unpleasant.

6 How does Tanya train for a dive?

A She goes on a diet.

B She swims up and down the pool with heavy objects.

C She lifts heavy objects underwater.

7 During her record dive, what did the other divers do?

A They sent signals to her.

B They checked her breathing equipment.

C They dived with her.

8 What does Tanya feel when she dives?

A The sea is looking after her.

B She has to fight against the sea.

C The sea contains spirits.

Try holding your breath. How long can you hold it for? 30 seconds? 45? If you can manage a minute, you're doing well. Now consider Tanya Streeter, the free diver. In July 2003 she broke the world record by diving to 121 metres on one breath which lasted her for 3 minutes, 38 seconds! Tanya's motto is 'redefine your limits', and she's certainly an amazing example of what a human being can achieve through courage, determination and intensive training. But I'm not sure I would like to follow her example: during the dive her heart rate slowed down to 15 beats a minute (60 to 100 beats is the normal rate for an adult); her lungs compressed like scrunched up plastic bags, and the blood stopped flowing to her hands and feet.

'Coming up by yourself is very difficult because you are not breathing, but your body is using up oxygen,' she says, which all sounds rather uncomfortable to me!

Mind you, Tanya always trains hard before a dive: for three months she builds up her physical fitness with a programme of exercise, which includes weight training – underwater! 'I take the weights down,' she says, 'then hold my breath and do as much as I can. I also swim up and down the pool underwater but without holding anything.'

There are strict safety procedures for every dive. For her record-breaking dive off the Turks and Caicos Islands in 2003, there were 14 other divers providing help and support. Some of them, wearing breathing equipment, took up positions at different depths in the water. During the dive, they banged on pieces of metal to let Tanya know what depth she had reached.

Tanya doesn't believe her achievements are only a matter of physical training: 'Ninety-five per cent of it is about mental strength. I have never let my mind dictate what my body can do.' And for her diving is almost a spiritual experience: 'I have an incredible sense of inner peace throughout a dive. I feel very protected when I'm underwater. I feel as though the sea is on my side and I've always been successful in that environment.'

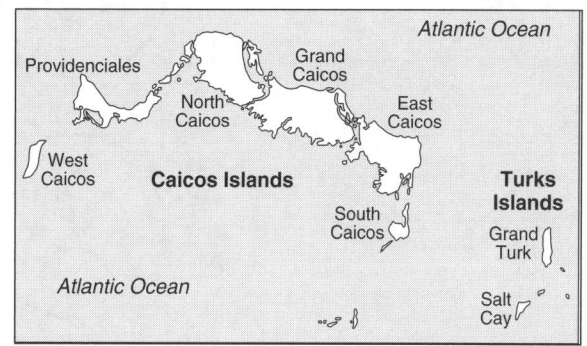

Quick on the draw

Warm up

Introduce the topic of drawing with these questions:
• *Who enjoys drawing?* • *Does anyone here feel that they are good at drawing?* • *How often do you draw these days? When? Why?* • *Did you draw when you were a (young) child? When? Why?* • *When did you stop drawing? Why?*

Next tell the students you would like them to draw a picture of a dog and that they shouldn't take longer than 3–4 minutes over it.

When they have finished the drawing, write these words on the board: *tail, fur, paws, hind legs*. Ask students to label their picture with these words.

NOTE: Students will want to see each other's pictures, but of course it is important not to force them to show their pictures, nor to pass judgement on their artistic skills. The labelling exercise is to intended to reassure: **drawing is a tool which can be used for many things, including learning vocabulary in a foreign language**. To emphasise the point, ask them now to modify their drawing to show the dog *barking*.

Now ask them to modify their picture again by showing that the dog is *wagging its tail*. Write on the board: *The dog is wagging its tail because …*

Students have to complete the sentence with a reason why the dog is happy. For example, *… its owner is going to take it out for a walk.*

Brainstorm some more ideas about how drawing pictures could be useful when learning a language (and make it more fun!).

Main activities

Students can do some of these activities in pairs or small groups.

1 Give out the activity sheets.
   Ask students to look at the drawings of dogs. Which one(s) do they like best, and why? Which one is the most dog-like?

2 Tell students they are going to read about an annual cultural event in Britain. Their first task is to decide what the purpose of the article is.

Answer
C

3 Students reread the article in sections, answering the other multiple-choice questions.

Answers
1 B   2 D   3 D   4 B   5 C   6 A

Follow up

Facial expressions

Give out the photocopies of the six facial expressions and words below. Ask students to match each of the expressions with one of the words (dictionaries may be useful for this task). They can then:

• try to draw the expressions from memory
• draw more empty circles, write different adjectives underneath each one (e.g. *tired, embarrassed, puzzled*), and then ask their partner to draw the expressions.

Answers
1 cruel   2 proud   3 worried   4 angry   5 excited
6 surprised

Pictographs

Give out the photocopies of the pictographs (on pages 139–140).

Pictographs can be used as a mnemonic for learning words but they are also an enjoyable and creative way of exploring words visually. You don't need particular skill at drawing, but you do need a playful imagination.

Once students have looked through the pictographs and done the puzzles (see answers below), ask them to think up more pictographs of their own, perhaps to illustrate vocabulary studied in recent lessons. Pictographs can be used to add a bit of visual interest to the students' own notebooks, or to make an attractive classroom display.

Answers
hear   boxing   selfish   handsome   wave
I'm looking forward to seeing you.

EXAM PART
Reading Part 4

EXAM SKILLS
Answering multiple-choice questions

TOPIC
Drawing

TIME
50 minutes

KEY LANGUAGE
Describing skills

Words for feelings

PREPARATION
One photocopy of the activity page for each student

Photocopies of the facial expressions and words on this page, and the pictographs on pages 139–140 for each student (for the **Follow up**)

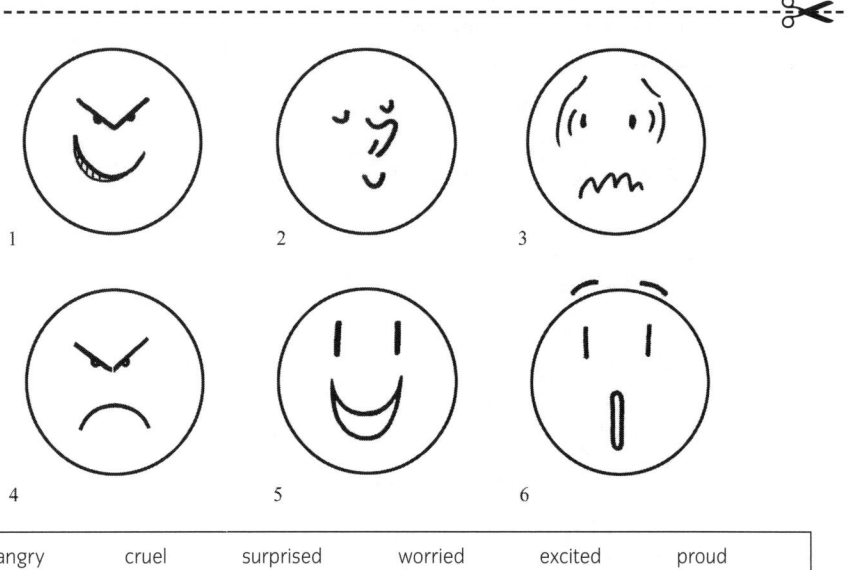

| angry | cruel | surprised | worried | excited | proud |

Quick on the draw

1

- How are the dogs different from each other?
- What is different about the style of drawing in each picture?
- Which do you like best, and why?

2 Read the article about the Big Draw. What is the writer's main purpose in this article?

A to advise us to take drawing lessons

B to describe the history of drawing

C to tell us about a cultural event

D to explain how children develop

Drawing is a universal language. It was probably our first form of self-expression when we were babies: long before we start writing, we're painting and scribbling, both in order to make sense of the world and because we enjoy it.

In the history of human culture, too, painting and image making came before writing or even simple mathematics: 30,000 years ago compared to 5,000. Yet after we leave school most of us never pick up a pencil again – willingly. If asked to draw something, most adults and many older children will shake their heads and say, 'Not me! I can't draw. I'm hopeless at it.'

When you think about it, this is very strange. Drawing involves coordinating the hand and the eye with the pencil. It's a basic skill, no more difficult to learn than 101 other amazing things that humans do, such as hitting a tennis ball over the net, zapping aliens on a computer screen or, indeed, writing our own name. There's no special talent involved. Anybody who can learn to write can learn to draw.

So, there you are – no excuse not to get out your pencil, pencil sharpener and rubber and take part in the **Big Draw**, a nationwide series of free art events taking place all over Britain next October. Everyone's welcome: all you need is a willingness to express yourself through drawing.

The **Big Draw**, now in its fifth year, has already achieved two world records: one for the longest drawing in the world (1 km) and the other for the greatest number of people drawing at the same time (7,000). This year, there will be an attempt to create a new Guinness World Record for the longest visitors' book: people will be invited to leave their name and a drawing on a three-kilometre piece of paper.

The theme this year is *Inside/Outside – People, Structures and Spaces*, and other events planned include drawing in the sand at Weston-super-Mare, and drawing self-portraits on helium balloons which will then be released to see how far they will travel.

The **Big Draw** is not about turning the nation into artists, it is about helping people to acquire this universal language of communication. Its greatest achievement next October will be to bring hundreds of thousands of people together to look, imagine, draw and *have fun!*

3 Read the article again in sections and choose the best option, A, B, C or D.

1 When we are babies we express ourselves by

A learning to write.

B making marks on paper. ✓

C painting pictures of the world.

D enjoying language.

2 What does the writer say about the history of culture?

A Writing is an older human activity than drawing.

B Mathematics is the oldest human activity.

C Drawing and mathematics developed at the same time.

D Drawing came before writing or mathematics.

3 What does the writer say about learning to draw?

A It requires special ability which only a few people have.

B It's easier than learning to write.

C You can do it if you keep your eye on the pencil.

D Anyone can do it.

4 Who is the Big Draw for?

A People who didn't draw when they were children.

B People who would like to try drawing.

C People who can't draw.

D People who want to create a world record.

5 The Big Draw already holds a world record for

A the length of time spent on a drawing.

B the number of visitors to the event.

C the number of people drawing at the same time.

D the number of balloons released on one day.

6 Which is the correct advertisement for this year's Big Draw event?

A
> Come and have fun practising your drawing skills. You'll get a chance to join lots of other people writing and drawing on an enormous piece of paper.

B
> Come and have fun practising your drawing skills. There'll be an exciting opportunity to travel in an air balloon with other artists.

C
> Come and have fun practising your drawing skills. You'll get a chance to work with lots of other people drawing enormous pictures on public buildings.

D
> Come and have fun practising your drawing skills as you explore the beautiful town of Weston-super-Mare.

Getting around

Warm up

- Draw a simple picture of a car on the board (or ask one of your students to draw it). Write the following words in a circle around the picture: *bonnet, windscreen, headlights, mirror, boot, number plate*, etc. Then ask students to come out and label the picture with the words.
  OR
- Ask students to look at a picture dictionary, if available, at the page showing the interior of a car, with the parts and features labelled. Put students in pairs, sitting side by side, like a driver and passenger. Ask those who can drive to 'teach' their partner step-by step how to start the car and move off into the traffic.
  OR
- Divide the class into two discussion groups; for larger classes, have an equal number of A and B groups.
  Group A has to think of as many reasons as possible for owning a car yourself. Group B has to think of as many reasons as possible for not owning a car yourself. One person in each group takes notes.
  After the discussion, one person from each group (probably the note taker) reads out their group's reasons.
  AND
- Hand out the photocopies of the driving questionnaire on page 141. Students interview each other in pairs using the questionnaire and write down their partner's answers.
  Form new pairs or groups of four for a reporting back phase. Write on the board some phrases for making comparisons:
  Marco drives once or twice a week whereas I never drive. Sema's family have a BMW whereas I drive a Nissan. I came to school on foot this morning, and so did Alejandro.
  However, the main aim of this phase is to prompt 'free' discussion on the merits and demerits of different forms of transport and makes and models of car.

Main activities

Students can do these activities in pairs or small groups.

1 Give out the activity sheets.
Students read the initial sentences and then the extracts and match them.

Answers
1 C   2 D   3 A   4 B

2 After students have answered the questions, you may want to discuss the differences in style and purpose of the extracts.

Answers
1 3   2 2,4   3 1   4 2,4   5 3   6 1

3
Answers
1 C   2 B   3 D   4 A

Follow up

Ask students to write either a letter to a newspaper about the transport problems in their area or to describe in detail a journey they make regularly, for example from home to school or work. They should write about 100 words and draw on their own experience and opinions. More confident students may like to try the letter, which requires a more controlled and formal style of language.

EXAM PART
Reading Part 4

EXAM SKILLS
Answering multiple-choice questions

TOPIC
Transport; driving

TIME
40 minutes

KEY LANGUAGE
Styles of writing

Vocabulary of cars and motoring

PREPARATION
One photocopy of the activity page for each student

Optional: One photocopy for each student of the driving questionnaire for the **Warm up** (page 141)

Getting around

1 Read extracts 1–4, which are all about different aspects of transport.

Which of sentences A–D is the first sentence of each extract? Write a letter in the box.

A My feeling is that you shouldn't spend your savings on a car right now, even if it is a bargain – and without seeing it, I can't be sure.

B Driving is an essential life skill that most of us want to learn as soon as we can.

C I strongly disagree with your correspondent who wrote that it's impossible to live without a car nowadays.

D The Rondo Circa 3000 is a wonderful example of stylish motoring.

1 ☐

My family and I live in Green Lea, 10 kilometres outside the city, and we work, go to and from school, shop and enjoy our leisure all without owning a car. We go by bicycle or we use the City Link bus service, which, though rather expensive, is at least regular and reliable. The children never complain about walking to friends' houses or to their various clubs and activities; what does annoy them, however, is the amount of traffic on local roads, which can make cycling unpleasant, and even dangerous.

2 ☐

It handles like a dream, whether you are driving in city traffic, on narrow country roads, or in the fast lane of a high-speed motorway. On longer journeys the supersoft upholstery and state-of-the art climate control will guarantee you a comfortable ride. And you can feel secure knowing that everything has been designed for maximum safety. What's more, we have six choices of engine and eight new colours to choose from. No wonder it was selected as Car of the Year by 50 of the top motoring journalists in Europe!

3 ☐

How many other students at college run a car? I'm sure that most of them couldn't afford it. It's one thing to buy a car, Jan, but remember you've then got to tax it and insure it, not to mention the running costs (and the price of petrol is going up again soon, I've

heard). I think you'd be much better off keeping your money in the bank and perhaps when you graduate in two years' time I can let you have my Fiat, which is in good condition, and a reliable little car. Anyway, we can discuss it when I see you at the end of the month ...

4 ☐

At Tootle School of Motoring we offer first class tuition by highly experienced instructors at a price you can afford. Whether you are a beginner who has never sat behind the wheel of a car before, or a practised learner driver preparing to take your test again, Tootle will provide both the expert advice and the sympathetic support you need. You can book individual lessons at times convenient to you, or you can take advantage of a special 10% discount on our one-week intensive driving courses (offer ends 12th April).

2 The extracts are written in different styles, for different purposes, with different readers in mind.

1 Which extract is from a personal letter?

2 Which extracts are advertising something?

3 Which extract disagrees with someone else's opinion?

4 Which extracts contain practical information?

5 Which extract contains advice?

6 Which extract describes a transport problem?

3 Read the four extracts again and answer the questions. Choose A, B, C or D.

1 What are the writer's children unhappy about?

  A the dangers of walking home alone

  B the efficiency of the bus service

  C the conditions for cyclists

  D the distance from Green Lea to the city

2 According to the extract, the Rondo Circa 3000

  A is good in all kinds of weather.

  B is nice and easy to drive.

  C is more colourful than other cars.

  D is safer on long journeys.

3 What does Jan want to do?

  A borrow some money to buy a car

  B buy her mother's Fiat

  C sell her car when she graduates

  D buy a car now

4 There is a 10% discount for customers who

  A take an intensive driving course.

  B book one lesson at a time.

  C take their driving test on April 12th.

  D pay within one week.

Exam-style task

Hints and tips for Reading Part 4

What you have to do

- Read a longer text and answer five multiple-choice questions.

- In each question you have to choose from four options.

- The first question is usually about the writer's purpose in writing the text, and the last question is about the general meaning of the text.

- The other three questions follow the order of information in the text and at least one will be about attitudes or opinions expressed in the text.

How to approach it

- Read the text fairly quickly, and think about the writer's purpose and the general meaning of the text.

- Read the text again, this time very carefully.

- Answer the questions, each time checking your answer by looking back at the text.

- It can be a good idea to answer the first question (writer's purpose) and the last question (general meaning) together.

- If you are not sure of the correct answer, cross out the answers that you know are wrong.

How to prepare yourself

- The texts in Part 4 are more than simply information about a topic: they will often express the attitudes, feelings and opinions of the writer or of other people mentioned in the text.

- These words are sometimes used to indicate the writer's purpose: *recommend, describe, explain, report, warn, advise, give an opinion.*

- Try to read a variety of texts that express opinions, attitudes, etc. Reading stories will help you: there are lots of excellent abridged and simplified readers in English, for learners at all levels. See www.cambridge.org/elt.

Who let the dogs out?

Red, a lurcher, opening a kennel

I've always known that dogs are intelligent animals, but even I was surprised when I heard about a dog called Red, at the Battersea Dogs' Home in London.

The Home has been caring for lost and unwanted animals for over 140 years. Recently, the staff there got a shock when they came to work in the morning. They found that some of the dogs had got out of their kennels during the night, opened cupboards and taken out food and toys. And it happened again, and again. The manager, Becky Blackmore, described how as many as nine dogs were escaping every night. 'We came in to chaos,' she said. 'Dogs were running around having fun and games and causing a lot of mess. We couldn't understand it.'

Someone or something was unlocking the kennels during the night. Becky decided that the only way to solve the mystery was to put in cameras to record how the dogs were getting out.

When she and her staff played back the recording, they saw Red, a three-year old lurcher, put his nose through the bars of his kennel and use his teeth to press the button that opened his door. That was clever enough, but Red did more: he unlocked the kennels next to his and let those dogs out too. The group went along the corridor, broke into cupboards and stole dog biscuits and toys to play with.

Becky Blackmore said, 'It's surprising, because lurchers aren't famous for their intelligence. It's amazing that he worked out how to open his own kennel, but also that he then let all his friends out.' Like most of us, I suppose, Red didn't like to party alone!

The story has a happy ending: after Red was shown on television, several people came forward and offered to give him a new home as a family pet. 'We are very pleased about this,' said a member of staff at the Dogs' Home. 'Lurchers are usually difficult to find homes for. When Red arrived here four months ago, he was very thin and in poor condition. Now he can look forward to a comfortable new life with an owner who wants him.'

PART 4

Questions 1–5

- Read the text and questions below.
- For each question, mark the letter next to the correct answer – **A**, **B**, **C**, or **D**.

1 What is the writer's main purpose in the text?

   A to describe the work done by the Battersea Dogs' Home

   B to give an example of how clever dogs can be

   C to complain about dogs escaping from the Dogs' Home

   D to ask people to look after unwanted dogs

2 What can readers find out from this text?

   A that Red didn't like being at the Dogs' Home

   B that Red and the other dogs escaped because they were hungry

   C that when Red and his friends escaped they had a good time

   D that Red and his friends enjoyed being recorded by the camera

3 What did Red do after he got out of his kennel at night?

   A He took biscuits and toys back to the other dogs.

   B He showed the other dogs how to unlock their doors.

   C He slept in a cupboard.

   D He released the other dogs.

4 How did Becky Blackmore feel about what Red did?

   A She was surprised because she didn't think lurchers were clever enough to do that.

   B She was angry because he ate the staff's biscuits.

   C She was pleased because he became a TV star.

   D She was worried because of the security problems it caused.

5 Which TV programme is about Red?

   A
Tonight on *Animal Matters*: how security cameras found a dog that went missing in London.

   B
Tonight on *Animal Matters*: a Dogs' Home that keeps its animals happy with night-time parties.

   C
Tonight on *Animal Matters*: the clever dog that could unlock doors.

   D
Tonight on *Animal Matters*: the dogs that rob people's houses during the night.

--✂--

Answers

1 B   **2** C   **3** D   **4** A   **5** C

All together now

EXAM PART
Reading Part 5

EXAM SKILLS
Reading for grammar
and meaning

Multiple-choice
questions

TOPIC
Families;
celebrations

TIME
50 minutes

KEY LANGUAGE
Lexical grammar
(modals, pronouns,
prepositions)

PREPARATION
One photocopy of
the activity page for
each student

Optional: bring in (or
draw) a map showing
the south-west of
England

Warm up

- Write the phrases *immediate family* and *extended family* on the board and ask students what they refer to. If it is needed, this can be an opportunity to revise the vocabulary of family relationships.
- Ask students about their own extended families – uncles, aunts, cousins, etc. How often do they meet? On what occasions?
- Put students into groups and ask them to list the advantages and disadvantages of belonging to a large extended family.
  OR
- Ask them to list the reasons why family members lose touch. (For example, because they move to different parts of the country.)

Main activities

Students can do these activities in pairs or small groups; exercise **4** is in small groups.

1 Give out the activity sheets.
Ask students to look at the photo in pairs and discuss their answers to the three questions. Briefly share answers in the whole group.

2 Students read the whole article fairly quickly in order to understand the main points. **They should read only the text in the shaded boxes for now and ignore the multiple-choice questions**. Check understanding with these questions:

1 *How often do the Gigg family meet up?*
2 *Where do they meet?*
3 *Who is George Gigg?*
4 *Who is Jack Greenfield?*
5 *What job does Faith have to do?*
6 *How has the event changed over the years?*
7 *Why did their family holiday tradition start?*
8 *What's special about next year's holiday?*

Answers
1 Once a year ('the annual holiday …')
2 Westward Ho! (in the south-west of England)
3 The head of the family / the oldest member of the family
4 The youngest member of the family / George Gigg's youngest great grandchild
5 She has to arrange all the holiday accommodation for the family.
6 The event has got bigger and bigger over the years.
7 George's wife, Stella, was ill and wanted to see all her family together in one place.
8 It will be George Gigg's 100th birthday.

3 Go through the instructions and advice for answering the multiple-choice questions. These are grouped according to the types of words being tested: questions 1–5 test collocations, 6–9 test 'grammatical' words, 10–13 test prepositions, 14–17 test verb forms and 18–20 test modals.

With less confident students, you might like to direct them to the example answers and ask them to circle these before going on to the remaining questions.

Answers
1 spend   2 tradition   3 world   4 way   5 distance
6 him   7 The   8 because   9 so   10 of   11 at   12 by
13 with   14 organised   15 wanted   16 died   17 have
18 can't   19 will   20 wouldn't

4 Tell students that they are going to give a talk lasting for 2 minutes about a holiday they have had with members of their own family. They should spend about 5 minutes silently planning what they are going to say (and it doesn't have to be true). Emphasise that they should not try to write a composition, but note down ideas in the form of key words and phrases.

Here are some questions to help them.
Who did you go with?
Who chose and organised the holiday?
Where did you go? How long did you stay?
What activities did you do together (with your relatives)?
What activities (if any) did you do separately?
How did you get on together?
*How would you rate the holiday for **fun** on a scale from 1 = boring to 5 = really great fun?*

Follow up

Tell students they are planning a big family party (they can decide the reason for the celebration). Working alone, they should write a guest list of family members they want (or ought!) to invite. Students then work with a partner. They show their guest lists to each other and explain who each person is and why they are invited. For example: *The next person is Lisa. She's a cousin of mine. My father's got a sister called Shirley and Lisa is her younger daughter. She's 21 or 22 and I like her a lot – she's really good fun. Then there's Uncle Maurice. He's my mother's older brother. He's not married. I don't see him very often, but I think he should be invited to the party.*

All together now

1 **Look at the headline and photo.**

A summer holiday with the family (all 109 of them)

- What do you think the article is about?
- Would you enjoy a holiday like this? Why/Why not?
- Imagine you are one of the people in the picture. Describe what was happening when the photo was taken.

2 **Read the text below quickly to get a general idea of the meaning. Don't try to do the multiple-choice questions yet.**

3 **Read the text again, carefully, and the advice at the beginning of each paragraph. This time choose the correct word from the alternatives in *italics*.**

In the first paragraph you need to think about how words **combine** in phrases. For example the answer to **1** is **spend**: you can *have*, *take* or *spend a holiday*, but you can't 'pass' or 'make' a holiday.

This summer the Gigg family met up to **1** *pass / make / spend* a holiday together at a resort called Westward Ho! in the south-west of England. Nothing unusual about that – except that there were 109 of them! The annual holiday is a family **2** *tradition / festival / time* dating back to 1969, and it draws members from all over the **3** *sea / England / world* including, this year, the United States, Africa and the Middle East. This summer's gathering was the largest yet, and one of the grandchildren, Timothy Greenfield, cycled all the **4** *way / travel / journey* from Manchester to be there, a **5** *length / distance / measurement* of over 420 kilometres.

In this paragraph you need to think about the **grammar** of the word in the sentence. For example, the correct answer to **6** is **him**: *him* is the object pronoun from *he* (referring to George Gigg). Here, it is the object of the verb *provided*.

The head of the family is 99-year-old George Gigg. His six children have provided **6** *he / him / his* with 31 grandchildren and 42 great grandchildren. **7** *The / A / One* youngest is 6-month-old Jack Greenfield. Jack's mother, Carol, said: 'It was a bit overwhelming when I first married Ed, **8** *although / but / because* I come from a small family, but everyone was **9** *such / too / so* friendly.'

In the next paragraph the missing words are all **prepositions**. For example, the correct answer to **10** is **of**. After a preposition we must use a gerund (a verb with the *-ing* form); the preposition *of* goes after words like *job*, *task* and *duty*.

Mr Gigg's daughter, Faith, has the difficult job **10** *of / to / in* arranging all the accommodation. The family stay **11** *on / at / to* a holiday park, where they occupy 20 chalets, each of which can take up to six people. The whole event is organised **12** *from / to / by* Mr Gigg's son-in-law, Peter. 'It's just got bigger and bigger,' he said. 'We all get together for some activities and the younger children play **13** *from / of / with* each other and have a great time. But we are also independent family units; we eat separately and do our own thing.'

Here you need to think about the form of the **verb** which is missing. For example, the correct answer to **14** is **organised**. The verb is in the passive form of the past simple tense. *Organise* is a regular verb, so the past participle ends with *-ed*.

Behind this happy annual event there is a sad story: the first holiday reunion was **14** *organise / organising / organised* in 1969 because George's wife, Stella Gigg, was very ill and she **15** *want / wanted / wanting* to see all her family together in one place. She **16** *died / dies / dead* later that same year. The Giggs **17** *has / have / had* come back to Westward Ho! ever since.

In these questions the missing words are all **modal verbs**. For example, the correct answer to **18** is **can't**: *some members of the family are not able to come*.

Naturally, there are a few members of the family every year who **18** *mustn't / wouldn't / can't* join the holiday because of work, study or illness. However, everyone **19** *shall / will / would* do their best to be there next August for the 100th birthday of their founding father. That's one celebration they **20** *wouldn't / mustn't / couldn't* want to miss!

4 **Work in small groups. Talk for 2 minutes each about a holiday you have had with members of your own family. You can invent details if you like.**

Sleep tight!

Warm up

Introduce the topic of sleep by asking one student the following questions:
How many hours did you sleep last night?
Was this more or less than normal?
Did you wake at all during the night?
Do you remember what you dreamed?
Did you feel tired or refreshed when you woke up?
Ask that student in turn to put the same questions to another student. Repeat the process a few more times.
Variation: Each time a student puts the questions they have to substitute one of the five with one of their own, **but on the same topic**. For example, instead of 'Did you feel tired or refreshed …' they ask, 'Do you ever have a nap during the day?'

Main activities

Students can do some of these activities in pairs or small groups.

1 Give out the activity sheets.

Ask students to note down their answers to each question. They could go through the questions alone before comparing with a partner, or they could discuss them in pairs or small groups.

Answers
1 FALSE A typical person spends *a third* (33%) of his/her life asleep.
2 FALSE Sleepwalking is more common among children than adults.
3 TRUE
4 FALSE Women are more likely than men to have bad dreams (or perhaps they are just more likely to *admit* it!).
5 TRUE
6 FALSE But it can be dangerous to let them walk near an open window!
7 TRUE But this is not REM sleep.
8 FALSE *Women* remember more of their dreams than *men*.

2 Ask students to complete the multiple-choice topic vocabulary exercise. A competitive element can be added by doing the exercise in pairs or teams, with a time limit. Teams then mark each other's papers and a winner is declared.

Answers
1 A   2 B   3 D   4 A   5 A

3 Introduce the text on powernaps by asking the students these questions:
How many hours do you usually sleep a night?
How do you feel if you don't get enough sleep?

Read the introduction aloud with the whole class. Discuss their answers to the three introductory questions *before* they go on to read the rest of the text. Students then read the text and answer the multiple-choice questions.

Suggested answers
Introductory questions
- Because they are busier and there are things to do and places to go 24 hours a day.
- We find it difficult to work or to concentrate and eventually our health is affected.
- Perhaps take a few minutes of complete rest in a quiet room, or go for a walk or jog to 'wake themselves up'.

1 C   2 A   3 D   4 C   5 B   6 A   7 D   8 C
9 A   10 C

Follow up

Write or dictate this letter from a 'problem page' in a magazine and ask students to write Susie's reply (in about 100 words).

Dear Susie,
I'm a student with a part-time job at a coffee bar during the day. Every time I sit down in the evening to study I feel very sleepy and often doze off over my books. I have some important exams in a few weeks, and I need to study. What should I do?

EXAM PART
Reading Part 5

EXAM SKILLS
Reading for grammar and meaning

Multiple-choice questions

TOPIC
Sleep; dreaming; tiredness

TIME
50 minutes

KEY LANGUAGE
Lexical grammar (collocations, word families, quantifiers)

Topic vocabulary

PREPARATION
One photocopy of the activity page for each student

Sleep tight!

1 Are these statements True or False?

		T	F
1	A typical person spends a quarter (25%) of his/her life asleep.	☐	☐
2	Sleepwalking is more common among adults than children.	☐	☐
3	REM sleep is the name used for the periods of sleep when we dream.	☐	☐
4	Men are more likely to have bad dreams than women.	☐	☐
5	An average person has more than 1,000 dreams every year.	☐	☐
6	It is dangerous to wake a sleepwalker.	☐	☐
7	The deepest sleep happens shortly after we fall asleep.	☐	☐
8	Men remember more of their dreams than women.	☐	☐

2 Read these sentences and choose the correct word, A, B, C or D for each space.

1 Are you children still awake? It's 10 o'clock. ....A........ to sleep at once!

   A Go ✓   **B** Make   **C** Have   **D** Take

2 These problems you are having could be caused by ....: you are simply not getting enough sleep.

   A tiring   **B** tiredness   **C** tire   **D** tired

3 If I drink coffee late in the evening it .... me awake.

   A makes   **B** gets   **C** lets   **D** keeps

4 Excuse me for yawning, but I didn't get .... sleep last night.

   A much   **B** many   **C** some   **D** a

5 'Is the baby still awake?' 'No, I'm happy to say she's fast ....'

   A asleep   **B** sleeping   **C** slept   **D** sleepy

3 Read the introduction to this article about powernaps.

> According to a recent report, we are getting less sleep than we used to – an average of 90 minutes less per night. Lack of sleep can cause all kinds of problems: it can make us less efficient and less creative; it can cause us to become bad-tempered, even depressed. In the longer term, say the researchers, sleep deficiency can lead to ill health, accidents and divorce.

- Why do you think people today sleep less than people in the past?
- What happens to us if we don't get enough sleep?
- What should busy people do if they feel tired during the day?

Read the rest of the text and choose the correct word, A, B, C or D for each space.

> So why are we sleeping (0) ....C........? The report blames our 24/7 society: the fact that people (well, some people) can work, (1) .... shopping or have fun 24 hours a day, 7 days a week.
>
> Supermarkets, bars, clubs and petrol stations stay open late, and there are TV and radio (2) .... broadcasting around the clock. So bedtime is when the club closes or the TV programme finishes, not (3) .... you feel tired.
>
> But the reality is, we need our sleep, and if we don't get enough of it, our performance at work or at school suffers, and so, eventually, does our (4) ....
>
> One American company has seen (5) .... business opportunity in this 'tired-out society'. Metronaps offers (6) .... New Yorkers so-called 'powernaps' – that is, short periods of sleep during the day which are supposed to refresh and re-energise them to (7) .... on working.
>
> After (8) .... $14 the customer goes into a darkened room and lies in a special bed called a 'sleeping pod' for 20 minutes, which is fine as long as you are (9) .... to fall asleep. The problem comes if you just lie (10) .... for the whole 20 minutes, worrying about having wasted $14!

0	**A** few	**B** not	**C** less ✓	**D** none
1	**A** make	**B** have	**C** go	**D** commit
2	**A** stations	**B** canals	**C** media	**D** emissions
3	**A** how	**B** that	**C** what	**D** when
4	**A** illness	**B** self	**C** health	**D** force
5	**A** one	**B** a	**C** an	**D** the
6	**A** busy	**B** occupied	**C** tiring	**D** broken
7	**A** increase	**B** continue	**C** get	**D** carry
8	**A** charging	**B** costing	**C** paying	**D** pricing
9	**A** able	**B** capable	**C** possible	**D** interested
10	**A** tired	**B** asleep	**C** awake	**D** refreshed

Many Happy Returns!

Warm up

- Introduce the topic by asking the students to stand up and get in a line **according to the month of their birthday**. In other words, the student with a birthday early in January will be at the front of the line, and the student with a birthday in late December will be at the end. They must find their places in the line by asking each other their birth dates **in English**. To liven up the activity, you could tell them the last class to do this took 3 minutes, that you are going to time them, and that you want them to do it faster than this.

  When they are in their right positions in the line, give the following instructions:

  Step out of the line if you had your last birthday at a weekend.

  Step out of the line if you had a special cake on your last birthday.

  Step out of the line if you were away from home for your last birthday.

  Step out of the line if you were given an unusual present on your last birthday.

  Step out of the line if you went out to a restaurant for your last birthday.

  Step out of the line if you stayed up late on your last birthday.

  When a student steps out of the line you, or their classmates, can ask them more detailed questions, for example: *Did you have candles on the cake? What colour were they?* etc.

  AND

- Hand out the photocopies of the birthday questionnaire on page 142.

  Ask students to complete the questionnaire for themselves. As they are doing it, help individuals with any problem vocabulary. For example: *fuss, apologise, remind, diary, hand-knitted, hurt, delighted, annoyed.* Alternatively, suggest they look in dictionaries.

  Ask different students to read aloud the scores and interpretations.

  Tell students to work out their scores and compare their answers in pairs. (Explain that it is 'fun' and not to be taken too seriously!)

  Ask a selection of students to say what their score was and if they agree with the interpretation.

Main activities

Students can do these activities in pairs or small groups; they start exercise **1** on their own.

1 Give out the activity sheets.

This exercise gives the students practice in verb + noun collocations. After matching a noun with each of the verbs, they put the actions in what they think is the most logical sequence by numbering them 1–10.

They compare and discuss their answers. Differences in their sequences should promote discussion. Note that the aim of the ordering exercise is to promote discussion and processing of the vocabulary – there is no single 'correct' sequence for the actions.

Answers and suggested sequence
send **invitations**   bake **a cake**   decorate **the room**
welcome **the guests**   offer **food and drink**
open **presents**   sing **a song**   blow out **the candles**
make **a wish**   take **photographs**

2 Before you start, ask for a volunteer to sing 'Happy Birthday To You' in English.

Ask students if they know which country the song comes from and how old it is.

Students then read the text quickly to find the answers.

Introduce the gap-fill task, which has initial letter clues.

Students read the text again carefully and fill the gaps. They can work in pairs or alone.

Answers
1 candles   2 blow   3 sung   4 many
5 composed   6 had   7 published / printed
8 sure   9 became   10 belong   11 earn   12 next

Follow up

Ask students to write a story of about 100 words with this title: *The perfect birthday present.*

EXAM PART
Reading Part 5

EXAM SKILLS
Guessing words from context

Multiple-choice questions

TOPIC
Birthdays

TIME
50 minutes

KEY LANGUAGE
Verb + noun collocations

Topic vocabulary

PREPARATION
One photocopy of the activity page for each student

Optional: One photocopy for each student of the birthday questionnaire for the **Warm up** (page 142)

Many Happy Returns!

1 **Look at how these verbs and nouns go together.**

You can **celebrate** a traditional festival or a birthday or an anniversary.

You can **give** or **receive** presents.

You can **play** or **listen to** music.

Match each verb with one of the nouns below.

Verbs

• offer • decorate • sing • welcome • send
• make • blow out • take • bake • open

Nouns

• invitations • the room • the guests • food and
drink • a wish • a song • photographs • a cake
• presents • the candles

Imagine you are having a birthday party. What is the most logical order for these actions? Number them from 1–10.

Work in pairs and compare your answers. Discuss any differences you find.

2 **Fill each gap in the text with one missing word. The first letter of the word is given to help you.**

The birthday cake is on the table; the (1) c_____ are lit. What are you going to do before you (2) b_____ them out and make a wish? Sing 'Happy Birthday' of course! Although it's (3) s_____ at birthday celebrations all over the world, how (4) m_____ of us ever stop to wonder where this popular tune came from?

Mildred J. Hill and her sister, Patty, were kindergarten teachers in Kentucky, USA. One day in 1893, Mildred (5) c_____ a melody on the piano. It sounded good, so she played it to Patty, who added some words. Soon they (6) h_____ made it into a simple song to greet the children as they came into class each day.

> Good morning to you
>
> Good morning to you
>
> Good morning, dear children
>
> Good morning to you.

Shortly afterwards the song was (7) p_____ in a book, Songs and Stories for the Kindergarten.

No one is (8) s_____ who took Mildred's melody and replaced Patty's words with 'Happy Birthday To You', or when it happened, but the new version quickly (9) b_____ popular through radio and the new medium of sound films.

The rights to the song now (10) b_____ to the huge media and entertainment group AOL Time Warner. 'Happy Birthday To You' is said to (11) e_____ about $2,000,000 a year in royalties. Sadly, Mildred Hill died in 1916, long before her song became world famous.

Think about her the (12) n_____ time you blow out the candles on your birthday cake!

Exam-style task

PART 5
Questions 1–10

- Read the text below and choose the correct word for each space.
- For each question, mark the letter next to the correct word – A, B, C or D.

Balmoral Castle

Scotland is a land famous for its old castles. One of the best known of (0) .... is Balmoral, on the river Dee in the north-east of the country. It (1) .... to the British Royal family, who have spent their summer holidays here (2) .... over 150 years. The (3) .... Queen's great-great-grandmother, Victoria, bought it in 1852.

She and her husband, Prince Albert, loved the (4) .... air, the wild countryside and the friendly local people. At Balmoral she could forget the worries and responsibilities of (5) .... both the Queen of England and also the ruler of the largest empire the world had ever seen.

In 1861, at the (6) .... of only 42, Prince Albert died. The Queen was heartbroken. She (7) .... black clothes for the rest of her life and (8) .... rarely seen to smile in public. However, she continued to return to Balmoral Castle, (9) .... she could walk or ride in the beautiful landscape of the Scottish Highlands and remember the happy times she (10) .... spent there with her husband.

Example answer:

0	**A** this	**B** that	**C** these ✓	**D** they
1	**A** owns	**B** is	**C** has	**D** belongs
2	**A** for	**B** since	**C** during	**D** from
3	**A** now	**B** today's	**C** actual	**D** present
4	**A** strong	**B** high	**C** fresh	**D** picturesque
5	**A** doing	**B** making	**C** having	**D** being
6	**A** years	**B** period	**C** age	**D** time
7	**A** dressed	**B** wore	**C** put	**D** invested
8	**A** was	**B** were	**C** had	**D** made
9	**A** why	**B** which	**C** where	**D** who
10	**A** has	**B** had	**C** did	**D** was

Hints and tips for Reading Part 5

What you have to do

- Read a text with ten gaps in it (and an example).
- Look at four multiple-choice items for each question and choose the correct word for the gap.
- The four multiple-choice options are generally the same category of word, e.g. they are all nouns or all prepositions.

How to approach it

- Before you answer the questions, read through the whole text so that you understand the topic and the general meaning.
- Look at the example answer (0).
- When you are choosing an answer you may need to read the whole sentence.

- If you are not sure of an answer, check each option: does it sound right in this space?

How to prepare yourself

- When preparing for Reading Part 5 (and Paper 1 in general) it is a good idea to learn words **in groups**, e.g. *to be interested in* history; *to change* your *mind*; *to work hard*.
- Reading Part 5 tests vocabulary, and also grammatical points such as prepositions, pronouns, connectors and quantifiers (words like *a, one, some, any*).
- Make your own 'gap-fill practice exercises'. Find a short text in English and select some words you want to test. Copy out the text, putting gaps in place of these words. Exchange exercises with other students, then correct each other's work.

Answers

1 D   2 A   3 D   4 C   5 D   6 C   7 B   8 A   9 C   10 B

In other words

Warm up

Write the following statements on the board:
Everybody needs to learn English these days.
It takes one year to learn English well.
The most difficult thing about English is the pronunciation.
It doesn't matter if you make mistakes when you speak English.
Grammar is boring and unneccessary.
It's important to learn to write well in English.
Students first decide on their own opinions, for example:
• *I agree* • *I disagree* • *I'm not sure.*
Then in small groups they compare opinions.

Write these pairs of sentences on the board:
I've got nothing to say. / I haven't got anything to say.
I can't remember your name. / I've forgotten your name.
Ask students if the second sentence means the **same** as the first, or the **opposite**.

Next, ask two students how far they live from the school. Write a comparative sentence on the board, for example:
Gustavo lives further away from the school than Anna.
Ask them if they can think of another way of saying this.

> **Answer**
> Anna lives nearer to the school than Gustavo. / Anna's house is not as far away from the school as Gustavo's. etc.

Write the title of this activity on the board and explain that they are going to practise sentence transformations, **in other words**, saying things in different ways.

Main activities

Exercise **1** starts as a whole class activity; exercise **2** can be done individually or in pairs.

1 *In advance*: Photocopy the activity page and cut exercise **1** up (or cover one version at a time) so there are equal numbers of Version A and Version B sentences for the class, plus exercise **2** and the **Follow up**.

Give out the activity sheets at random. The aim is for students to find the sentences that match their own in meaning. Students walk around the room with their lists; when you clap your hands they have to find the nearest person with a different version of the sentences from their own. They then have to find matching pairs and write the missing versions on their paper. **They should do this by dictating the sentences to each other rather than by simply copying them**. After a minute (more or less), clap your hands again. At this signal the students must start circulating again, **whether or not they have finished dictating a matching sentence**. After 5 seconds or so of circulating, clap your hands again. Students must find a *new* partner. The process is repeated until everyone has all the other versions of their sentences. Students who have finished the task must sit down and try to *learn* the alternative versions of the sentences.

In pairs, students discuss how far they agree or disagree with the opinions expressed in the sentences. Each student then chooses the best (i.e. the truest and most useful) **for them**. Suggest that they copy these sentences out neatly on some surface where they will see them frequently – the cover of an exercise book, for example, or on a piece of card, with a decorative border, to be put on the classroom wall.

Test the sentence pairs at the end of the lesson or at the beginning of the next lesson.

The matching pairs

Nobody likes grammar. / Everybody dislikes grammar.

Listening is more difficult than grammar. / Grammar is not as difficult as listening.

I enjoy reading stories in English. / Reading stories in English is enjoyable.

We shouldn't translate. / It's better not to translate.

Having an English-speaking friend could help us. / It could be helpful to have an English-speaking friend.

Watching films in English can teach us a lot. / We can learn a lot from watching films in English.

You get better at a language by using it. / You won't get better at a language if you don't use it.

This activity isn't very difficult. / This activity is quite easy.

My English has improved during the last six months. / My English is better now than it was six months ago.

2 Students can do this on their own or in pairs.

Answers

1 don't **2** is spoken **3** 've (have) been **4** more than **5** can get **6** learn **7** this word pronounced **8** do you say **9** you repeat that **10** I had read

Follow up

Remind students that they are writing a *letter* and that their answers to the friend's questions should be incorporated into an appropriately friendly, natural-sounding communication.

EXAM PART
Writing Part 1

EXAM SKILLS
Sentence transformations

Identifying synonymous expressions

Rephrasing and reformulating information

TOPIC
Language learning

TIME
40 minutes

KEY LANGUAGE
Mixed structures

PREPARATION
One photocopy for each student of exercise 1 Version A OR Version B, plus exercise 2 and the Follow up

In other words

- ✂ - - -

1 Find students who have Version B of these sentences. Find the matching sentences and write them down.

Version A

Nobody likes grammar.

- -

Listening is more difficult than grammar.

- -

I enjoy reading stories in English.

- -

We shouldn't translate.

- -

Having an English-speaking friend could help us.

- -

Watching films in English can teach us a lot.

- -

You get better at a language by using it.

- -

This activity isn't very difficult.

- -

My English has improved during the last six months.

- -

- ✂ - -

1 Find students who have Version A of these sentences. Find the matching sentences and write them down.

Version B

It could be helpful to have an English-speaking friend.

- -

Everybody dislikes grammar.

- -

It's better not to translate.

- -

My English is better now than it was six months ago.

- -

This activity is quite easy.

- -

We can learn a lot from watching films in English.

- -

Reading stories in English is enjoyable.

- -

You won't get better at a language if you don't use it.

- -

Grammar is not as difficult as listening.

- -

- ✂ - -

2 For each question, complete the second sentence so that it means the same as the first using no more than three words.

1 I haven't got an English dictionary.

I - own an English dictionary.

2 People speak English all over the world.

English - - - - - - - - - - - - - - - - - - - all over the world.

3 I started learning English a year ago.

I - learning English for a year.

4 I prefer science to languages.

I like science - - - - - - - - - - - - - - - - - - - languages.

5 I'm learning English in order to get a better job. I'm learning English so that I - - - - - - - - - - - - - - - - - - - a better job.

6 I'm thinking of learning Japanese next.

I might - - - - - - - - - - - - - - - - - - - Japanese next.

7 How do you pronounce this word?

How is - - - - - - - - - - - - - - - - - - - ?

8 What's the English word for *martello*?

How - - - - - - - - - - - - - - - - - - - *martello* in English?

9 Would you mind repeating that, please?

Could - - - - - - - - - - - - - - - - - - - , please?

10 How many English books have you read?

She asked me how many English books - - - - - - - - - - - - - - - - - - - .

Follow up

Here is an extract from a letter you have received from an English-speaking friend:

> I hear you're studying English at the moment. That's great! Is it difficult to learn? What do you do to practise the language? Is there anything I can do to help you?

Write your reply, answering your friend's questions. Write about 100 words.

After the show

Warm up

Write these mixed up questions on the board.

kind your favourite of what's music?
music day do to you every listen?
any English sing can songs in you?
to you a been live have concert ever?

Students work in pairs and have to unscramble them. Make it a race by giving a time limit of 1 minute, or stop when one pair have the correct questions.

Students then ask and answer the questions across the classroom for practice. Encourage them to develop their answers, e.g. *Yes, I listen to music every day – in the morning when I'm getting dressed, then when I'm out walking or jogging, and sometimes when I'm in bed, before I go to sleep. Also when I meet friends we often play music CDs while we're talking.*

> **Answers**
> What's your favourite kind of music?
> Do you listen to music every day?
> Can you sing any songs in English?
> Have you ever been to a live concert?

Main activities

Students do some of these activities alone and the others in pairs or small groups.

1 Give out the activity sheets.

Ask students to describe what is happening in the three pictures. They should cover up the rest of the sheet in order not to see the 'answers' beforehand.

Ask students for examples of what they have written about the pictures. They should try to justify what they have written by referring to how the characters might be feeling.

2 Students read the dialogue silently. Then ask them to look again at the three pictures in **1**. What were the characters *actually* saying in the pictures?

Check students' understanding of the dialogue with the following questions:

1 Why does Sara want to leave now?
2 Why doesn't Jeff want to leave?
3 How long have they been at the concert?
4 What do you think *the support band* means?
5 What does Sara think of the band they're watching now?
6 Why does Sara wish they had left the concert earlier?
7 Why don't they take a taxi?
8 Why doesn't Jeff lend Sara his mobile phone?
9 What does Sara ask Max?
10 Why doesn't Max take Jeff in his car?

NOTE: Answering these questions correctly will give students valuable oral practice of typical PET-level structures.

> **Answers**
> 1 Because if they leave now they'll catch the last bus.
> 2 Because the band are still playing.
> 3 For three hours / since 9 pm.
> 4 The musicians who perform first, before the main band.
> 5 She thinks they're not as good as the support band.
> 6 Because they have missed the bus.
> 7 Because finding one this late / at this time is difficult.
> 8 Because he has left it at home.
> 9 She asks if he can give them a lift (to Grendon).
> 10 Because there is only room for one other person in the car.

3 Students familiarise themselves with the structures in the dialogue by reading it aloud in pairs. They should be encouraged to make their reading as natural and fluent as possible, as follows:

First read the sentence you are going to say.
Think about the feeling or attitude expressed in the sentence.
Remember the sentence as a whole.
Look up, make eye contact with your partner, and speak the whole sentence.

4 Students who are already familiar with Writing Part 1 sentence completion exercises should immediately 'get the point' of this task. Others will be helped by trying to anticipate the kind of differences in wording they might hear, for example the adjective/adverbial pair in *is a good guitar player = plays the guitar well.*

▶▶▌ Play the recording of the second version of the dialogue. **See page 124 for the Tapescript and Answers.**

Rather than crossing out words in the first version, students should underline where the words are different and write the alternative phrasing just above.

Play the recording as often as necessary for students to complete the task. You may want to give out photocopies of the Tapescript so they can check their answers.

5 Using as prompts the unaltered sentences in their printed version of the dialogue, students complete this exam-style task.

> **Answers**
> 1 we'll miss   2 been here for   3 a louder
> 4 as good as   5 going to do   6 taking   7 agree with
> 8 to phone   9 brought / got it with   10 room for two

Follow up

Students work in groups of three and practise the *alternative* version of the dialogue. That is, they must read the amended sentences from the recorded version *and* the transformations in exercise **5**. This will be slow, but will effectively reinforce the different structures.

EXAM PART
Writing Part 1

EXAM SKILLS
Sentence transformations

Identifying synonymous expressions

Rephrasing and reformulating information

TOPIC
Leisure activities: music

TIME
50 minutes

KEY LANGUAGE
Mixed structures

Expressing opinions; agreeing and disagreeing

Oral fluency practice

PREPARATION
One photocopy of the activity page for each student

Optional: photocopies of the Tapescript for exercise 4 (see page 124)

After the show

1 Look at the pictures. What is happening in each one? Where are the boy and girl? Why do you think the girl is pointing to her watch and then covering her ears?

2 Read the dialogue. Then answer your teacher's questions.

SARA: If we leave now, we'll catch the last bus.

JEFF: But the band are still playing.

SARA: Well, it's midnight now and we arrived here at 9 pm.

JEFF: But, Sara, we have to stay until the end.

SARA: This is definitely the loudest band I've ever heard!

JEFF: But Rory is a really good guitar player, isn't he?

SARA: He's all right, but I think the support band were better.

Jeff and Sara have now left the concert and are outside in the street.

JEFF: Look! The bus has just gone. What shall we do now?

SARA: I wish we'd left the concert half an hour earlier.

JEFF: Why don't we take a taxi?

SARA: Finding a taxi at this time isn't going to be easy.

JEFF: Mmm. You're right.

SARA: We'll have to walk home.

JEFF: You'd better phone your parents. You know how strict they are.

SARA: You're right. Can I borrow your mobile?

JEFF: Yeah, of course … Oh, no! I've left it at home.

SARA: Oh look, there's Max. Perhaps he'll take us home in his car. Hi, Max! Any chance of a lift to Grendon?

MAX: Glad to. But there's only enough room for one, I'm afraid.

SARA: (*Jumping in*) Thanks, Max. Sorry, Jeff! But you know how it is: my Mum and Dad are stricter than yours.

JEFF: Sara!!!

3 Work in pairs. Read the conversation aloud (one of you will also play the third character, Max). As you do so, try to lift your eyes from the page sometimes and speak the words *to your partner*.

4 ▶▶|Listen to the conversation on the recording. Some of the wording is different this time, but the meaning is the same. As you listen, note on the dialogue the words that are different.

5 Look at the sentences in the conversation that you didn't change and complete these sentences *so that they mean the same*. Use between one and three words for each answer.

1 Unless we leave now .... we'll miss .... the last bus.

2 Well, it's midnight now and we've .... three hours!

3 I've never heard .... band than this.

4 In my opinion they're not .... the support band.

5 Look! The bus has just gone. What are we ....now?

6 What about .... a taxi?

7 Mmm. I .... you.

8 You ought .... your parents.

9 Yeah, of course … Oh, no! I haven't .... me.

10 Glad to. But there isn't .... , I'm afraid.

Follow up

Work in groups of three. Taking the parts of Sara, Jeff and Max, practise the second version of the conversation.

Structure Bingo

Warm up

Explain how the game of Bingo works. Each player has a card with numbers on it. Someone (the 'Bingo caller') calls out numbers and players mark any of those numbers that they have on their card. The first person to mark all the numbers on his/her card wins the game (usually by calling out 'Bingo!').

In this version of the game, the numbers refer to sentences that students have to match with other sentences read out by the teacher.

Main activities

Exercise **1** is a team game; students can do exercise **2** in pairs.

1 **How to play Structure Bingo**

There are two lists of sentences, one on the activity page, and the other below. Your list contains rewordings of all the sentences in the students' list, but **they are presented in a different order**. Also, **there are ten extra sentences in the students' list that serve as distractors**. The purpose of the game is for students to score points by calling out the number of the sentence on their sheet that corresponds in meaning to the sentence you have just read.

Give out the activity sheets.

Students get into teams of three or four. They have 3 minutes to read their list of sentences, and to discuss with each other the meanings of any problematic sentences. Don't help them too much at this stage, otherwise it will take away the competitive element of the game.

To begin the game, read your list aloud, slowly, with short pauses between each sentence. After each sentence from your list, any student can call out a number from their list. If that sentence is the same in meaning as the sentence on your list, that student gets a point for his/her team.

However, if a wrong number is called, that team loses a point and the chance passes to the other team(s). Your list of sentences provides the correct corresponding numbers so you can check the answers quickly.

If two or more students call out the correct number at exactly the same time, the point is given to the student who can repeat your original sentence correctly.

If no one calls out a number, write the sentence from your list on the board to prompt an answer.

To aid learning, each time a student calls out a correct number, ask him/her to read the sentence aloud as well.

In order to establish which team is the winner, you will need to keep a tally as the teams score points.

Teacher's sentences

NOTE: The correct numbers of the sentences from the students' list are given.

Come on time.   **7**

I haven't got any brothers or sisters.   **19**

He left a moment ago.   **13**

This is yours.   **6**

Can I help you?   **27**

We've never tried this before.   **4**

Let's ask him.   **14**

Can I borrow your bike?   **1**

There are no sweets left.   **12**

She's younger than she looks.   **25**

I can't wait to see you again.   **17**

How tall are you?   **21**

They're too small.   **9**

Could you say that again?   **11**

What's the title?   **20**

Shall I drive?   **26**

Don't look sad!   **3**

It's a question of price.   **28**

She's pregnant.   **18**

We make it.   **8**

2 Briefly introduce the topic of films by asking students if they have seen any recent film releases. If more than one person in the class has seen the same film, get them to compare their opinions on, for example the story, the actors, the filming, special effects, etc.

Ask students to read the conversation between Pilar and Dasha. They complete the sentences by writing one or two words in the space. Remind them that the two friends always agree.

After checking answers, students should read the conversation in pairs for practice.

Suggested answers
1 seen better   **2** confusing   **3** was paid
4 more popular   **5** acts   **6** more than   **7** shorter
8 bored by   **9** left   **10** seen worse

Follow up

Find out how well students remember the Structure Bingo sentences on their sheet. You can do this by asking two people to come out to the front of the class. They take it in turns to read aloud the sentences from the teacher's page – *but not the number!* (They can be read in any order.) Their classmates must try to recall the corresponding sentence from the activity page, without looking at it. Points can be awarded for each correctly remembered sentence.

EXAM PART
Writing Part 1

EXAM SKILLS
Sentence transformations

Identifying synonymous expressions

Rephrasing and reformulating information

TOPIC
Mixed topics; films

TIME
40 minutes

KEY LANGUAGE
Mixed structures

Expressing opinions; agreeing

PREPARATION
One photocopy of the activity page for each student

Structure Bingo

1 You are going to play this game in teams. Listen to your teacher and follow the instructions.

1 Can you lend me your bike?

2 It's not sweet enough.

3 Cheer up!

4 This is the first time we've tried this.

5 We've already tried this.

6 This belongs to you.

7 Don't be late.

8 It's made by us.

9 They're not large enough.

10 What's your name?

11 Would you mind repeating that?

12 The sweets have all gone.

13 He's just left.

14 Why don't we ask him?

15 She asked me for help.

16 What's your weight?

17 I'm looking forward to seeing you again.

18 She's expecting a baby.

19 I'm an only child.

20 What's it called?

21 What's your height?

22 He ought to leave.

23 How much does it cost?

24 She's just had a baby.

25 She's not as old as she looks.

26 Would you like me to drive?

27 Can I give you a hand?

28 It depends on the price.

29 I feel happy.

30 I haven't seen you for ages.

2 Two friends, who always agree with each other, are talking about a film they have both seen. Fill in the gaps so that the two friends' sentences always mean the same. **Use** one **or** two **words each time.**

PILAR: It wasn't the best film I've ever seen.

DASHA: I agree. I've (1) ...._seen better_.......... films.

PILAR: The story confused me a bit.

DASHA: Yes. I found the story a bit (2) .... too.

PILAR: They paid Tim Swift a million for it.

DASHA: Really? Tim Swift (3) .... a million for it?

PILAR: Yes, he was.

DASHA: I'm surprised, because he's much less popular nowadays.

PILAR: You're right. He used to be a lot (4) ....

DASHA: Mind you, he's still a good actor.

PILAR: Oh, yes, he still (5) .... very well.

DASHA: Did you prefer this film to his last one?

PILAR: Pardon?

DASHA: Did you like this film (6) .... his last one?

PILAR: No, I didn't. For one thing, it's much too long.

DASHA: You're right – it should be a lot (7) ....

PILAR: And I thought the battle scenes were very boring.

DASHA: Yeah. I was very (8) .... the battle scenes too.

PILAR: I didn't stay until the end.

DASHA: Nor me. I (9) .... before it finished.

PILAR: But it wasn't the worst film I've ever seen.

DASHA: Oh, no. I agree. I've (10) .... films.

Exam-style task

Hints and tips for Writing Part 1

What you have to do

- You must write an answer that is between one and three words.
- You must write only the missing words on your answer sheet.
- The sentences are all about one topic.

How to approach it

- Try to identify what is being tested. Is it verb forms? Comparisons? Direct to indirect speech, etc.?
- No marks will be given if a word is misspelt, so check carefully!

- When you have completed the second sentence, check that it means the same as the first sentence.

How to prepare yourself

- Look at the grammar syllabus for a PET level coursebook. A good example is the Map of the Student's Book on pages 4–7 of *Objective PET* (Cambridge University Press). Have you practised all these grammatical areas?
- Work with a friend and test each other on irregular verbs. There is a list of these on page 208 of *Objective PET*.

PART 1

Questions 1–5

- Here are some sentences about a person's grandfather.
- For each question, complete the second sentence so that it means the same as the first, **using no more than three words**.

Example:

Although my grandfather is 73, he still works full time.

Although my grandfather is 73, he still

does a .... *full-time job* ....

---

1 He sells old furniture and clocks.

He has a shop .... **old furniture and clocks.**

2 He's had the shop for nearly 34 years.

He bought the shop nearly

....

3 The shop is open from Monday to Saturday.

The shop .... **on Sundays**.

4 Some of the clocks in his shop are very valuable.

Some of the clocks in his shop are

.... **a lot of money**.

5 But making money doesn't interest grandfather.

But grandfather's not ....

money.

--- ✂ -

Answers

1 selling / that sells / which sells / where he sells

2 34 years ago

3 closes / shuts / is closed / is shut / isn't open (is not open) / doesn't open (does not open)

4 worth

5 interested in making

Message in a bottle

Warm up

Give out the activity sheets.

Ask students to look at the cartoon strip of the man on the desert island. Ask them about his situation, for example:

What has happened to the man?
Why is he writing a message?
What does he want?
Who do you think wrote the reply?

Ask one student to tell the story in his/her own words.

Main activities

Students can do these activities in pairs or small groups, though they should do the writing on their own.

1 The discussion in the **Warm up** should generate some ideas for this first writing task, but obviously there will be differences between the messages written by students. Ask a few individuals to read their messages aloud to the class. Write them on the board, helping to correct or improve the wording as you do so.

Here is a sample message:

Help! I'm stranded on a desert island in the South Pacific, Latitude 31° S, Longitude 178° E. Please send a helicopter to rescue me.

(Obviously, a geographical reference isn't necessary, but it adds a bit of 'realism'!)

2 Exercise **1** involved a message written in a very improbable context. This exercise looks at a variety of different notes and messages that people write in real-life contexts.

Once you have been through the answers, reinforce learning by asking students to work in pairs. Student A covers the extracts 1–8. Student B reads the first part of the message and Student A must try to remember the second part of the message (a–h). They change roles and repeat.

Answers
1 d   **2** h   **3** a   **4** f   **5** b   **6** c   **7** e   **8** g

3 Students will become familiar with some of the functional language used for such messages by matching the extracts with the functions A–H.

Answers
A 8 + g   **B** 1 + d   **C** 4 + f   **D** 7 + e   **E** 5 + b
F 2 + h   **G** 6 + c   **H** 3 + a

4 This exercise focuses more closely on the exam task. Support is given in that the sentences needed to complete the task are given, but in a list with additional and unnecessary information. Students have to select from the 12 sentences the ones most appropriate for writing the reply **within the 35–45 word limit**. They should write the reply out in full, and not simply tick the sentences they want to include.

Suggested answer
Thanks very much for the invitation. Unfortunately, I'll be away on holiday on 6th June. But I want to buy you a present. Do you have a wedding list of things that you need? Please let me know.
Speak to you soon.
[42 words]

Follow up

Ask students to choose one of the extracts in exercise **2** and expand it into a longer note or message. They should write 35–45 words.

EXAM PART
Writing Part 2

EXAM SKILLS
Thinking about different types of notes and messages

Selecting the important information

TOPIC
Mixed topics; invitation to a wedding

TIME
50 minutes

KEY LANGUAGE
Functions: invitations, apologies, requests, arrangements, thanks, etc.

PREPARATION
One photocopy of the activity page for each student

Message in a bottle

1 Look at the picture story. Write the man's message for him, this time in English!

2 Look at these extracts from notes and messages. Match the openings 1–8 with the second part of each message a–h.

1 | Jack called.　d

2 | I hear you've passed the PET exam.

3 | Thanks for answering my questions.

4 | Sally's asked me to play tennis with her this afternoon.

5 | Sorry to hear you've been ill.

6 | Preheat the oven to 180° C …

7 | I'll buy the tickets …

8 | We're having a little party on Saturday.

a | It was very kind of you to help me.

b | Get well soon.

c | … and bake for 45 minutes.

d | He said can you call him back after 8 pm?

e | … and I'll wait for you in front of the station.

f | Could you lend me your tennis racket?

g | It would be lovely if you could come.

h | Well done!

3 Now match the messages 1–8 and a–h with the descriptions A–H.

A an invitation 8 + g
B a message about a phone call
C a request to borrow something
D a note making an arrangement
E a message to someone who is ill
F a message congratulating someone
G instructions on how to do something
H a note thanking someone

4 You have just received this invitation to a wedding. Unfortunately, you can't go because you have booked a holiday for the first two weeks in June.

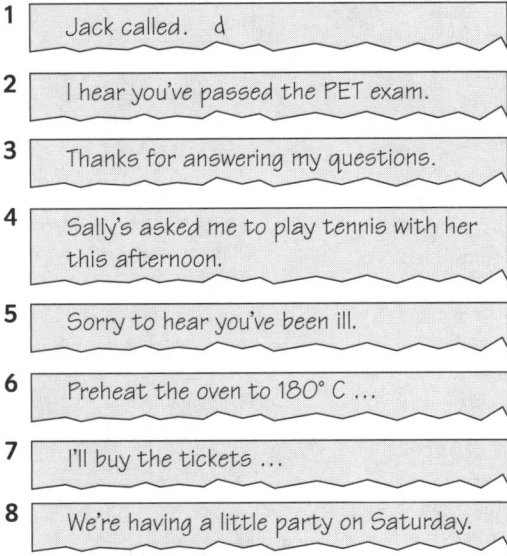

Wedding invitation

Dear

Great news – we're getting married at last! We hope you'll be able to come to the wedding, which will be at Graveney Registry Office on Saturday 6th June at 2.30 pm, and to join in the celebrations afterwards at Al Dente Restaurant, Severn Street.

Jess and Matt

Write your reply to the invitation. In it you should:

• thank them for the invitation
• explain that you can't come
• tell them that you would like to buy them a present and ask them what they need.

Your reply should be 35–45 words.

Write your answer by choosing from the sentences below (you will not need to use them all).

It was lovely to hear from you again.

Thanks very much for the invitation.

I'm really sorry, because I love weddings.

I can't believe you're getting married after all this time.

Unfortunately, I'll be away on holiday on 6th June.

I'm going to Spain with my friend Carol.

But I want to buy you a present.

I don't want to waste time buying something you already have.

Do you have a wedding list of things that you need?

I'll be thinking of you on 6th June.

Please let me know.

Speak to you soon.

All the very best

Warm up

If possible, show students one or two samples of greetings cards to prompt the discussion. Ask the class to suggest different occasions when people send each other greetings cards.

You may want to tell them that in many English-speaking countries greetings cards are a popular way of sending messages. In Britain, for example, you can buy cards for people when:

- they have a birthday or anniversary
- they are ill
- they are leaving a job
- they have graduated from college or university
- someone close to them has died
- you want to thank them for something
- you want to congratulate them on something, e.g. getting married
- there are special festivals, e.g. Christmas, Eid-ul-Fitr.

Write two or three of their suggestions on the board. Ask them to work in pairs and think of a suitable message to write *inside* each of the cards, with a maximum of two sentences.

Students read their messages aloud and the rest of the class discuss how appropriate they are.

Main activities

Students can do these activities in pairs or small groups, though they should do the writing on their own.

1 Give out the activity sheets.

In this exercise there are six messages that might be found in greetings cards. Each message consists of two sentences. One word in the message has 'strayed' into the wrong sentence. Students have to find the stray word and insert it into the right place in the other sentence.

Answers

1 Sorry to hear about your accident. Get **well** soon.
2 Sorry you're **leaving** us. All the best in your new job.
3 Good luck in your new home. I hope the move **went** well.
4 Congratulations **on** the birth of your baby girl. I can't wait to see her.
5 Best wishes on your birthday. I can't believe **you're** 18 already!
6 Wishing you a **Merry** Christmas. I hope to see you again in the New Year.

2 Students match the six messages to 'typical' greetings card artwork.

Answers

1 c   2 a   3 e   4 d   5 f   6 b

3 This exercise gives more practice in formulaic greetings.

Answers

1 luck A   2 wishes D   3 hope B
4 regards E   5 of A   6 soon C   7 Remember E
8 seeing C   9 enjoy B   10 great happiness D

4 Hand out slips of blank paper (see Preparation). Students match the requests and replies first, and then write a one-sentence request on any topic, starting with one of the polite phrases given, on one of the slips of paper.

Collect the requests and redistribute them. Students write their reply to the request on the same slip of paper, using one of the polite phrases given.

Give students a time limit to write and reply to as many requests as possible.

You may want to give the replies back to the students who wrote the requests before asking a selection of students to read out their requests and the replies.

Answers

1 D   2 A   3 C   4 E   5 B

Follow up

Ask students to look again at the pictures in exercise **2**. Discuss the appropriateness of these pictures to the messages being sent. What other pictures could illustrate the same messages?

Tell students they are going to send a card with a message inside it to one of their classmates or to someone they know outside the classroom. They should think about the type of message they want to write. Look at the examples in exercise **1** and the sentences in **3** used for wishing people well.

To make the card, they simply fold a piece of paper in half, draw a simple picture on the front, e.g. if it's a get well card it might be a picture of a bunch of flowers or a smiling patient in a hospital bed.

They should write a draft message on scrap paper first and show it to you. When it's correct, they copy it into their card and then send or give the card to someone.

Variation: They could make a display of their cards on the classroom noticeboard.

EXAM PART
Writing Part 2

EXAM SKILLS
Writing greetings and short messages

TOPIC
Messages in greetings cards; polite requests

TIME
50 minutes

KEY LANGUAGE
Fixed phrases for greetings

Phrases for polite requests and refusals

PREPARATION
One photocopy of the activity page for each student

Optional: one or two samples of greetings cards for the **Warm up**; slips of paper for exercise **4**

All the very best

1 In each of the messages 1–6, one word is in the wrong place. Find the word and put it in the right place.

1 Sorry to hear (well) about your accident. Get soon!

2 Sorry you're us. All the best leaving in your new job.

3 Good luck went in your new home. I hope the move well.

4 Congratulations the birth of your baby girl. I can't wait to see on her.

5 Best wishes on your you're birthday. I can't believe 18 already!

6 Wishing you a Christmas. I hope to see you Merry again in the New Year.

2 Match the messages 1–6 above with the pictures a–f.

a  b  c

d 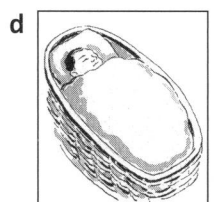 e  f

3 In most cases the main purpose of a greetings card is to show the person that you are thinking of them and to wish them well. Here are some expressions that help to do this. Choose the correct word in *italics* and then match the expression with one of the people A–E.

1 Good (luck) / wishes.

2 Best *luck* / *wishes* for the future.

3 I *wish* / *hope* you have a great time.

4 Give her my *salutations* / *regards*.

5 I'll be thinking *of* / *for* you.

6 Hope to see you *soon* / *after*.

7 *Remind* / *Remember* me to Tom.

8 Look forward to *seeing* / *see* you again.

9 Hope you *enjoying* / *enjoy* the break.

10 Wishing you both *the great happiness* / *great happiness*.

A For someone who is taking an exam

B For someone who is going on holiday

C For someone you expect to meet again

D For a couple who are getting married

E For another person that both of you know

4 Read the requests 1–5 and match each one to a reply A–E.

1 Do you think you could clean my shoes?

2 Would you mind buying lunch for me today?

3 Could you possibly sing a song for us?

4 I wonder if you could come and help clean my flat as it's very untidy at the moment?

5 Would you mind doing my English homework for me?

A I wish I could but I haven't got any money on me.

B I'm afraid I can't because my level is so bad.

C I'm sorry but I've got a sore throat today and I can't sing.

D I'd like to, but I haven't got any shoe polish.

E I'd like to help but I'm not very good at housework.

Now write your own one-sentence request of any kind on a piece of paper. Use your imagination and sense of fun – requests can be humorous or fantastic, but they must be expressed politely. Begin each request with one of these polite phrases:

Do you think you could …?

Would you mind …?

Could you possibly …?

I wonder if you could …?

Another student will receive your request and you in turn will receive one. You must write a reply politely refusing the request and giving an excuse or reason for your refusal. In each of your replies you should use one of these phrases:

I'm afraid I can't because …

I'm sorry but …

I'd like to help but …

I wish I could but …

Continue the activity by writing and replying to as many requests as you can.

Instant PET by Martyn Ford © Cambridge University Press 2007 **PHOTOCOPIABLE**

Getting the message

Warm up

Give out the activity sheets.

Look at exercise **1** and tell students this is a typical rubric for PET Writing Part 2. Elicit from them what problems candidates might have with this task in the actual exam. What kind of mistakes might they make? Here are some examples:

Their message is too short.
Their message is too long.
They don't cover all three points in the rubric.
Their message contains irrelevant material.
The information in their message is in the wrong order.
Their message is difficult to understand because of basic errors.

Tell them they are going to look at four Writing Part 2 tasks and sample answers to the tasks. Each sample answer has something wrong with it that needs to be corrected.

Main activities

Students can do these activities in pairs or small groups, though they should do the writing on their own.

1 The fault in the first message is in the sequencing. The writer needs first to state what she wants to tell the teacher about the lesson, i.e. that she will have to miss it; second, the reason for this, and thirdly what she intends to do afterwards. The three comprehension questions are intended to direct students to this more logical order.

2 The fault in the second message is the length. Students can simply cross out the sentences that are not necessary for the task (they don't have to do any actual rewriting).

NOTE: Cutting can be difficult where all the material is stylistically right for the communication, and students may differ in the way they edit this text. But they should keep in mind the three points for inclusion listed in the rubric and be ruthless about cutting other material. Obviously, care should be taken not to cut material in a way that affects coherence.

3 The fault in the third message is in the accuracy of the language. Students should discuss the mistakes in pairs, noting them on the sheet, and then rewrite the whole message.

4 The fault in the fourth message is that it has not answered all parts of the question. Tanya doesn't actually invite Becky or suggest a time for her to come and see the puppy.

5 Give out photocopies of the model answers on this page for students to check and revise their own work.

Follow up

The following exercise gives students freer practice in writing short messages of different types. For example, they can be invitations, arrangements to meet, requests, apologies, congratulations or thank you notes.

*   Give each student four or five small pieces of paper. These should be large enough for a short message (35–45 words) plus a reply of the same length.
*   Students write a different message on each piece of paper. The messages shouldn't be addressed to a named individual and students shouldn't sign them.
*   As soon as they have written their messages, they fold them and put them on your desk. As

they do so, they pick up other notes from the desk and reply to them (again, they needn't sign their name).

*   They put their replies back on the desk and collect the replies to their notes.
*   Selected students read their messages aloud to the whole class, who have to guess what the reply was. The student then reads out the reply given.

✂----

Model answers

1   Dear Mrs Judd,

I'm sorry, but I have to miss your lesson today. My mother has a doctor's appointment and so I have to go home and look after my little sister. I'll get the important notes and homework topic from one of my classmates tomorrow.

Kitty   [43 words excluding names]

2   Hi Hilary,

Nice to hear from you. It would great to see you again, but I'm afraid Saturday 8th April is not possible as I'm going to a wedding that day. What about Sunday 9th instead?

Could you let me know?

Cheers,

Andrew   [40 words excluding names]

3   *Susie,*

Thanks for returning my DVD, but I think you've made a mistake – the box is empty! Could you look for my disk at home, please? I'll bring the empty box to school tomorrow. Hope you can find it!

Ivan   [38 words excluding names]

4   Becky,

Hi! Guess what – I've just been given a beautiful puppy. He's a golden labrador and he's so sweet. You'll love him, I'm sure. Would you like to come round and see him? How about Friday after school, if you're free?

Love,

Tanya   [40 words excluding names]

✂----

Getting the message

1
You have to leave school early and will miss an important lesson. Write a note for the teacher. In your note, you should
- apologise for missing the lesson
- give your reason
- explain what you will do about the work that you miss.

Write 35–45 words.

Read this sample answer.

Dear Mrs Judd,
I'll get the important notes and homework topic from one of my classmates tomorrow. My mother has a doctor's appointment and so I have to go home and look after my little sister. I'm sorry, but I have to miss your lesson today.
Kitty

- What does Kitty want to tell the teacher about the lesson?
- Why does she have to look after her little sister?
- What will Kitty do about the work she has missed?

The information in Kitty's letter is in the wrong order. Using your answers to the questions, rewrite it in the correct order.

2
A friend has sent you an email asking if he can come and visit you for the day. You would like to see him, but the date he suggests is not convenient. Write a reply. In your email you should
- thank him for his message
- explain that the date he suggests is not convenient
- suggest an alternative date.

Write 35–45 words.

Look at this sample answer. Which sentences can you cut to make it less than 45 words?

Hi Hilary,
Nice to hear from you. We haven't seen each other since Judy's party last Christmas. (Have you heard from her, by the way?) It would great to see you again, but I'm afraid Saturday 8th April is not possible as I'm going to a wedding that day. I'm not the bridegroom, don't worry! It's my cousin Laura, who's marrying an airline pilot from Sri Lanka. What about Sunday 9th instead? I don't have anything to do that day, and I'll be able to tell you how the wedding went. Could you let me know?

Cheers,   [95 words excluding names and opening and
Andrew   closing salutations]

Work with a partner. Read each other's messages and compare how you have cut the text. Which version works better?

3
Your friend has returned a DVD she borrowed from you, but the box is empty. Write a note to her. In it you should
- thank her for returning the DVD
- point out her mistake
- ask her to look for it.

Write 35–45 words.

Look at this sample answer. There are no problems with the length and content, but there are ten grammar and spelling mistakes. Underline all the mistakes and rewrite the corrected message.

Susie,
Tanks for return my DVD, but I think you've done a mistake — the box it is empty! You could look for my disk in home, please? I bring the empty box at school tomorow.
Hope you can to find it!
Ivan

4
You've just been given a new pet. Write an email to your friend Becky. In it you should
- tell Becky the news about your new pet
- invite her to come and see it
- suggest a day and time for her to come.

Write 35–45 words.

Look at this sample answer. What's missing? Rewrite it so that it answers all three parts of the question.

Becky,
Hi! Guess what — I've just been given a beautiful puppy! He's a golden labrador and he's so sweet. You'll love him, I'm sure. I haven't thought of a name for him yet. Oops! Must go — he's trying to eat one of my shoes!
Love,
Tanya

5 **Your teacher will give you model answers to exercises 1–4. Correct or revise your own answers if necessary.**

Missing pieces

Here are two examples of questions for PET Writing Part 2. (Remember, in this question the answer should be 35–45 words.)

1 It's your last day at school. A classmate you really like is absent so you can't say goodbye to her. Write her a note. In it you should

- say you're sorry not to have seen her today
- tell her how much you have enjoyed studying with her
- wish her good luck and suggest that you both keep in touch.

2 Some friends lent you their summer house for a holiday. Write a note to them. In it you should

- thank them for their kindness
- say something about your holiday
- invite your friends to come and visit you.

Two incomplete model answers to these questions follow.

Here are *two* of the *four* points needed to complete the messages. Copy these into the right parts of each answer. Then write the other missing points to complete each message.

I visited lots of the places you recommended and I had a really great holiday.

Sorry to have missed you today.

1

Hello Maya,

-- It's my last day at school and I wanted to say goodbye.
-- Good luck with everything, and let's keep in touch, shall we? Take care.

Love,

Karin

2

Dear Paolo and Francesca,

It was so kind of you to lend me your summer house.
-- You must come and visit me soon. ---

Best wishes,

Nazim

Exam-style task

Hints and tips for Writing Part 2

Hints and tips for Writing Part 2

What you have to do

- You must write a message to someone. It may be a note, a card or an email.
- The instructions tell you who you are writing to and why.
- Your message must include the three points listed.
- Your message must be 35–45 words in length.

How to approach it

- Think about the question carefully and plan what to include in your answer.
- You will not lose marks for minor errors but your message must be clear and well organised.
- Check that you have included each of the three points in the list.

- Check that you have kept to the word limit: answers that are too long or too short will probably lose marks.

How to prepare yourself

- It is important to understand the following verbs: *apologise, ask, explain, invite, suggest, tell* and *thank*.
- Work on your punctuation and spelling. See *Objective PET* page 21 and *Insight into PET* page 51, published by Cambridge University Press.
- Practise writing messages that are between 35 and 45 words long, giving yourself a time limit.
- Work with another student and compare what you have written. Rewrite your messages to improve them.
- If you can, practise outside the class by writing short emails in English to other students.

See page 143 for the Answers.

PART 2

A month ago your friend, David, borrowed your tent to go on a camping holiday. He still hasn't returned it and you want to use it yourself next week for a camping trip.

Write an email to David. In your email, you should

- ask him about his camping holiday
- explain that you need your tent
- suggest a time tomorrow when you could come and collect it.

Write **35–45 words**.

I'd be lost without it

Warm up

Optional: Show the class a personal possession you have brought in. Don't say too much about it but get them to ask you questions about it. For example:
How long have you had it?
Did you buy it or did someone give it to you?
Why is it important to you?
Guide and correct as you go along.
AND/OR
Introduce the idea of personal possessions and how to describe them by reading out the **riddles** below. Each riddle describes someone's most important possession. Each one consists of three sentences, containing three clues. The third clue is the easiest, so the challenge for the students is to guess the object with the first or second clue. You can emphasise the game-playing element by adding a scoring system:
FIRST clue = 3 points; SECOND clue = 2 points; THIRD clue = 1 point.
Students only have one guess after each sentence.

Riddles

They easily fit into my bag or pocket.
They are made of plastic and a small amount of metal.
I need them every day to see what I'm doing.
Answer = glasses

It's made of plastic.
I keep it in my wallet.
I use it when I pay for things.
Answer = a credit card

It's long and thin and made of wood, metal and nylon cord.
I hang something from the end of it.
I take it to the river to practise a particular sport.
Answer = a fishing rod

It's soft and furry.
It was given to me by my grandparents when I was two years old.
It's an animal, but not a real one.
Answer = a teddy bear

Main activities

Students can do these activities in pairs or small groups, though they should do the writing on their own.

1 Give out the activity sheets.

The emphasis in this writing activity is on *fluency and quantity*. Tell students not to worry about mistakes at this stage, as the important thing is their ideas. Discourage them from stopping to look words up in the dictionary or checking spelling.

Students may want further clarification of what is or is not a personal possession (though this is dealt with in more detail in exercise **2**).

Stop them after 3 minutes.

Don't discuss what they have written yet, but ask them to put it aside for later in the lesson.

2 Go through the examples first.

Answers

Possessions (✓): a ring my grandmother gave me, my car, my pet snake, Zsa Zsa (though this is debatable), my saxophone, my computer, a silver cup I won in a swimming race

Not possessions (✗): playing basketball, my family, the sports club I go to, Christmas

3 Again, it may help if you go through the examples first.

Suggested answers

1 saxophone **2** tennis racket, car, saxophone, computer
3 tennis racket, car, saxophone, computer **4** tennis racket, car, saxophone, computer, pet snake **5** ring, car, saxophone, computer, cup **6** all **7** ring, cup **8** car, computer, tennis racket **9** ring **10** all

4 Go through the dialogue before asking students to complete the answers.

Suggested answers
1 I'm not sure how valuable it is, but it may be worth a few hundred euros.
2 I don't know who made it, but I don't think it was anyone famous.
3 I'm not sure what it's made of, but I think it may be bronze.
4 I don't know why he gave it to me, but I'm very grateful to him!
5 I'm not sure who it is, but it could be an athlete.
6 I don't know how long it's been in the family, but my grandfather got it from his father.

5 In this guided speaking activity, students look back at the short texts they wrote at the beginning of the lesson, and they read them aloud in pairs or small groups. (If they are diffident about the quality of their writing – which was done quickly without any emphasis on accuracy – they can paraphrase what they wrote.)

The other group members ask questions (they can use those in exercise **3** and add their own as appropriate).

Follow up

For this exam-style task, students can write about the same possession they described in exercise **1**, or a different one.
This time, accuracy and organisation of ideas will be as important as fluency. With this in mind, it may be helpful to give them these check questions:
What is your Canadian friend's most important possession? (Mobile phone)
Why is it important/special? (He/She wouldn't be able to keep in touch with friends without it)
What possession are you going to write about in your reply?
How many words should your letter be? (100)

I'd be lost without it

1 Choose any personal possession you have at home. You have 3 minutes to write as much as you can about it. Keep your writing for later.

2 A group of students was asked the question *What is your favourite possession?* Here are their answers. However, some of them are not possessions. Which ones? Put a tick (✓) or a cross (✗).

my tennis racket ✓ Reason – you can own a tennis racket

my boyfriend ✗ Reason – you can't own a person

a ring my grandmother gave me

my car

playing basketball

my family

my pet snake, Zsa Zsa

my saxophone

the sports club I go to

Christmas

my computer

a silver cup I won in a swimming race

3 Look again at the items with a tick (✓). Which of the following questions can you ask about them? (Some questions can be asked about more than one item.)

1 How often do you play it?   saxophone

2 Was it new or second-hand when you got it?
tennis racket, car, saxophone, computer

3 Does anyone else use it?

4 Was it a present or did you buy it yourself?

5 Is it in good condition?

6 Where do you keep it?

7 Is it valuable?

8 What make is it?

9 What's it made of?

10 Is it the first one you've ever owned?

4 Sometimes we don't know the answer to a question, or we are not sure about it. It's important to say that, too! Look at this dialogue. Note the position of the subject pronoun and the verb in the answers (shown in bold).

A: *My most important possession is this little statue.*

B: Where did it come from?

A: *I don't know **where it came from**, but it was given to me by my grandfather.*

B: How old is it?

A: *I'm not sure **how old it is**, but I think it's at least a hundred and fifty years old.*

Now complete the answers to these questions, each time using *I don't know …* or *I'm not sure …*

1 **B**: How valuable is the statue?

A: ...., *but it may be worth a few hundred euros.*

2 **B**: Who made it?

A: ...., *but I don't think it was anyone famous.*

3 **B**: What material is it made of?

A: ...., *but I think it may be bronze.*

4 **B**: Why did your grandfather give it to you?

A: ...., *but I'm very grateful to him!*

5 **B**: Who is the figure?

A: ...., *but it could be an athlete.*

6 **B**: How long has it been in the family?

A: ...., *but my grandfather got it from his father.*

5 Now work in pairs or groups of three. Read to each other the description you wrote at the beginning of the lesson. Using the list in exercise 3, ask and answer questions about each other's possessions.

Follow up

This is part of a letter you receive from a Canadian friend.

My mobile phone is my most important possession. I use it every day to call or text my friends and if I lost it I wouldn't be able to keep in touch with them. What about you? What's your most important possession and why is it special to you?

Now write a letter telling your friend about your most important possession. Don't forget to say why it's special to you. Write about 100 words.

Fighting fit

EXAM PART
Writing Part 3

EXAM SKILLS
Writing a letter to
a friend

Keeping to the
required length
(100 words)

TOPIC
Diet and health

TIME
50 minutes

KEY LANGUAGE
Food and drink
vocabulary

Talking about habits

Comparing and
contrasting

PREPARATION
One photocopy of
the activity page for
each student

Optional: bring in
examples of food
packaging for the
Warm up

Warm up

Introduce the topic with these questions:
How many meals a day do you usually have? Which is the biggest meal?
What time do you usually have your main meal?
Are there any foods you can't eat, for example because you are allergic to them?
AND/OR
Try this 'Calorie quiz'. Tell students that calories are units used to measure the energy value of foods. People who are on diets try to eat foods that don't contain many calories. To give students some help, tell them there are 143 calories in a banana weighing 150 grams.
NOTE: Diet, health and body shape can be very sensitive topics for teenage learners. If this quiz and any resulting discussion could prove difficult for some individuals in your class, it may be advisable to omit it.

Calorie quiz
How many calories do you think there are in the following? (The correct answers are given in **bold**.)

1	A medium-sized egg weighing 57 grams	62	**84**	121
2	A chocolate bar weighing 65 grams	**294**	332	415
3	An apple weighing 112 grams	29	40	**53**
4	100 ml of whole milk	**64**	73	93
5	A Big Mac weighing 215 grams	373	**492**	605
6	100 grams of chips	213	**294**	38
7	100 grams of mushrooms	52	94	**157**
8	1 slice of wholemeal bread weighing 36 grams	39	56	**79**

Optional: Show students the food packaging you have brought in. Ask them to guess the number of calories in them. Once you have given out the activity pages, you could ask them to rate the foods using the scale in exercise **1**.

Main activities

Students can do these activities in pairs or small groups, though they should do the writing on their own.

1 Give out the activity sheets if you haven't already done so.
To help students with this task, write *Breakfast, Lunch, Dinner* and *Snacks* on the board.
Explain *nutritious* and *in moderation*.
Help students negotiate any difficult vocabulary in this production phase. In monolingual classes some translation may be necessary.
NOTE: A pairwork discussion of lists and results is possible at this point. However, diet and health can be a sensitive topic. If such a discussion may prove difficult for some individuals in the class, then leave the results for private reflection and move on to **2**.

2 Before they write their alternative menus of healthier options, ask students to think about which foods and drinks in Paul's diet are not very healthy, and why. For example: *Too much coffee is not good for you; a lot of sugar is unhealthy; a piece of cake contains fat and sugar but not many vitamins.*
Their alternatives will probably include more fresh fruit and vegetables, fish, chicken, nuts, and so on, though you might like to suggest that Paul be allowed one or two 'treats' in his new regime!
When they've written the alternative menu, the pairs can form groups of four. They read each other's menus and discuss their suggestions.

3 Present the task and check students' understanding with questions 1–4.
You can ask students what they would put in their reply, though this phase should be brief and should not distract from the main aim, which is looking at how to approach and organise a letter for Writing Part 3.

Answers
1 given up　**2** diet　**3** fizzy　**4** avoid

4 The best opening is **B**. It retains the friendly style of the original letter and starts with a general response to it. **A** and **C** sound too abrupt and introduce detail too soon. 'What about you?' is not appropriate so early in the reply.

5 Students read the reply carefully. It answers the question but goes into too much detail. Their task is to edit it down from 210 words to around 100 (this includes opening **B** but not the closing salutation).

Suggested answer
Nice to hear from you. I'm sure you're doing the right thing, though it's difficult, isn't it?
I think I have quite a healthy diet. I eat a large portion of salad every day and I enjoy fruit of all kinds. I have fast food meals occasionally with friends, but I don't think it's a problem. I haven't put on weight recently, and I feel fit and well.
No, there aren't any things I particularly avoid. On the other hand, I think I eat a bit too much chocolate. I don't want to give it up completely, but I think I should cut down a bit.
Keep in touch.
Cheers,
Jess
[109 words]

Follow up

This choice of tasks may be done for homework or as a timed practice in class.

Fighting fit

1 Make a list of everything you ate and drank yesterday. You have 2 minutes.

Give the items on your list a Health and nutrition rating from 0–3.

0 = not very healthy or nutritious

1 = OK if eaten in moderation

2 = good for you

3 = very healthy

Add up your Health and nutrition score.

2 Paul doesn't have a very healthy diet. This is what he eats and drinks on a typical day. Work in pairs. Write out an alternative menu of healthier options.

7.30	Two cups of strong coffee with sugar
11.00	A cup of coffee; a chocolate bar
12.30	Cheeseburger and fries; a can of coke
4.30	A cup of tea; a piece of cake
8.00	Macaroni cheese with broccoli and carrots; ice cream
9.30	A bag of salt and vinegar crisps; a glass of warm milk

Now work with another pair. Read each other's menus.

- Which menu do you think is healthier?
- Which would you *enjoy* more?

3 This is part of a letter you receive from an English friend.

> I've given up fast food and fizzy drinks and I'm trying to have a healthier diet. What about you? Are you careful about what you eat and drink? Are there any things you avoid?

Find the word or phrase in the extract that means the following.

1 stopped having ..given up........

2 everything you usually eat and drink

....

3 (of drinks) with bubbles in ....

4 don't have / keep away from ....

4 Here are different openings for the reply. Which do you prefer and why?

> **A** *No. I eat anything I want. I don't like tomatoes, though.*
>
> **B** *Nice to hear from you. I'm sure you're doing the right thing, though it's difficult, isn't it?*
>
> **C** *Every day for breakfast I have a glass of orange juice and a piece of toast. What about you?*

5 Here is the rest of the reply.

> *I think I have quite a healthy diet. I'm not very keen on cooked vegetables, but I eat a large portion of salad every day. I enjoy fruit of all kinds and I know that it's very good for you. For breakfast I usually have chopped fruit like apples, dates and bananas with my muesli, and I always take an apple to eat after lunch. At home we often have fruit as a dessert: my favourites are grapes and watermelon.*
>
> *You mentioned that you've given up fast food. I have fast food meals occasionally at weekends, when I'm out in town with my friends, but I don't think it's a problem. I mean, I haven't put on weight recently, and I feel fit and well.*
>
> *In answer to your other question: no, there aren't any things I particularly avoid. On the other hand, I think I eat a bit too much chocolate. It's such a temptation when you feel hungry and need a bit of energy quickly. I have a bar nearly every day on my way home from school. I don't want to give it up completely, but I think I should cut down a bit and maybe have it only once or twice a week.*
>
> *Keep in touch.*
>
> *Cheers,*
>
> *Jess*

The letter answers the question, but it is too long (210 words). Can you cut it down to about 100 words?

Follow up

This is part of a letter you receive from a friend in the United States.

> I've recently started going to cookery classes and I'm really enjoying it. As well as trying out meat and fish recipes from all over the world, we're learning how to bake our own bread and cakes. Are you interested in cooking? What do you like making? Who is the best cook in your family?

Write the reply, answering your friend's questions about cooking. Your letter should be about 100 words.

OR

Write a story beginning with this sentence:

> It was my best friend's birthday and so I decided to bake a cake for her.

Your story should be about 100 words.

What happened next?

Warm up

A story circle

This activity may not produce writing of a very high *quality* but it is a fun, collaborative way into a skill that many students feel is difficult and even dull. It frees the imagination, encourages fluency and can generate a lot of laughter too!

Students all need a sheet of lined paper to write on. Arrange the students in circles of 4–6.

Dictate **one** of these opening sentences to the class:

I was on my way to interview one of the most famous movie stars in the country. OR

The next time I saw George, he looked completely different.

Each person has to write the **second** sentence of the story.

They then pass their paper to the next person in the circle.

Everyone reads the two sentences and then adds a third and passes the paper on.

This continues until each paper has come back to its owner.

It is important that everyone is in step, so you may need to give students a time limit of 1 or 2 minutes for each sentence.

When everyone has their own paper back, they have to read the whole thing and add a concluding sentence. Students then take it in turns to read the resulting stories (which will probably be fairly crazy!) aloud to the class.

Main activities

Students can do these activities in pairs or small groups, though they should do the writing on their own.

1 Rather than giving out the activity sheets immediately, you may want to write the opening sentence on the board and elicit questions and answers from the students.

They may suggest further questions like these:

Who will be at the party? Children, teenagers, adults, people of all ages?

Why doesn't the narrator want to go to the party?

Why does the narrator have to go?

What happens at the party? Something bad (which is what the narrator expects) or something good (which the narrator did not expect)?

Then give out the activity sheets and go straight to exercise **2**.

2 Read the three possible ways this story could develop. Ask students which they prefer. Invite other ideas for development.

Students then write their own fourth scenario.

Ask students to compare their results with a partner. Or you may prefer to ask a few individuals to read their scenario aloud to the class.

3 The aim is for students to think quickly but also to consider different options (one of the things that can go wrong in writing a story in the exam is embarking too quickly on an unpromising route, and then finding it difficult to develop or finish the story).

Students will probably come up with questions of this kind:

Why were you surprised? What was the sport? Were you good at it or not? What team was it? Were they going to play an important game? Why did they choose you? What happened next? How did the game go? Did you play well? What was the result? How did you feel?

4 Working in groups of three or four, students make a compilation of all the different questions that were written. Monitor the groups to make sure incorrect or inappropriate sentences are rewritten or discarded.

Students create a mind map like the one in exercise **2**, with the opening sentence *I was very surprised when I was chosen to play for the team* in the middle and their alternative development ideas around it.

5 Working alone, students choose **one** of the alternative development ideas in the mind map (if possible, a different one for each member of the group).

They write the rest of the story.

Follow up

Students read each other's stories and discuss any interesting differences that they notice.

You could ask them to nominate 'best **closing** sentences', which you write on the board.

EXAM PART
Writing Part 3

EXAM SKILLS
Writing a story

Opening sentences

Developing a story

TOPIC
Parties; sports

TIME
50 minutes

KEY LANGUAGE
Questions

Past tenses in narrative

PREPARATION
One photocopy of the activity page for each student

Optional: extra writing paper for the **Warm up**

What happened next?

1

> I didn't want to go to the party but I had to.

This opening sentence could develop into many different stories. First we need to ask ourselves some questions about the situation. For example:

Who is the narrator (the person telling the story)? Male or female? A child or an adult?

Whose party is it?

Think of some more questions to ask, beginning with *who*, *why* and *what*.

2 Here are three different ways the story could develop. Think of a fourth idea of your own and write it in the box.

I was six years old. I knew that older, bigger children were going to be there. I knew they were going to play party games that I didn't like. I was scared.	I knew that my ex-boyfriend, Matt, would be there and I didn't want to see him, specially as he would be with his new girlfriend, Jane. I hated her!

> I didn't want to go to the party but I had to.

I didn't know any of the people who were going to the party. I knew I'd end up sitting on my own while everyone else was chatting happily.	

3 Here is the opening to another story:

> I was very surprised when I was chosen to play for the team.

Write as many questions as you can about the situation (look back at the questions in exercise 1 for ideas).

4 Work in small groups. Read out all the *different* questions you have written about the story in exercise 3. Discuss the different possible answers.

Design a mind map like the one in exercise 2, with the opening sentence of the story in the middle and your alternative development ideas around it.

5 Choose one of the alternative development ideas in the mind map (it's a good idea if each member of the group chooses a different one).

Write the rest of the story, using about 100 words.

Follow up

Read each other's stories.

Never mind!

1 **Work with a partner. Look at the pictures and put them in the best order to make a story by numbering them 1–6.**

What happened? Tell the story to each other.

Now work with another pair and listen to their version of the story.

2 **Read this example answer to exercise 1. Fill the gaps with one of the phrases below.**

It was a Saturday afternoon ..and I was at home with my younger brother, Daniel. We couldn't go outside

_____ , so we decided to play football in the sitting room. The score was

3–2 _____ . Unfortunately, I kicked the ball too hard, hit the old silver clock

above the fireplace _____ . We thought our mother would be furious, but

all she said was, 'Oh well, _____ ! I never liked that clock, anyway.' She

even let us continue with our game, _____ !

and broke it into pieces	though this time it was volleyball, using a balloon
because it was raining	never mind, it can't be helped
and I was at home with my younger brother, Daniel ✓	and I was trying to equalise

Exam-style task

PART 3

Answer one of the following questions (1 or 2).

Question 1

- You have to write a story for your English teacher.
- Your story must have this title:

A meeting on the beach

- Write your **story** in about 100 words.

Question 2

- This is part of a letter you receive from an English-speaking friend.

> *I live in a three-bedroom house with a small garden. The area's quiet, and a bit far from the city centre, but my neighbours are friendly. Where do you live? What's the area like? Do you know your neighbours?*

- Now write a letter answering your friend's questions.
- Write your **letter** in about 100 words.

Instant PET by Martyn Ford © Cambridge University Press 2007   **PHOTOCOPIABLE**

Hints and tips for Writing Part 3

What you have to do

- Choose between two writing tasks, a letter and a story.

- Write about 100 words.

- For the story, you are given either the first sentence or a title. You may need to write in either the first person (*I* …) or the third person (*he/she* …).

- For the letter, you are given an extract from a letter which you must imagine is written to you. It will usually contain a few questions and you should answer these in your reply to the letter.

How to approach it

- Write about the topic or title given – don't include material you have prepared in advance.

- If you choose the story, ask yourself *who, what, when, where* and *how*? This will help to give you ideas.

- If you choose the letter, write your reply in a natural, informal style.

- Make sure you write around 100 words. You may lose marks if your answer is too short.

- Leave enough time to read your answer carefully. Check for verb tenses, vocabulary, spelling and punctuation. Ask yourself: 'Does it clearly communicate the message?'

How to prepare yourself

- Look at some sample compositions for this part of the test. (See page 51 of *Insight into PET*, published by Cambridge University Press; there is also a checklist of six questions to ask yourself when writing a letter.)

- Practise writing stories and letters of about 100 words with a time limit of about **20 minutes**.

- Find texts in English that interest you and bring them to class to share and discuss.

- Read graded readers and write short reviews of them. There are lots of excellent abridged and simplified readers in English, for learners at all levels. See www.cambridge.org/elt.

- If possible, exchange emails or letters with English-speaking friends.

Answers

It was a Saturday afternoon **and I was at home with my younger brother, Daniel**. We couldn't go outside **because it was raining**, so we decided to play football in the sitting room. The score was 3–2 **and I was trying to equalise**. Unfortunately, I kicked the ball too hard, hit the old silver clock above the fireplace **and broke it into pieces**. We thought our mother would be furious, but all she said was, 'Oh well, **never mind, it can't be helped!** I never liked that clock, anyway.' She even let us continue with our game, **though this time it was volleyball, using a balloon!**

[110 words]

EXAM PART
Listening Part 1

EXAM SKILLS
Matching short texts
to correct pictures

Listening for specific
information

Eliminating
distractors

TOPIC
Descriptions of
people
(appearance)

TIME
40 minutes (60
minutes with the
Warm up role-play)

KEY LANGUAGE
Vocabulary for
physical appearance,
including clothes and
accessories

PREPARATION
One photocopy of the
activity page for each
student

Optional: bring in
photographs of people
cut out of newspapers
or magazines for the
Warm up, or ask your
students to bring them
in. They can be famous
or unknown but should
represent a variety of
human types, ages and
styles of dress. It's a
good idea if some of the
pictures show full-length
figures.

Optional: photocopies
of the Tapescript for
exercise **2** (see page
124)

Distinguishing features

Warm up

- Working in pairs, students stand back to back and describe each other out loud. This can include such things as height (*you're taller than me*), eye colour, hair type, clothes and accessories. Then they turn round and face each other and talk about what they didn't (or couldn't) describe, or what they remembered wrongly.
  OR
- For this activity you need to know something of the content of the photos you or the students have brought in. Give one photo to each student. They then stand in a circle, holding their pictures. Give instructions as follows, based on details in their photos:
  Stand in the middle if your person has dark hair.
  Stand in the middle if your person is smartly dressed.
  Stand in the middle if your person is smiling.
  And so on.
  As the students come into the middle, ask them to hold their photo up so everyone can see it. Compare and contrast.
  OR
- **Role-play** Students work in groups of three. Two of them work as detectives in a **Missing persons bureau**. The third plays the client, who is searching for a missing relative or friend.
  (Time permitting, discuss the different reasons why a person might go missing.) Give each of the clients one of the photos to look at and ask them to withdraw while they look carefully at it. They should try to remember as much as possible of the physical appearance of the person in the picture. They should also think of a name for the person and decide on their relationship to him/her. More confident students may also like to improvise some details about the missing person's life and the circumstances surrounding their disappearance.
  While the client is preparing this (2–3 minutes), ask the remaining students – who are going to play the detectives – what questions they are going to ask the client about the missing person. For example:
  How old is he/she?
  What does he/she look like?
  What was he/she wearing when you last saw him/her?
  Use this opportunity to revise vocabulary for physical appearance, dress, etc. (For further practice on this topic, see **Speaking Part 3 Activity 3**.)
  Bring back the clients and take the photos from them. Form groups of three. The detectives now have to get as much information about the missing person as possible.
  Meanwhile, place all the photos on the floor, at some distance from the students.
  When they are ready, ask one of the detectives in each group to describe, in a few sentences, the person they are looking for.
  Finally, ask the detectives to come and find the missing person from amongst the photos on the floor. (It obviously helps if there are a few extra photos to serve as distractors.)

Main activities

Students do some of these activities alone and the others in pairs or small groups.

1 Give out the activity sheets.
Encourage students to describe the people in the picture as fully as they can. Partners shouldn't forestall the description by immediately jumping in with a guess.

2 ▶▶| Play the recording. Students listen and draw lines from the names to people in the picture. Make sure they know what a *distractor* is. **See page 124 for the Tapescript**.

Answers
Top row: Hiro, distractor; Peter, distractor; distractor, Sophie
Bottom row: distractor, Clara; Antonio, distractor; distractor, Esra; Anna is not mentioned.

3 ▶▶| Play the recording after students have labelled the items in the pictures. **See page 124 for the Tapescript**.

Answers
1 Luke   2 Will   3 Michelle

4 ▶▶| Play the recording. **See page 124 for the Tapescript**. When students are ready, they will want to compare their drawings.

Answer

Follow up

Students choose a photo of a person they know, or a picture of someone cut from a magazine. They attach it to a piece of paper (or stick it into their exercise book) and underneath, in approximately 50 words, they write a description of that person.
For ideas, give them a photocopy of the tapescript for exercise **2**. Ask students to list all the words and expressions that refer to: height/build, facial features, hair, expression and personality, clothes and accessories. Students then suggest more vocabulary to add to these categories.

Distinguishing features

1 This is a picture of Cristina's English class.

Anna   Antonio   Clara   Esra   Hiro   Peter   Sophie

Work with a partner. Take it in turns to describe some of the people in the picture. Your partner must point to the person you are describing.

2 ▶▶|Listen to Cristina talking about her classmates. Draw a line from the name of the student to the correct person in the picture. There is one extra name. To get the right answer you have to hear the important clues and avoid the *distractors*.

3 Three children, Will, Luke and Michelle have drawn pictures of pirates. Label these items in the pictures.

spotted scarf   earring   bushy beard   parrot

1 ....   2 ....   3 ....

▶▶| Listen to the recording. Under each picture write the name of the child who drew it.

4 ▶▶| Listen to the recording and draw the rest of this pirate.

How do you know?

Warm up

Give out the activity sheets.

Ask students to look at the pictures of buildings. Discuss the following questions:

What do you call these places?

Why do people go to these places? What happens there?

What different jobs do people do there?

Have you been to any of these places? What did you see or do there?

During the discussion, elicit (or supply) topic vocabulary related to each place, and write it on the board, under the appropriate heading. For example:

Art gallery

paintings   sculpture   works of art   exhibition   styles and periods   appreciate   boring (!)

Afterwards, rub out the new vocabulary but leave the headwords for a recall exercise later in the lesson.

Main activities

Students do some of these activities alone and the others in pairs or small groups.

1 ▶▶| Play the recording. Students write the number by the appropriate picture. There are two extra pictures that serve as distractors. **See page 125 for the Tapescript**.

Go over the answers to the exercise and then play the recording again. Stop after each section to ask:

How do you know the answer? What clues are there in the listening text?

Optional extension: Make one photocopy of the Tapescript (see page 125). Blank out ten key identifying words or expressions, e.g. *creature, cage = zoo*. Make photocopies for the whole class. Students listen again and fill in the blanks.

Answers

1 Hospital	**2** Hotel	**3** Post office	**4** Zoo	**5** Airport
6 Swimming pool		

2 ▶▶| In this exercise, students get further practice in matching short recorded texts to visuals. This time the vocabulary area is objects and their functions. Play the example first and then the other seven sections. **See page 125 for the Tapescript**.

Answers

1 C   **2** A   **3** C   **4** B   **5** A   **6** A   **7** B

3 ▶▶| This exercise gives students more focused practice in listening for identifying words or expressions. Play the recording for exercise **2** again, stopping after each section to discuss the words they have written down and why they chose them.

Go through the **example** with them first.

Key words or expressions: *smell* – flowers smell, but so does perfume and so do some vegetables; *from ... garden* – flowers grow in a garden, but so can vegetables; *vase* – this word tells us that **C** is the correct answer – you don't put vegetables or perfume in a vase!

Follow up

Game: What on earth ...?

Students work in pairs. Give each pair a cue card with a topic for conversation (see below). Their task is to improvise a simple conversation about the topic *without giving away exactly what it is*. Allow them a few minutes to prepare what to say, and then ask a pair of more confident students to come to the front and sit facing the others, like the panel in a TV discussion show. They begin their 'secret conversation'. When someone in the audience thinks they know what the topic is, they put their hand up. The class only has three guesses, and they must get the exact wording on the card. If all three guesses are incorrect, the pair speaking are the winners. Repeat the process with the other pairs.

Here is an example:

A: *Have you got one?*

B: *Yes, I have. I used it last summer.*

A: *Why? Where did you go?*

B: *I went to England. What about you – have you got one?*

A: *Yes. It's got an awful photo of me inside, which was taken five years ago.*

B: *A friend of mine lost hers while she was on holiday in America. She had to get a special document from our embassy.*

C: *I think you're talking about passports.*

Suggested topics

Dancing   Brothers and sisters   Fast food   Cartoons films (e.g. Tom & Jerry, The Simpsons)   Homework   Swimming in the sea   Pets   Hospitals   My neighbours   Motorbikes   Rain

---

EXAM PART
Listening Part 1

EXAM SKILLS
Matching short texts to correct pictures

Listening for specific information

Identifying a topic from key vocabulary

TOPIC
Descriptions of places and objects

TIME
50 minutes

KEY LANGUAGE
Vocabulary in context; collocations, e.g. *ride a bicycle, boil an egg*

PREPARATION
One photocopy of the activity page for each student

Optional: photocopies of the Tapescript for exercises 1 and 2 (see this page and page 125)

Optional: a cue card for each pair for the **Follow up** game

How do you know?

1 ▶▶| You will hear people talking about six of these places. Listen and write the appropriate number by the picture.

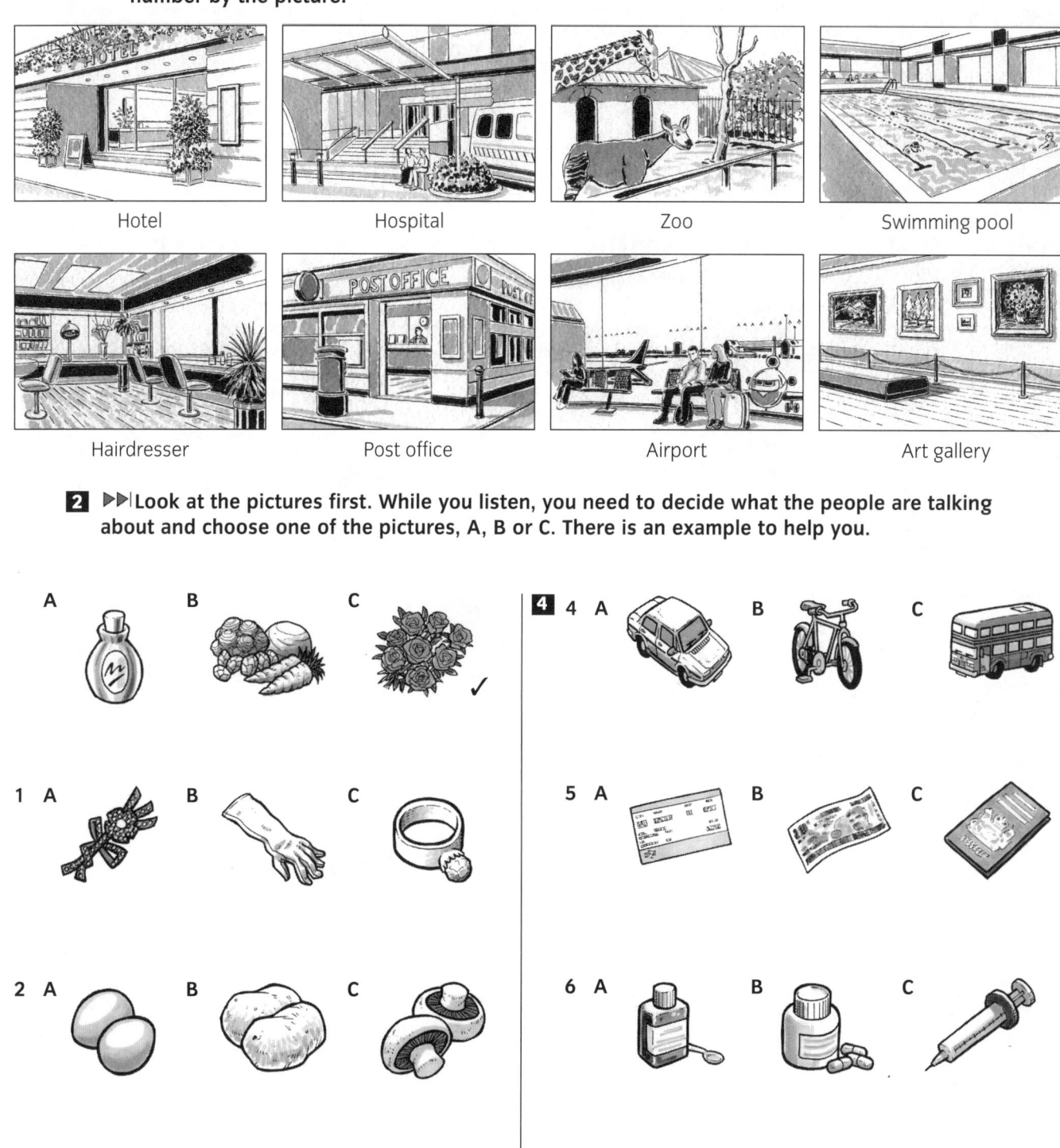

Hotel   Hospital   Zoo   Swimming pool

Hairdresser   Post office   Airport   Art gallery

2 ▶▶| Look at the pictures first. While you listen, you need to decide what the people are talking about and choose one of the pictures, A, B or C. There is an example to help you.

3 ▶▶| Listen to the recording again, and this time write down the key words or expressions that helped you to identify the correct subject in each section.

Look at the time!

Warm up

Tell students that in Listening Part 1, they may have to identify the correct time or the correct description of the weather from three possibilities on the recording, so both are covered in these two activities.

Introduce the topic of time by asking these questions:
What time is it now?
What time will it be in half an hour?
What time did you go to bed last night?
What time did you get up this morning?
What time of the day is noon?
What day and time is your favourite television programme?

Main activities

Students do some of these activities alone and the others in pairs or small groups.

1 Give out the activity sheets.
▶▶| Before you play the recording the first time, check that students understand *am* and *pm*.
See page 125 for the Tapescript.

Answers
The times: 10.20, 11.50, 2.35
The plane took off at 11.50.

2 Students can discuss the questions in pairs or small groups. If you have a group discussion, one member of each group should make a note of the main points of agreement and/or disagreement and then summarise them using this model:
We agreed that …
We didn't agree that … (A) thought that … , whereas (B) thought that …
▶▶| Play the recording after the discussion.
See page 125 for the Tapescript.

Answers
1 9 o'clock (pm)   **2** 7 o'clock (7 am)   **3** 10 (pm)

3 ▶▶| Play the recording. **See page 125 for the Tapescript.**

Answer
A

And now for the weather

Warm up

Introduce the topic by revising weather vocabulary. These questions provide a starting point for this:
What's the weather like here today?
What do you think the weather is like in these places at the moment? Note down at least three words for each place.
San Francisco   London   Moscow   Singapore   Cape Town

Main activities

1 This drawing/writing exercise is an opportunity to elicit or teach some more vocabulary relating weather to visuals. Students who are reluctant to draw will probably enjoy writing and reading out their artwork briefs for pictures B and C. For example: *Picture B shows a big sun in a clear blue sky. A girl is sitting on the beach wearing a bathing costume and sunglasses. She's eating an ice cream.*

2 ▶▶| Give students time to read the extract before you play the recording. The Tapescript is on the activity page.

Answers
B

the snow storms and freezing temperatures of the past ten days have come to an end; the bad news is that there is heavy rain, with the possibility of flooding in some areas.

3 ▶▶| Play the recording. You may want to tell students that this question follows the format of the exam. **See page 125 for the Tapescript.**

Answer
C

Follow up

Before students start writing, give out photocopies of the Tapescript for exercise **3** (or copy it onto the board) with blanks for the following words: *cloudy and cold, didn't have a drop of rain, wasn't hot, blue skies and sunshine.*
▶▶| Students fill in the gaps. Play the recording again and check their answers. This text and the text in exercise **2** will provide models for their writing.

Look at the time!

1 ▶▶I**Listen to the recording. Three times are mentioned. Draw hands on the clocks showing the three different times.**

A ☐   B ☐   C ☐

▶▶I**Listen again. What time did the plane take off? Tick the correct box.**

2 • What time in the evening do you think a 15-year-old girl should have to come back home?

• Should that time be different for a 15-year-old boy?

▶▶I**Listen to the conversation on the recording and answer these questions.**

1 What time must Tamsin come home this evening?

2 What time does Tamsin have to get up in the morning?

3 What time do her friends have to come home in the evening?

3 ▶▶I**Listen to the recording. What time should the woman take the cake out of the oven?**

A ☐   B ☐   C ☐

And now for the weather

1 **Describe picture A. What do you think pictures B and C will show? Make notes in the boxes or, if you prefer, quickly draw the pictures.**

A *Wet and windy*   B *Warm and sunny*   C *Wet but not windy*

2 ▶▶I**Read and listen to this extract about the weather.**

> I think a lot of us in Britain at the moment wish we could be with our friends in Australia, who are lying on the beach, enjoying temperatures of over 35 degrees. Lucky people! The good news here is that the snow storms and freezing temperatures of the past ten days have come to an end; the bad news is that there's heavy rain, with the possibility of flooding in some areas.

What is the weather like in Britain at the moment?

A snowy and cold ☐

B very wet ☐

C hot and sunny ☐

Underline the key words in the text that direct you to the correct answer.

3 ▶▶I**Listen to the recording. What kind of weather did the man have on his holiday?**

A ☐   B ☐   C ☐

Follow up

Write a weather forecast for tomorrow for *your* city or region. Use the texts in this activity as models to help you.

OR

Write a composition with this title:

The good and bad points of sunshine (or rain or snow). (Choose **one** of these.)

Write about 100 words.

Exam-style task

Hints and tips for Listening Part 1

What you have to do

- Listen to seven short recordings.

- For each recording, look at the question and the three pictures, A, B and C.

- Choose the picture that best answers the question about what you have heard.

How to approach it

- There are pauses in the recording during which you should look carefully at each question and the three pictures that go with it.

- You will hear each recording twice. The first time, listen for general meaning.

- The second time, listen for specific information and match it to one of the pictures. All the options will be mentioned in the text but only one will be the answer to the question.

How to prepare yourself

- The listening texts can be dialogues or monologues, for example, conversations – at home, at school, in the street – announcements on the radio, and extracts from talks. If you are studying in an English-speaking country, try to listen to as many of these varieties of English as possible. Also, try to listen to different voices and styles of speaking.

- If you are not studying in an English-speaking country, try to listen to English language broadcasts on the internet. Some of these are available as 'podcasts', which can be downloaded onto your computer and played on a portable MP3 player. Find programmes or podcasts about subjects you are interested in and listen to them when it suits you. It will also be helpful for you to watch films with an English language soundtrack. DVDs offer you the opportunity to choose the language you want to hear or to read subtitles to help understanding.

PART 1

Questions 1–7

- There are seven questions.
- For each question there are three pictures and a short recording.
- Choose the correct picture and put a tick (✔) in the box below it.

Example: Which is Isabel's favourite band?

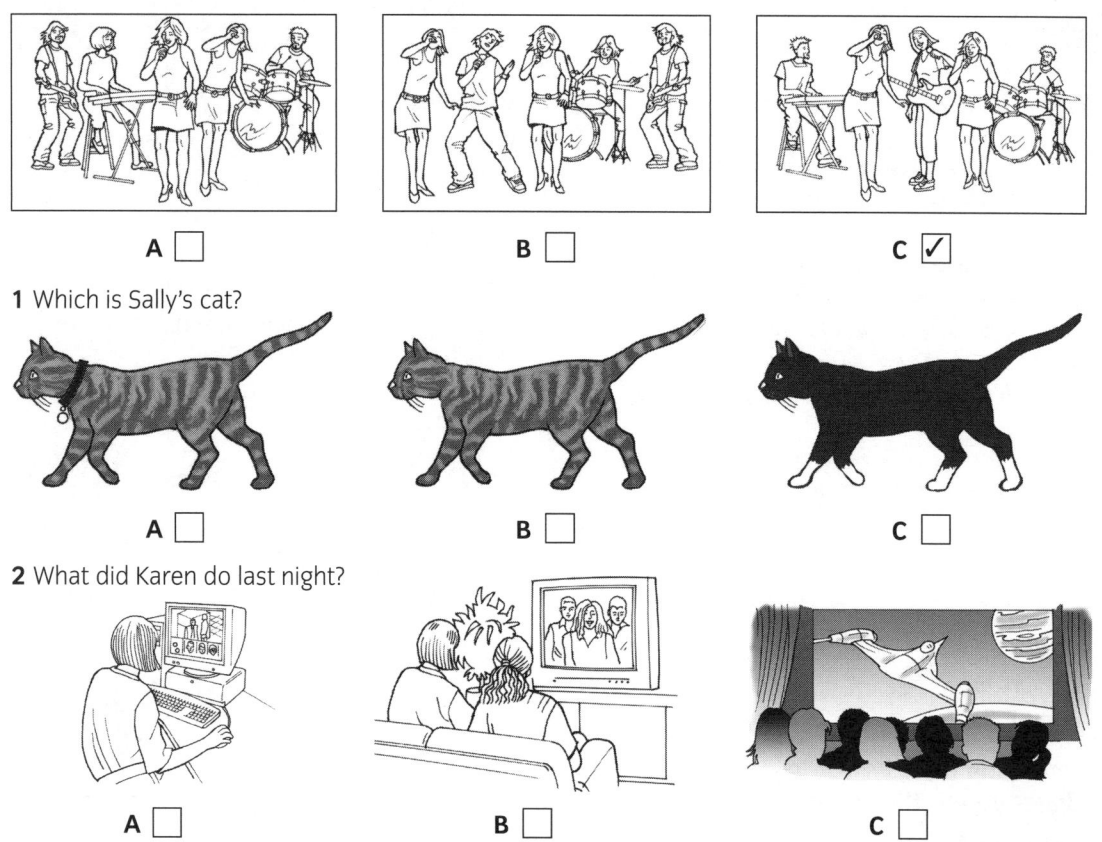

A ☐   B ☐   C ✔

1 Which is Sally's cat?

A ☐   B ☐   C ☐

2 What did Karen do last night?

A ☐   B ☐   C ☐

Instant PET by Martyn Ford © Cambridge University Press 2007 **PHOTOCOPIABLE**

3 What time did Tom catch the bus this morning?

A ☐

B ☐

C ☐

4 What is the best present for the man to buy?

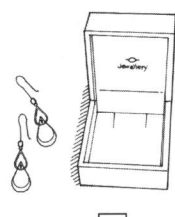

A ☐

B ☐

C ☐

5 What does the woman have?

A ☐

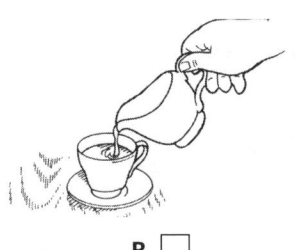

B ☐

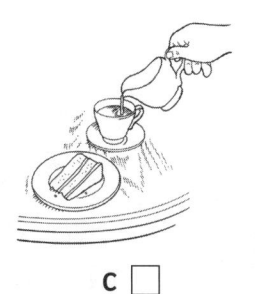

C ☐

6 Which book is Mandy looking for?

A ☐

B ☐

C ☐

7 Which computer game is the boy talking about?

A ☐

B ☐

C ☐

- ✂ - - -

Answers

1 B   **2** A   **3** C   **4** A   **5** C   **6** B   **7** B

See page 126 for the Tapescript.

EXAM PART
Listening Part 2

EXAM SKILLS
Multiple choice

Listening to a longer monologue

TOPIC
Radio broadcast

Tourist attractions

Shops and other amenities

TIME
50 minutes

KEY LANGUAGE
Vocabulary in context

PREPARATION
One photocopy of the activity page for each student

Optional: bring in maps, guides, flyers, etc. for your town; photocopies of the Tapescript for exercise **2** for the **Follow up**

The place to be

Warm up

Raise the subject of tourism with the students. It is an important part of the economy of many towns and cities, and there is a lot of competition between these places to attract visitors.
Write on the board this list of 'typical' tourist attractions:
A modern shopping centre with lots of fashionable shops
A historic town centre with old buildings of architectural interest
A public park with trees and flowers
Ask students if their town/city/village has any of these.
Students work in pairs or threes. They have to add as many visitor attractions as they can think of in 2 minutes.
Here are some suggestions:
Plenty of good hotels and restaurants
A large indoor sports and leisure centre
A nice beach nearby
Attractive tree-lined streets with pavement cafés
A traffic-free centre
A good museum and art gallery
Varied nightlife (clubs, discos, cinemas, theatres, concert halls)
Special annual events, e.g. a festival
Add their suggestions to the list on the board. In groups, or as a whole class, discuss:
Which of these would attract you to a place (choose three)?
Which three would be most attractive to these people?
Families with young children
Single people in their late teens/early twenties
Couples over 65

Main activities

Students do some of these activities alone and the others in pairs or small groups.

1 Give out the activity sheets.
Discuss the title with students. The answer is **C**.
Ask students to look at the map of the Quarter. Invite them to speculate about what different shops might sell and what they might find at a flea market.
▶▶| Students read and listen to the introduction to the feature and do the multiple-choice question (the Tapescript is on the activity page). This is to establish the purpose or rationale of the text and to prepare them for the longer listening tasks in **2** and **3**. The answer is **B**.
Check *how* they arrived at their answer. These questions may tease out any problems in comprehension:
What has happened to the Quarter over the last five years?
Which word in the text has the same meaning as quarter?

2 Students discuss the list of possible topics. (NOTE: There are no absolute correct answers to this pre-listening task. Its purpose is to familiarise them with the whole listening text and get them thinking about the topic.)
Invite their suggestions. This phase should be very brief.
▶▶| Students listen to the recording and amend their list accordingly. **See page 126 for the Tapescript**.

Answers
The feature talks about: The kind of things you can buy in the Quarter; Restaurants and cafés; Discounts for students; The kind of people you see in the Quarter.

3 ▶▶| Explain that these questions test their detailed understanding of the recording. **See page 126 for the Tapescript**. Classes in need of a challenge at this point can try it straight through. Classes needing more support can do it

one question at a time: pause to check answers and focus on tricky areas of comprehension. For example, check questions for question 1:
Where is the railway station?
Where are the big stores?

Answers
1 C   2 A   3 C   4 A   5 C   6 A

Follow up

Ask students to prepare a short talk. Tell them to think of an interesting place they know where they can go shopping and eat, drink and enjoy the surroundings. They should imagine that a local radio station has asked them to present a short piece (lasting only **1** minute) in which they describe this place. Give them these suggestions:
Make notes about the place you have chosen.
Does the place/area have a name?
Where is it?
Describe it (e.g. Are the streets wide or narrow? Are the shops large or small?)
What sort of people go there?
Describe one or two of the shops and cafés or restaurants.
What is the place/area like at different times?
They should then write their piece.

As it is for broadcasting on local radio, it is important that once you have corrected it, they practise reading it aloud with a partner. When practising, they should time themselves to make sure the talk is about 1 minute. To give them extra help in the form of a model, give them photocopies of the Tapescript (see page 126). If it is possible to record their 'broadcasts', this will give them an excellent incentive to work on their pronunciation. In this case, listen to their recordings and mark, on their written texts, any significant problems with pronunciation and sentence rhythm. There should, ideally, be a second 'take' where students can try again in the light of this feedback.

The place to be

The title of this activity, *The place to be,* means

A the place where you normally live.

B a place that hasn't been built yet.

C a fashionable, interesting place you would probably like.

▶▶|**Read and listen to this extract from a local radio programme, then answer the question.**

▶ ▶ ▶ ▶ ▶ ▶ ▶ ▶ ▶

Hello, there. You're listening to Radio Southcliffe FM. It's 12.20 and I'm Mark Wharton with our regular *In Town* feature on what to do and where to go. This week I'm talking about the *Quarter*, which over the last five years has become the fashionable area of our town for young people to shop, or eat and drink, or just hang out with friends.

▶ ▶ ▶ ▶ ▶ ▶ ▶ ▶ ▶

This part of the radio programme is about

A fashion over the last five years.

B a particular area of Southcliffe.

C the eating habits of young people.

2 **What do you think the rest of the radio feature will talk about? Tick your choices.**

The kind of things you can buy in the Quarter
Restaurants and cafés
Social problems in Southcliffe
Discounts for students
Hotel prices
How to make new friends
The kind of people you see in the Quarter
Nightclubs and discos

▶▶|**Listen and check your ideas.**

3 ▶▶|**Read the questions, then listen to the recording again. Choose the correct answer A, B, or C.**

1 The Quarter

  A has a railway station.

  B has famous name stores.

  C has many small shops.

2 On Tuesday afternoons Dave and Miranda

  A show people how to make kites.

  B show people how to fly kites.

  C give away free kites.

3 *Dressed to Kill* and *Togged Up* are popular because

  A the sales assistants are students.

  B they sell the top designer clothes.

  C their clothes are not very expensive.

4 When can you buy things at the *Flea Market*?

  A on Sunday mornings.

  B all day on Sunday.

  C six days a week.

5 The speaker says that the buskers

  A earn too much money.

  B sit on the pavement.

  C are good musicians.

6 The *Medina Barbecue*

  A has cheaper prices on certain days.

  B only serves takeaway meals.

  C only gets busy on Friday, Saturday and Sunday.

Sweet memory

Warm up

Discuss these questions with the students:
Did you get any pocket money when you were a child?
At what age did you start to get pocket money?
Did you / do you have to do any jobs in return for the money?
What did you / do you spend your pocket money on?
Were there any shops you liked to go to spend your pocket money?
Were you / are you good at saving money?

EXAM PART
Listening Part 2

EXAM SKILLS
Multiple choice

Listening to a longer monologue

TOPIC
Childhood memories
Generations

TIME
50 minutes

KEY LANGUAGE
Would and *used to* for describing events in the past

PREPARATION
One photocopy of the activity page for each student

Main activities

Students do some of these activities alone and the others in pairs or small groups.

1 Give out the activity sheets.

Students look at the pictures and speculate what Helen's 'sweet memory' might be about.

2 ▶▶| The first listening enables students to get a general idea of the whole passage and relate its content to the pictures. **See page 127 for the Tapescript**.

Answers
1 Her father 2 Her brother 3 A local shop 4 Sweets
5 Football cards

3 Encourage discussion while students decide on the order of the illustrations.

Answers
1 Father giving pocket money to Helen and Bernard
2 Helen going to the shop
3 The tray of sweets
4 Bernard with football cards
5 Helen in her room
6 Helen having to share her sweets with Bernard

4 ▶▶| You will need to play the recording section by section for this exercise. **See page 127 for the Tapescript**. Tell students the task will vary for each section and remind them that they are not expected to understand every word. You may want to ask these check questions when going through the answers to the first two sections.

Answers and check questions

1 **A** Yes **B** No **C** No
   A Why did she like Saturday mornings? Which phrase expresses a similar idea to *like*?
   B How much of her pocket money did Helen take to the shop? What did she do with the rest?
   C Which word means *the area very near where you live*? Were there supermarkets when Helen was a child?

2 **A** fewer **B** although **C** usually
   A What does *varieties* mean? Are there more varieties of sweets on sale nowadays, or fewer?
   B Why did the children think the tray was wonderful? (NOTE: It's not necessary for students to know what *barley sugar, liquorice, aniseed balls*, etc. are, but it is important they understand that these are types or varieties of sweets.)
   C Which phrase here means *she was patient*? Which phrase means the same as *if*? What do you think happened when there were grown-up customers waiting?

3 **A** The newsagent's was in the opposite direction to Bartlett's.
   B Bernard only bought football cards at the newsagent's.
   C Bernard spent all his pocket money.

4 **C**

Follow up

This can be done for homework.

Sweet memory

1 In this recording, Helen, aged 70, remembers her childhood and how she used to spend her pocket money. Look at the pictures. What do you think she talks about?

2 ▶▶|Listen to the recording and note down short answers to these questions.

1 Who gave Helen her pocket money?

2 Who is Bernard?

3 What was Bartlett's?

4 What did Helen spend her pocket money on?

5 What did Bernard spend his pocket money on?

3 Look at the pictures again. What parts of Helen's story do they illustrate? Put them in the correct order by numbering them 1–6.

4 ▶▶|Listen to Helen's story again, in four sections, and answer the questions.

1 Choose **Yes** if the sentence is correct, and **No** if it is incorrect.

A Helen liked Saturday mornings. Yes / No

B Helen took all her pocket money to the shop. Yes / No

C Helen's neighbours bought their food from a supermarket. Yes / No

2 Underline the correct word in italics in each sentence.

A When Helen was a girl, there were *more / fewer* sweets for children to buy.

B The children loved to look at the tray *because / although* there weren't a lot of things on it.

C Mrs Bartlett *usually / always* waited patiently for the children to choose their sweets.

3 These sentences are all untrue. Write the correct sentence.

A The newsagent's shop was next to Bartlett's.

B Bernard bought sweets and football cards at the newsagent's.

C Bernard saved half of his pocket money every week.

4 Choose the correct answer.

A Helen felt sorry for her brother because he hadn't got any sweets.

B Helen felt angry with Bernard because he had hidden her sweets.

C Helen felt unhappy because she had to give her brother some sweets.

Follow up

Write about a childhood memory. Choose from the following titles:

Pocket money

Saturday mornings

My brother/sister and I

A favourite toy

You should write about 100 words.

Nick Chandler, spider man

Warm up

Give out the activity sheets.

Ask students to look at the pictures, and then discuss these questions with them:

How many of you are afraid of spiders? Can you explain why?

How do you feel when you see a spider?

What do you do if you see a spider at home?

Who can pick up a spider without feeling afraid?

Has anyone seen (or even perhaps held) a big spider, such as a tarantula?

Main activities

Students do some of these activities alone and the others in pairs or small groups.

1 Before starting the quiz, check whether students understand the words *species* (= variety or type) and *leg span* (width from leg to leg at the widest point, see illustration). Don't explain *arachnid* at this stage, as it is the answer to the second question.

To introduce a collaborative or competitive element, you could split the class into teams. Team members work together to make their choices.

Answers
1 B **2** C **3** C **4** B **5** B **6** C **7** A **8** C

2 ▶▶| Tell students they are going to listen to an interview with an expert on spiders. They will hear the recording twice. The first time they must identify the topics the interviewer asks about. **See page 127 for the Tapescript**.

Answers
The interviewer asks about:

A spider Nick has with him; Dangerous spiders; People's fear of spiders; Spiders as pets.

Optional extension: Having checked this exercise, see what else students can remember from their first listening. For example:

What does Nick Chandler say about these numbers?

300   40,000   800   8

Did you learn any new facts about spiders? What?

Answers to optional extension
He has **300** spiders in his collection.

There are **40, 000** known species (types) of spiders in the world.

There are **800** species of tarantulas in the world.

Spiders have **8** eyes as well as **8** legs.

3 ▶▶| In this exercise, students practise the kind of listening skills they need for the examination such as word spotting, synonym spotting and paraphrasing. Question 4 is a shortened exam-style task.

Tell them they are going to listen to the interview again, this time in four sections. The task will vary for each section. **See page 127 for the Tapescript**.

Answers
1 **A** Since he was a boy

  B Not exactly (because new species are being discovered all the time)

  C Brazil

  D They can't see very well (even with eight eyes)

2 **A** to bite   **B** kill   **C** moved

3 **A** There are very few dangerous spiders in the world.

  B The bite of the funnel web spider is / can be very serious.

  C Most spiders are harmless to people.

4 1 A   2 C   3 B

Students may need further input on the use of the form *moved* (inflected like the past tense of the verb) in question 2 C.

Follow up

Discussion

Students may know the story of Arachne from Greek mythology: she is turned into a spider by the Goddess Athena, who is jealous because Arachne can weave better than she can. They may know the delightful story of the prophet Mohammed who hides from his enemies in a cave and is saved from detection by a spider that spins a web to cover the entrance. They probably won't know the story of Scottish king Robert the Bruce (also on the run from his enemies), who is inspired by the industry and perseverance of the spider to return to the fray and defeat his enemies.

Explain the word *justified*. Nick Chandler's account of tarantulas and other spiders makes it clear that our fear/dislike of spiders is not justified by the degree of danger they actually pose to us. And fear is very often based upon ignorance.

Other animals students may cite: snakes, sharks, crocodiles, insects of various kinds.

Encourage students to describe what is interesting and impressive about these creatures and to learn more about them.

Writing

Students can do this as homework.

EXAM PART

Listening Part 2

EXAM SKILLS

Multiple choice

Listening to a longer interview

Word spotting; synonym spotting; paraphrasing

TOPIC

The natural world (spiders)

Looking after pets

TIME

50 minutes

KEY LANGUAGE

Present simple; present perfect (simple and continuous)

Modal verbs *would, could, might* for degrees of probability

First and second conditionals

PREPARATION

One photocopy of the activity page for each student

Nick Chandler, spider man

House spider

Tarantula

Leg span

1 **Try this short quiz on spiders.**

1 How many legs do spiders have?
   A six ☐ **B** eight ☐
   C more than eight ☐

2 Spiders are:
   A insects ☐ **B** mammals ☐
   C arachnids ☐

3 What do spiders eat?
   A the leaves of plants ☐ **B** fruit ☐
   C insects and small animals ☐

4 What do most spiders make?
   A nets ☐ **B** webs ☐ **C** strings ☐

5 The leg span of the biggest spider in the world is about
   A 14 cm ☐ **B** 28 cm ☐ **C** 42 cm ☐

6 How many different species of spider are there in the world?
   A about 10,000 ☐ **B** about 25,000 ☐
   C about 40,000 ☐

7 The most dangerous spider (for people) lives in:
   A Australia ☐ **B** Africa ☐
   C South America ☐

8 Some of the larger spiders can live as long as
   A 5 years ☐ **B** 10 years ☐
   C 20 years ☐

2 ▶▶|**Listen to a radio interview. Which of these topics does the interviewer ask about? Put a tick by them.**

A spider Nick has with him ✓
Nick's travels around the world
Dangerous spiders
Spiders as pets
What spiders eat
People's fear of spiders

3 ▶▶| **Listen to the interview again in four sections and answer the questions.**

1 Write short answers to these questions.
   A How long has Nick been interested in spiders?

B Do scientists know exactly how many species of spider there are in the world?

C Nick is holding a spider in his hand. Where is it from?

D What does Nick say about spiders' eyes?

2 Complete each sentence with one or two words to make a true statement.
   A It's unusual for a tarantula .... a human being.
   B A bite from a tarantula wouldn't .... you.
   C The spider might be afraid if you .... suddenly.

3 These sentences are wrong. Correct them.
   A There are a lot of dangerous spiders in the world.
   B The bite of the funnel web spider is not serious.
   C Most spiders are harmful to people.

4 For each question, put a tick (✓) in the correct box.
   1 Before buying a pet tarantula you should
      A learn how to take care of them. ☐
      B look for one that will live a long time. ☐
      C remove any cats or dogs you have in the house. ☐
   2 What does Nick say about bees?
      A They live in dark holes. ☐
      B They often sting spiders. ☐
      C They kill more people than spiders do. ☐
   3 What advice does Nick give to people who are frightened of spiders?
      A The more you hold them, the more you will learn about them. ☐
      B If you learn more about them you are less likely to fear them. ☐
      C People who hold spiders never feel frightened. ☐

Follow up

Discuss these questions in small groups:

• Do you know any stories about spiders? Do these stories present spiders as 'good' or 'bad' creatures?

• Can you think of any other animals that are often feared or disliked? Are these feelings justified?

OR

Write a story of about 100 words which begins with this sentence:

Kate's friends were very surprised when they saw her new pet.

Exam-style task

PART 2
Questions 1–6

- You will hear a man called John Miller talking about his new book, *The Story of Ice Cream*.
- For each question, put a tick (✓) in the correct box.

1 What was in the ice cream eaten by the ancient Romans?

   A fruit and syrup   ☐
   B cream and snow   ☐
   C fruit and ice   ☐

2 In France in 1775 ice cream

   A was too expensive even for rich people.   ☐
   B was eaten by most of the population.   ☐
   C was an unusual luxury.   ☐

3 What was different about 'hokey pokey'?

   A A lot of ordinary people could afford to buy it.   ☐
   B It was made in Italy.   ☐
   C It was served in clean glasses.   ☐

4 What does the interviewer think is a 'typical' ice cream?

   A an ice cream with different flavours   ☐
   B an ice cream in a cone   ☐
   C an ice cream with a wafer biscuit stuck in the top of it   ☐

5 What was Ernest Hamwi selling at the St Louis World Fair?

   A a kind of cake   ☐
   B a kind of ice cream   ☐
   C cones for ice creams   ☐

6 What problem did the ice cream seller have?

   A He lost his glasses.   ☐
   B Nobody wanted to buy ice cream.   ☐
   C He had nothing to serve his ice creams in.   ☐

Hints and tips for Listening Part 2

What you have to do

- Listen to one longer recording.

- Read six multiple-choice questions and choose from three options, A, B and C.

How to approach it

- You have 45 seconds to read the questions before the recording starts. Read the questions carefully: the different options A, B and C will probably be mentioned in the recorded text, but only one of them is the answer to the question.

- The first time you listen to the recording, listen for the general meaning. As you do so, choose the best option for each question. As you listen for the second time, check carefully that your answers are correct.

- If you are confused by any of the three options, think how you would answer the question in your own words. Then look again at the three options and choose the one that best matches your own answer.

How to prepare yourself

- The recorded text may be an interview or a monologue and will probably contain factual information. For example: an extract from a radio programme in which someone talks about their interests or experiences or a recorded announcement or message giving factual information. Questions can be about specific information in the text; occasionally a question will be about the attitude or opinion of the speaker.

- If you are studying in an English-speaking country, try to listen to radio or television broadcasts, particularly interviews, and to recorded announcements giving factual information.

- If you are not studying in an English-speaking country, try to listen to English language broadcasts on the internet. Some of these are available as 'podcasts' that can be downloaded onto your computer and played on a portable MP3 player. Find programmes or podcasts about subjects you are interested in and listen to them when it suits you. It will also be helpful for you to watch films with an English language soundtrack. DVDs offer you the opportunity to choose the language you want to hear and to read subtitles to help understanding.

Answers

1 C   **2** C   **3** A   **4** B   **5** A   **6** C

See page 128 for the Tapescript.

Time and place

EXAM PART
Listening Part 3

EXAM SKILLS
Filling gaps in a text

Distinguishing
essential information
from distractors

Predicting words
from context

TOPIC
Practical
information: days,
dates, times,
numbers

Travel; wonders of
the world

TIME
40 minutes

KEY LANGUAGE
Spelling

Numbers

PREPARATION
One photocopy of
the activity page for
each student

Warm up

Ask students to do some or all of these short revision exercises. They can be done around the class or in small groups.

- Say the days of the week in English from Monday to Sunday and then again backwards.
- Count backwards from 20.
- Count backwards in tens from 100–0.
- Count in ordinal numbers from first to twenty-first. OR Find out the order of everyone's birthdays. Students have to say: *I was born first/second/third/fourth*, etc.
- Check the spelling and pronunciation of *fourth, fourteenth, thirteenth, thirtieth*.
- Student A says 'January'; Student B has to spell it and then say the name of the second month in the year; Student C has to spell that word correctly and then say the name of the third month, and so on, round the class.
- Each student has to say, in full, a date which is important in his/her life.
- As long as body size is not an issue, ask students how much they weigh and how tall they are.
- Ask students one or two general knowledge questions involving large numbers, for example: *How old do scientists think our Earth is?* **Answer**: about four and a half billion years old. *How high is Mount Everest in the Himalayas?* **Answer**: 8,848 metres.

Main activities

Students do some of these activities alone and the others in pairs or small groups; exercise **3** can be done in teams.

1 Give out the activity sheets.

Emphasise to students the importance (in all parts of the Listening paper) of reading any accompanying text. This exercise practises prediction (what *kind* of word are you listening for?).

Answers
1 a day of the week, for example Wednesday
2 a day of the week
3 a time of the day and/or a date
4 a historical date
5 a time, a day of the week, a month or a date
6 a number
7 a large number
8 a number
9 a historical period, for example a century
10 a number
11 a number
12 a series of digits (rather than an arithmetical number)

2 ▶▶| Students listen to the recording once. In most cases their task is to distinguish the item required for the answer from other items mentioned in the recording. **See page 128 for the Tapescript**.

Answers
1 Thursday
2 Wednesday
3 23rd November
4 (August) 1822
5 31st January
6 11 / eleven
7 65 million
8 700
9 20th century
10 7.5
11 52
12 07952 396755

3 You could do this in teams. Give students a time limit of 1 minute to decide on the countries.
▶▶| Play the recording so students can check their answers. **See page 129 for the**

Tapescript. Write the correct spellings of the countries on the board. An acceptable spelling earns one point. A winning team is declared.

Answers
1 Italy 2 Egypt 3 China 4 India 5 England
6 Australia

4 Students look at the questions to try to predict the kind of item needed to fill the space.
▶▶| Play the recording again and check the answers. **See page 129 for the Tapescript**.

Answers
1 An outdoor theatre
2 Four statues (of the King, Ramses II)
3 Three roofs
4 His (dead) wife
5 (over) 4,000 years
6 Denmark

5 Students read the gapped text quickly to get an idea of the subject. They try to guess what the missing words might be. They should look for and underline contextual clues, for example: for gap 2 the clue is the numbers 38,000 and 50,000. They should make a note of their guesses on a separate piece of paper. You may want to discuss their guesses with the whole class.

6 ▶▶| Play the recording. Students write the exact words they hear in the spaces in the text. Check their spelling afterwards. (The Tapescript is on the activity page.)

Answers
1 country 2 population 3 tourists 4 church
5 shopping 6 countryside

Follow up

Ask students to do one or more of these activities.

- Write down some dates that are important in the history of your country. For each one, explain in a sentence why it is important.
- Write down some dates that are important in your life (apart from your birthday) or that of your family. For each one, explain why it is important.
- In exercise **3**, people were asked to choose the man-made wonder of the world that impressed them most. Which would *you* choose? Explain why.

Time and place

1 Read the sentences. What *kind* of word is needed for the space? (There may be more than one possible answer.)

1 Maths is every .... morning.
   a day of the week, for example Wednesday

2 Lisa works from .... afternoon until Friday.

3 The office will not be open on Wednesday
   ....

4 The poet, Shelley, died in ....

5 You have to send off your college application by ....

6 There are .... players in a cricket team.

7 Dinosaurs became extinct .... years ago.

8 About .... athletes take part in the summer Olympics.

9 The furniture at the exhibition was made during the early part of the ....

10 It takes 15 years for an oak tree to grow .... metres.

11 The speaker now weighs .... kilos.

12 Dan's new telephone number: ....

2 ▶▶|Listen to the recording and fill in the missing information in exercise 1, using one or two words.

3 Look at this list of man-made 'wonders of the world'. Do you know which country they are in?

1 The Colosseum .... *Italy* ....
2 The Temple of Ramses ....
3 The Temple of Heaven ....
4 The Taj Mahal ....
5 Stonehenge ....
6 The Sydney Opera House ....

▶▶|Listen to six people talking about the 'wonder of the world' that most impressed them when they were travelling. Check your answers about which countries the 'wonders' are in.

4 Look at the following questions carefully and think about what kind of word is needed for the answer.

▶▶|Listen to the recording again and write down the answers.

1 What was the Colosseum 2,000 years ago? *An* ....

2 What can you see on the outside of the temple of Ramses? *Four* ....

3 What can you see on the top of the Temple of Heaven? *Three* ....

4 Who did Shah Jehan build the Taj Mahal for? *His* ....

5 How old is Stonehenge? .... *years*

6 Where did the architect, Jorn Utzon, come from? ....

5 Here is a text about a fictitious town. Read it carefully and then try to guess the missing words. In many cases there is more than one possible answer. Write your guesses on a separate piece of paper.

The historic town of Guerston is in the south-west of the [1] .... *country* .... The [2] .... of the town is around 38,000, rising in the holiday season to about 50,000.

This is because Guerston is a popular destination for [3] .... from all over the world, many of whom come to see its famous old buildings.

The most splendid of these is probably St Thomas's [4] ...., which was built in the 14th century and has a beautiful dome designed by the 17th century architect, Sir Charles Sparrow.

There's a modern part of the town too, including a covered [5] .... centre with branches of many famous name stores. There you can buy everything from hi-fi equipment to wedding dresses.

It's a short walk out of the town centre into lovely unspoilt [6] .... where, in fine weather, there are lots of places to have a picnic.

6 ▶▶|Now listen to the recording and fill in the gaps with the words you hear.

Please speak after the tone

Warm up

Tell students of the importance of accurate spelling in the exam. For the answers in Listening Part 3, recognisable spellings can be acceptable, unless the word is very common (for example, a day of the week) or it is spelt out. In general, occasional minor errors in spelling and punctuation won't stop students from getting full marks – the important thing is that the message is clear and easy to understand.

Action spelling test – What am I doing?

Tell students you are going to mime a series of actions. They must try to guess what the word for the action is. If they think they know, they must not *say* the word but write it down. All the words end in -*ing*, but some have a double consonant in the middle and some do not. Demonstrate this with a few examples:

What am I doing? (sit) Write it. What have you written? You should have written **sitting**.
What am I doing? (walk) Write it. What have you written? You should have written **walking**.
Actions: swimming, writing, hopping, cutting, smiling, pulling, pushing, sleeping, falling, phoning, driving, running
Introduce the topic of the activity by asking these questions:
Do you have an answering machine at home? What is the recorded announcement on it (translated into English!)? If you have a mobile phone, what does your voicemail announcement say?
How do you feel when you have to leave a message on someone's answerphone?
Can you give some examples of recorded information services, e.g. where you have to press numbers for different options? Why do organisations have these? Do you like them?

Main activities

Students do some of these activities alone; exercises **2** and **3** are done in pairs.

1   Give out the activity sheets.
▶▶| You may need to pause the recording after each speaker to allow students time to write their answers. **See page 129 for the Tapescript**.

Answers

Caller's name	Paul	Sue	Mike Marston	Francesca	Carol
Subject	bowling	shopping	job interview	dinner	babysitting
Day and time	Friday, 7.30	Saturday, 10.45 am	Tuesday, 4.15	next Wednesday, 8 pm	Saturday, 8.45 pm
Place	Cool Zone	Black Cat Café	the shop	Solo Restaurant	her house

2   Students work in pairs, A and B. Hand out the photocopied answerphone messages (on page 143) to each pair. They sit back to back, and take it in turns to read their message to each other. While they are listening, they note down the information in the table on their activity sheet.

Answers

	Student A	Student B
Caller's name	Anna Marshall	David Saunders
Subject	interview	International Club
Day and time	Friday 11th April, 10.20 am	Sunday 19th March, 3.45 pm
Place	Newbury School of Business	Linford Hall

3   In pairs, students improvise their own messages based on the models supplied.

4   ▶▶| Students should read the programme for the Pantheon Arts Centre before you play the recording. They write their answers in the spaces. **See page 129 for the Tapescript**. Play the recording again and check their answers. You may want to give out photocopies of the Tapescript.

Answers

1 models   **2** families   **3** charities   **4** postponed
5 education   **6** training   **7** B13   **8** Canada
9 8.30 pm   **10** sold out   **11** February
12 www.pantheonarts.org

Follow up

Ask students to write a story in about 100 words. Give them a choice for the first sentence:

* *Last week I received an answerphone message that made me very, very happy.*

  OR

* *When Susan came home and listened to her answerphone messages, she had a big surprise.*

EXAM PART
Listening Part 3

EXAM SKILLS
Filling gaps in a text

Distinguishing essential information from distractors

Predicting words from context

TOPIC
Answerphone and voicemail messages

TIME
30 minutes

KEY LANGUAGE
Spelling

Numbers

PREPARATION
One photocopy of the activity page for each student

One photocopy per pair of the answerphone messages on page 143 for exercise **2**

Optional: photocopies of the Tapescript for exercise **4** (see page 129)

Please speak after the tone

1 ▶▶|Listen to five answerphone messages for Julia. Write the missing information in the spaces.

Caller's name	Paul				
Subject	bowling				
Day and time	Friday, 7.30				
Place	Cool Zone				

2 Work in pairs. Your teacher will give each of you a different answerphone message. Sit back to back and take it in turns to read out your message to your partner and write the information in the spaces.

Caller's name	
Subject	
Day and time	
Place	

3 Write an answerphone message for your partner. In it, suggest an activity to do together and a time and place for it.

Then sit back to back again. In turn, read your messages aloud, spelling the name of the place. While you are listening, note down the information in the spaces. Then look at each other's information and check the spelling.

Caller's name	
Subject	
Day and time	
Place	

4 ▶▶|Listen to the recording and fill in the missing information.

PANTHEON ARTS & LEISURE CENTRE

Programme for week beginning 15th September

Tuesday *The World in Miniature*: Hundreds of fascinating [1]........................ of cars, trains, ships and aircraft. Reduced price tickets for students, over 60s, and [2]........................ .

Wednesday For **one night** only, at 7.45 pm: *Double Trouble*. (All profits from this performance will go to help local [3]........................)

Mind Games with TV magician and illusionist, Sebastian Walker, [4]........................**until next April.**

Thursday & Friday Conference on Computers in [5]........................ and [6]........................ .

SPECIAL FREE EXHIBITION: Interactive Learning Technology, Room [7]........................ . All welcome.

Saturday From [8]........................, the sensational rock band, *Storm Warning*. The band will start playing at [9]........................ .

SORRY – THIS CONCERT IS NOW [10]........................**, BUT THE BAND WILL BE BACK AGAIN IN** [11]........................ .

For more information on future events at the centre, visit our website: [12]........................ .

Home, sweet home

Warm up

Revise the following vocabulary used to describe homes: *ground floor flat, six-storey block, detached/semi-detached house, bedroom, bathroom, kitchen, reception rooms* (i.e. *sitting room, dining room,* etc.), *balcony, terrace,* also *painting, decorating, redecorating*.

Ask students to say in which room of a house they would expect to find the following things: *a fridge, a television, a pillow, a towel, a sink, a radiator, a washbasin, a wardrobe, a computer, a sofa*. (There is more than one possible answer, of course, but students should try to explain their choices.)

Explain that in the UK about 70% of people own their own home. This is above average for the European Union, but Italy, Greece and Spain have a higher proportion of homeowners. 80% of UK homes are houses or bungalows (as opposed to flats).

Ask students if they know how much the following might cost to buy or to rent (in their own country):

a two-bedroom flat in or near the centre of their capital city
a three-bedroom house with a garden in a nice suburb of the city.

Main activities

Students do some of these activities alone and the others in pairs or small groups.

1 Give out the activity sheets.

Explain to students that in Britain an *estate agent* is someone who works for a company that sells houses and land for other people. The estate agent advertises that the house is for sale and shows it to people who may want to buy it. If he/she sells the house, he/she receives a fee, which is usually a percentage of the selling price.

▶▶| Students should look at the estate agent's form before you play the recording. **See page 130 for the Tapescript.** You may want to give out photocopies of the Tapescript when you check the answers.

Answers
Conrad and Sally Gould; a flat; two bedrooms; one reception room; £150,000–£165,000; a terrace or balcony; near the station (and on a bus route to city centre); before (or by) the end of September

2 ▶▶| Explain that in the recorded message the estate agent describes three possible flats for Conrad and Sally. Students have to fill the gaps with the missing information. Before you play the recording, they should read through the three flyers about the properties. **See page 130 for the Tapescript.** You may want to give out photocopies of the Tapescript when you check the answers.

Answers
1 Northbrook; two; three-storey; balcony; 30 minutes; £160,000; end of October
2 Bridge; third; reception; terrace; on foot; £165,000; now
3 Valley; 130 years; garden; redecorating; by car; £155,000; mid-September

3 Students compare the three properties, look again at the estate agent's form in exercise **1**, and decide which flat is the most suitable for Conrad and Sally.

Answer
Bridge House: two bedrooms; a large terrace; near the station; in their price range (their maximum price). Also, Sally wants to move 'as soon as possible' and Bridge House is available now.

Follow up

If students write the description of their home, they should include the kind of information that interested Sally and Conrad: the type of home it is; the number of rooms; any special or interesting features; the location and access to public transport; the decorative order of the property.

If they opt to write the story, encourage them to use their imaginations.

EXAM PART
Listening Part 3

EXAM SKILLS
Filling gaps in a text

Distinguishing essential information from distractors

TOPIC
Buying property

Homes

TIME
50 minutes

KEY LANGUAGE
Describing homes

Numbers, prices

PREPARATION
One photocopy of the activity page for each student

Optional: photocopies of the Tapescript for exercises **1** and **2** (see page 130)

Home, sweet home

1 ▶▶|**Sally and Conrad want to buy a flat, so they go to an *estate agent*. This is a person who will try to help them find the right flat. Listen to their conversation with the estate agent and fill in the form.**

Fraser & Sons Estate Agents

Name of clients: ...... Conrad and Sally Gould ......

Type of property wanted:

....

Number of bedrooms:

....

Number of reception rooms:

....

Price range:

....

Special features:

....

Location:

....

Date needed:

....

2 ▶▶|**A few days after their visit, the estate agent phones them and leaves a message. He describes three different flats. Listen and complete the three information sheets.**

3 **Which of the three flats do you think Conrad and Sally will choose, and why?**

Follow up

Imagine that you want to sell your home. In about 100 words, write a description of it for an estate agent's advertisement. Make it sound attractive!

OR

Write a story in about 100 words that begins with this sentence:

When I saw our new home for the first time I couldn't believe my eyes.

1

Flat 3, 11 .... Gardens

An attractive ....-bedroom flat in a ....–........................ block

One large reception room plus kitchen and bathroom

The whole interior was redecorated only two months ago.

It has a small .... with room to dry washing.

There's a good bus service to the station and town centre shops: journey time about

....

Price: £ ....

Available from the ....

2

Flat 1, ... House

A two-bedroom flat on the .... floor of a new four-storey development

It has two .... rooms, a kitchen and a bathroom. The property also has a large .... with plenty of space for a table, chairs and plants.

The flat is on a bus route to the city centre and the station can be reached .... in only ten minutes.

Price: £ ....

Available: ....

3

Flat 2, ... Court

On the ground floor in a beautiful three-storey building over .... old. The flat has two bedrooms, two reception rooms, kitchen and bathroom, and there's an attractive .... at the back.

The interior of the flat is full of character but needs .... The station and town centre shops can be reached .... in about 15 minutes.

Price: £ ....

Available: ....

Exam-style task

Hints and tips for Listening Part 3

What you have to do

- Listen to a longer monologue (only one speaker).
- Read a short text about the monologue.
- Fill in six numbered gaps in the text with words from the monologue.
- The answers can be single words, numbers or short phrases. You will not have to write a long answer.

How to approach it

- You have 20 seconds to look at the text and the gaps. You can probably guess what kind of words you need to listen for.
- The questions are in the same order as the information on the recording.
- The words you must write in the gaps are the same as those you hear on the recording, but the context (the words around the gaps) may be different.

- Don't worry if you miss something the first time – you will hear the recording again.

How to prepare yourself

- The monologues contain information. They can take the form of recorded messages, announcements, extracts from talks and radio programmes. Try to listen to recordings of a variety of voices speaking English.
- Practise reading short texts with gaps and predicting the kind of word that is missing (see *Insight into PET* pages 68–71 and *Objective PET* pages 20, 120 and 158, published by Cambridge University Press).
- You may lose marks on this part of the test if you spell common words wrongly. Work with a friend and test each other's spelling of familiar everyday vocabulary such as the days of the week and the months of the year.

PART 3

Questions 1–6

- You will hear a man talking on the radio about a writing competition.
- For each question, fill in the missing information in the numbered space.

SHORT STORY COMPETITON

Up For It

FIRST PRIZE

An all-expenses-paid trip for two people across the Russian Federation, from north to south.

CONDITIONS

Entrants should write a story called (1) .... Adventure, which describes a difficult but exciting journey.

The story should be no longer than (2) .... words, and it must be all your own work. Only one entry per person, please.

The last date for entries is (3) ....

Please write your full name and address on the back of each page of your story.

Stories must be sent to Chris (4) ...., *Up For It*, Radio Nova, 33–41 Saxon Court, London EC2 4AW.

There are additional prizes of rucksacks and (5) .... for the 25 best stories.

If your story wins it will be read out on air in December. And you'll be invited onto the programme so we can (6) .... you.

--- ✂ ----

Answers

1 Holiday / holiday

2 1,000 / a thousand / one thousand

3 13th October / 13 October

4 Berwick

5 T-shirts

6 interview

Time off

Warm up

Introduce the topic of absenteeism in a fun way: first call the attendance register in the normal way, with students responding to their names with 'here' or 'present'. Then explain to students that you are going to call it again, but this time each student has to say *how* present they are: 25%? 50%? 75%? 100%? Students quickly recognise the notion that of course physical presence in a classroom doesn't mean total 'presence' in the sense of engagement with the lesson and the other people in the room. When you have taken this 'alternative register' students must explain their responses: if a student says that 25% of him/herself is not present in the classroom, then *where exactly* is he/she? For the brief period of the discussion, you will usually find that everyone is fully present!

Main activities

Students do some of these activities alone and the others in pairs or small groups.

1 Give out the activity sheets. They can do this vocabulary exercise quite quickly.

Answers
1 different (*to have a day off* means to have a day of holiday)
2 same
3 different (*minor* means *not* very important)
4 same
5 different (*to rise* means, here, to increase or get more)

2 ▶▶| Students read and listen to the four quotes and underline the words and expressions listed in exercise **1**. (The Tapescript is on the activity page.) Then they read the texts again and decide if they agree or disagree with the opinions expressed.

When they are discussing their opinions, encourage students to explain their views and add examples from their own experience.

3 Explain that these are true and false questions, similar to Part 4 in the exam.

Answers
1 No   2 Yes   3 Yes   4 No

4 ▶▶| After students have listened to the recording, they discuss their answers in pairs or small groups. **See page 131 for the Tapescript.**

Possible answers
1 He doesn't feel well. / He feels ill. / He's got a cold.
2 She wants him to stay at home / take a day off school.
3 He wants to go to school even though he is feeling ill / in spite of his cold.
4 *Open question*

5 ▶▶| Students read the true and false sentences before they listen to the recording again. **See page 131 for the Tapescript**. You may want to give out photocopies of the Tapescript when you check the answers.

Answers
| 1 No | 2 Yes | 3 No | 4 No | 5 No | 6 Yes | 7 Yes |
| 8 Yes | 9 No | 10 Yes | | | | |

Follow up

If students opt to make up their own dialogue, they could work in a group of three, with the role of a doctor added to the sketch. You may want to give them this example:

The 'child' has a reason for not wanting to go to school and invents an illness. The sceptical parent questions him/her about the symptoms to determine if he/she is telling the truth. In a group of three, the doctor could see if the child is telling the truth. The dialogue must end with a decision: either the child goes to school, or the child is allowed to stay at home (on what conditions?).

Pairs and groups take it in turns to act out their dialogues for the class, if they are happy to.

EXAM PART
Listening Part 4

EXAM SKILLS
True or false questions

Interpreting attitudes and opinions in a longer dialogue

TOPIC
Absenteeism from school and work

TIME
50 minutes

KEY LANGUAGE
Expressing opinions; agreeing and disagreeing

If clauses

PREPARATION
One photocopy of the activity page for each student

Optional: photocopies of the Tapescript for exercises **4** and **5** (see page 131)

Time off

1 **Do these words and expressions mean the same or are they different?**

1   to have a day off / to have a bad day (at work or school)   *different*

2   to feel proud / to be pleased with yourself about something

3   minor / very important

4   spread something around / to pass it to others

5   to rise / to get less

2 ▶▶|**Read and listen to what these people say about taking time off work or school. Underline the words and expressions you find from exercise 1.**

> **1**   Some people take a day off work just because they feel a bit tired. I think that's irresponsible because it means that other people have to do their work for them.

> **2**   I think that if you've got a bad cold you shouldn't go to school because you'll only spread it around, and before long everyone in the class will be ill.

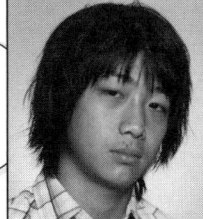

> **3**   I feel proud of the fact that I haven't missed a day of school this year. I think too many of the kids in my class are absent for really minor things, you know, like a sore throat or a slight cough.

> **4**   I noticed that the number of sick days taken by staff in our department rose by 60% during the World Cup. In my opinion there's no excuse for taking time off work to watch a football match, even if your national team is playing.

Read the four texts again and write A if you agree with something that is said, and D if you disagree. Discuss your opinions with other students.

3 **Now read these sentences about what the speakers say. If a sentence is true for that speaker write YES next to it, if it is false write NO.**

1   She says that responsible people should not do the work of a sick colleague.

2   He thinks you shouldn't go to school when you are ill because other people may catch the illness from you.

3   She thinks that some absent children are probably well enough to come to school.

4   He thinks that some of his colleagues were ill during the World Cup.

4 ▶▶|**Listen to the conversation between Simon and his mother and answer the questions. Then discuss your answers with other students.**

1   What is the matter with Simon?

2   What does his mother want him to do?

3   What does Simon want to do?

4   Have you ever been in a situation like this? What happened?

5 ▶▶|**Look at the sentences below, and then listen to the conversation again. Decide if each sentence is correct or incorrect. If it is correct, write YES. If it is not correct, write NO.**

1   Simon wants to go to school today because he likes geography lessons.   NO

2   His mother thinks he will get better more quickly if he stays at home.

3   Simon has already had breakfast.

4   He is often absent from school.

5   Ella is a girl in Simon's class.

6   Simon is worried about what the geography teacher will think.

7   Simon is good at geography.

8   Simon asks his mother to take his project to school for him.

9   She offers to go to the school and speak to the teacher today.

10   Simon decides to stay at home.

Follow up

Read the opinions in exercise **2** again. What do you think about taking time off school or work? Write about your own experience and opinions (50–70 words).

OR

Working in pairs, make up a dialogue between a parent and a child who does or doesn't want to go to school. Your dialogue must end with a decision: does the child go to school, or is he/she allowed to stay at home, and on what conditions?

What's your point?

Warm up

Write this question on the board: *What are your favourite spare time activities/interests?*
Ask students to predict what would be the top five activities/interests amongst the people in their class. Write their suggestions on the board.
Ask everyone to list their own top five spare time activities/interests. Write their answers (or a selection of them) on the board. Then compare their predictions with their actual individual choices.
Tell students that this question was put to a sample of British teenagers (aged between 14 and 16). In what way do they think the answers of the British teenagers might be like theirs?
In the British survey, the results for girls and boys showed very different interests. Here are the five choices of each group put together:
Friends/socialising   Music   Skateboarding   Fishing   Cinema   Going to the gym   Using the internet   Football   Shopping   TV programmes
Write the list on the board and ask students to separate the items into two groups: Girls and Boys.
Here is the actual breakdown:
Boys: Music, Skateboarding, Fishing, Using the internet, Football
Girls: Friends/socialising, Cinema, Going to the gym, Shopping, TV programmes
Discuss the reasons for the differences between the lists.

Main activities

Students do some of these activities alone and the others in pairs or small groups.

1 Give out the activity sheets.
Ask students to look at the picture. What has happened? Why do the young people look so happy?
Explain *GCSE*.

> *GCSE* stands for General Certificate of Secondary Education. GCSEs are public examinations taken by secondary school students at or around the age of 16 in the UK.
> - Most pupils take GCSEs in most of their subjects.
> - It usually takes two years to study for a GCSE. Coursework is part of most GCSEs: work done over an extended period, which could include essays, field work reports, art work, making products or doing investigations.
> - GCSEs are graded A* to G. The grade a student gets will depend on coursework and exam marks.

Ask students to read the article about UK school examination results for 2005 and to discuss the questions.

2 ▶▶| Before you play the recording, make sure students realise that only one sentence in each pair is correct. **See page 132 for the Tapescript.** You may want to give out photocopies of the Tapescript when you check the answers.

Answers
Correct sentences: Sarah B   Graham A   Liz B
Shareen B   Alan A

3 Students should discuss the questions in small groups. Give them a time limit (e.g. 5 minutes). They should choose a spokesperson who will summarise the views of the group at the end. At the end of the discussion, give each spokesperson a maximum of 1 minute to sum up the opinions of the group.
Optional extension: Students take part in an extension of the phone-in programme.
They prepare what they are going to say by making notes. You play the role of the show's host and invite in turn a selection of students to add their point of view to the debate, speaking or reading aloud. If practicable, they could be recorded (a motivation to enhance their performance).

Follow up

You could also ask students to write questions about differences between girls and boys, and then interview a selection of people in or out of the classroom, making notes on the views expressed. They report back to the class on their findings. They could also write a summary of the views expressed.

EXAM PART
Listening Part 4

EXAM SKILLS
True or false questions

Interpreting attitudes and opinions in a longer dialogue

TOPIC
Learning styles of girls and boys

TIME
50 minutes

KEY LANGUAGE
Expressing opinions; agreeing and disagreeing

PREPARATION
One photocopy of the activity page for each student

Optional: photocopies of the Tapescript for exercise **2** (see page 132)

What's your point?

1

Read this news report.

GCSE results rise at all grades

GCSE results for England, Northern Ireland and Wales have improved at all grades for the first time since 1996.

The overall pass rate rose from 97.6% of the exam entries to 97.8%.

And 61.2% were awarded the higher grades, A* to C, up two whole percentage points on last year – the biggest rise since 1992.

But concern has been expressed about the decline in entries for modern languages, and whether GCSE students have essential basic skills.

Entries: 5.74 million (down 2.4%)

Pass rate: 97.8% (up 0.2)

A*–C grades: 61.2% (up 2)

A*/A grades: 18.4% (up 1)

A* grades: 5.9% (up 0.3)

As usual, overall, girls outperformed boys, and students in Northern Ireland achieved higher grades than those elsewhere.

GCSE Grades A*–C

England: 60.8%

Northern Ireland: 71%

Wales: 61.3%

All boys: 57%

All girls: 65.2%

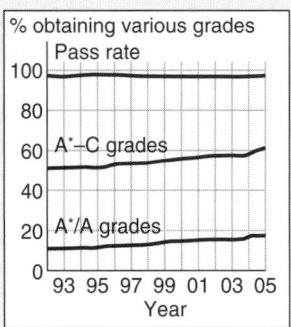

% obtaining various grades

Do these British examination results surprise you?

How do they compare with national exam results in your country?

2 ▶▶ **You are going to hear a radio phone-in programme on the subject of boys' and girls' performance at school. Listen to five people and decide which of the sentences A or B is correct for each speaker.**

A **Sarah** thinks men make better teachers than women. ✗

B **Sarah** thinks boys need male teachers as well as female teachers. ✓

A **Graham** thinks there is an 'anti-school culture' which boys are afraid to challenge.

B **Graham** doesn't like studying because he thinks it isn't 'cool'.

A **Liz** says that boys are better at building things than girls.

B **Liz** says that boys can be quick learners especially if they have to do something as part of their learning.

A **Shareen** says it's natural for boys to be lazy and that parents should accept this.

B **Shareen** says that parents have different standards for boys and girls.

A **Alan** thinks the success rates of girls and boys are always changing.

B **Alan** thinks that in his school girls and boys are all at the same educational level.

3 **Discuss these questions in small groups.**

- How do you explain the examination marks of girls and boys in the UK?
- Do you think that boys and girls learn in different ways? Can you give some examples?
- Is it better for boys to have male teachers?
- Do you think there is a 'negative, anti-school culture' among some students? Can you give some examples?
- In your opinion, are boys given more freedom than girls?
- Should boys and girls be treated exactly the same by parents?

Follow up

Write a summary of the views expressed in your discussion.

What do you feel?

Warm up

Write these adjectives on the board:
cheerful   tired   snobbish   surprised   shy   impatient   friendly   frightened   polite   rude
Ask the students to greet you or each other (*Hello. How are you?* etc.) expressing one of the moods/feelings on the board. The others in the class have to say which one it is.

Main activities

Students do some of these activities alone and the others in pairs or small groups.

1 Give out the activity sheets.

Students look at the cartoon pictures and match the feelings to the characters.

They try to explain why the characters feel as they do. ('Some people are worried about going to the dentist, others don't care ...' etc.)

Explain the different uses of adjectives ending in -*ed* (feelings) and adjectives ending in -*ing* (situations). Use the cartoons for examples: 'Describe the man on the left.' 'He's <u>embarrassed</u>.' 'So what kind of situation is it?' 'An <u>embarrassing</u> situation.' And so on.

Answers
a embarrassed, annoyed   **b** relaxed, worried   **c** excited, disappointed

Suggested answers
a One man looks **embarrassed** because he has splashed sauce over the other man. The other man is **annoyed** because he has sauce on his face.
b The man with the magazine looks **relaxed** because he is not worried about seeing the dentist. The other man looks **worried** because he is nervous about seeing the dentist.
c One man looks **excited** because his team has just scored a goal. The other man looks **disappointed** because the other team has just scored a goal.

2 Students read what the woman said and answer the questions.

Answers
1 B   **2** <u>didn't live up to our expectations</u>   **3** A
4 <u>we found it rather dull</u>

3 Discuss with students the language functions and situations in the questions.

Explain that they are going to listen to 12 short extracts and they have to listen for 'clues' about the situation in each one.

▶▶| Play the recording of the example and point out the clues in the text. You may need to pause the recording while you play the other extracts, to allow students time to write their answers.
See page 132 for the Tapescript.

Answers
1 J   **2** K   **3** F   **4** B   **5** D   **6** H   **7** A   **8** G
9 E   **10** L   **11** C   **12** I

4 Explain what a *riddle* is. Tell students that when they guess what the answer is, they shouldn't call it out but write the word in their notebooks and wait, so more of the class have a chance to think about the puzzle. Ask the *last* student who 'got' it to give the answer.

Answer
The 'it' is *money*.

5 ▶▶| Before you play the recording, you may want to pre-teach these collocations: *to pay for something, to pay someone back, to take money out (of an account), to be careful with (your) money*. Also check understanding of *bargain, debt, overdrawn* and *budget*. **See page 133 for the Tapescript**. You may want to give out photocopies of the Tapescript when you check the answers.

Answers
1 NO   **2** YES   **3** YES   **4** NO   **5** NO   **6** NO
7 YES   **8** NO   **9** YES   **10** NO

Follow up

Ask students to write about the topic of money in relation to themselves and their lives. Brainstorm some sub-topics, as appropriate for your class, for example:
Do you get pocket money?
Do you earn any money?
Do you have a bank account, credit card, etc.?
What do you spend your money on?
Have you ever lent money to friends?
Have you ever borrowed money?
Did you pay it back?
Do you manage to save money? What for?
What would you like to buy that you can't afford?

EXAM PART
Listening Part 4

EXAM SKILLS
True or false questions

Interpreting attitudes and opinions in a dialogue

TOPIC
Holidays; money

TIME
50 minutes

KEY LANGUAGE
-*ing* and -*ed* adjectives (*interesting, interested,* etc.)

Words for feelings

Mixed functional language: complaining, complimenting, warning, etc.

Listening for synonyms

PREPARATION
One photocopy of the activity page for each student

Optional: photocopies of the Tapescript for exercise **5** (see page 133)

What do you feel?

a

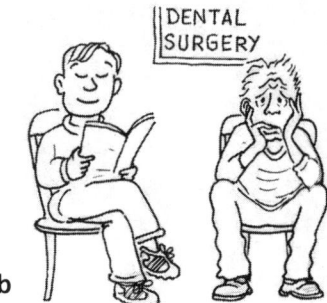
DENTAL SURGERY
b

c

1 **Look at the pictures. Match these feelings to the men in the pictures.**

excited   worried   annoyed   disappointed
relaxed   embarrassed

In each case, explain why the man feels like that.

2 **Read what this woman said about her holiday, and answer the questions.**

> The holiday didn't live up to our expectations at all. Everyone had told us it was a really exciting place, but to be honest with you we found it rather dull.

1   How does the woman feel about her holiday?
    A pleased ☐   **B** disappointed ☐
    C excited ☐

2   Underline the expression that tells us how she feels.

3   What did she think about the place they stayed at?
    A It was boring. ☐   **B** It was exciting. ☐
    C It was tiring. ☐

4   Underline the word(s) that tell us what she thinks.

3 ▶▶ **You are going to listen to 12 short extracts. First, read the questions. Then read and listen to this example.**

I'm <u>fascinated by</u> robots, how they are designed and built. I really <u>want to find out more about them</u> and maybe build one myself one day.

The words that are underlined tell us that the speaker is *interested in* robots.

Now listen to the extracts and write the appropriate letter A–L by each question.

1   Who's in a hurry?
2   Who's in trouble?
3   Who's missing something?
4   Who's lost something?
5   Who's warning someone?

6   Who's complimenting someone?
7   Who's interested in something? A
8   Who's complaining about something?
9   Who feels relieved?
10 Who feels hurt?
11 Who's asking for advice?
12 Who's asking for directions?

4 **Here is a riddle. What is meant by 'it'?**

> Be careful how you lend it, be careful how you spend it.
>
> Wise folk work to earn it, fools go out and burn it.
>
> Some of us try to save it; all of us crave* it.
>
> No one ever says 'Enough!'
>
> What is this stuff?
>
> *crave: to want or need something very strongly

5 ▶▶ **Jenny and Harry are two university students on holiday abroad together. Read the sentences below. Listen to their conversation and decide if each sentence is correct or incorrect. If it is correct, write YES. If it is not correct, write NO.**

1   Harry has spent all his holiday money.   NO
2   Jenny thinks that Harry spent too much money in the first week of their holiday.
3   Last night they ate at a rather expensive restaurant.
4   Harry thinks Jenny paid too much for her carpet.
5   Jenny wants to take some more money out of her bank account.
6   Harry says that his father will pay Jenny back.
7   Harry wants to buy presents to take home.
8   Jenny agrees that their friends will expect presents.
9   In the end they agree to make their money last.
10 Harry seems to be more careful with money than Jenny is.

Exam-style task

Hints and tips for Listening Part 4

What you have to do

- Listen to a longer dialogue between two people (usually male and female).
- At the same time look at six statements about the dialogue.
- Decide if the statements are correct or incorrect.
- Tick the box for YES or NO.

How to approach it

- You have 20 seconds to look at the questions.
- The statements are in the same order as the information on the recording.
- Read the instructions. They will tell you **who** the speakers are and **what** they are talking about.
- The six statements are usually about the **attitudes** and **opinions** of the speakers.
- Underline key words in the statements that indicate these. For example: *Lynn's father*

refuses to let her...; *Lynn decides to record ...*

- If you are unsure whether a statement is correct or not, try turning it into a question. (For example: question 4 *Who is going to show the viewers how to make fish soup?*)
- Don't worry if you miss something the first time – you will hear the recording again.

How to prepare yourself

- Listen to examples of informal dialogues in which the speakers talk about their opinions, attitudes and feelings.
- Notice the verbs which indicate such opinions and attitudes. For example: verbs such as *advises, agrees, believes, encourages, hopes, suggests, wonders, worries*; adjectives such as *annoyed, embarrassed, grateful, pleased, sorry, surprised, unsure.*
- Further practice can be found in *Insight Into PET* pages 72–75 and *Objective PET* pages 96, 146 and 196, published by Cambridge University Press.

PART 4

Questions 1–6

- Look at the six sentences for this part.
- You will hear a conversation between a girl called Lynn and her father, about what programmes are on television and what they might like to watch.
- Decide if each sentence is correct or incorrect.
- If it is correct, put a tick (✔) in the box under **A** for **YES**. If it is not correct, put a tick (✔) in the box under **B** for **NO**.

		A YES	B NO
1	*Is Anyone There?* is a factual programme.	☐	☐
2	Lynn thinks that *Emergency* is educational.	☐	☐
3	Lynn's father refuses to let her watch *Emergency*.	☐	☐
4	In this week's *What's Cooking?* Tim Fielding is going to show the viewers how to make fish soup.	☐	☐
5	Instead of watching *What's Cooking?*, Lynn's father decides to use the computer.	☐	☐
6	Lynn decides to record the medical drama and watch it later.	☐	☐

- ✂ - -

Answers

1 A   **2** A   **3** B   **4** B   **5** B   **6** A

See page 133 for the Tapescript.

Breaking the ice

Warm up

Circle game

You will need a soft ball for this game. Ask the class to stand in a circle. Tell students that they are going to ask and answer questions following a simple rule that you will give them, for example: 'All questions must begin with *What …?*'

The person with the ball must: think of a question beginning with *What …?*; choose a person in the circle; say that person's name; throw the ball to them; ask the question; listen to the answer and repeat it, for example:

Cristina. What did you have for breakfast?

I had coffee with milk and a brioche.

OK, you had coffee with milk and a brioche.

This goes on, round the circle, until you change the rule. Every time you want to change the rule, it's a good idea to get the ball back and give the students your own example.

Here are some suggested rules to impose:

* questions must use the **past tense**
* questions must begin with **Why ...?**
* questions must be about **family/hobbies/school**, etc.
* questions must be **negative**, e.g. *Why didn't you throw the ball to Petra?*
* questions must consist of **four words** only.

Main activities

Students do some of these activities alone and the others in pairs or small groups.

1 Give out the activity sheets.

Divide the class into pairs or groups and assign one picture to each pair or group. They must think of as many questions as they can that they could ask the person or people in their picture. Remind them that their questions must begin with the words in the list. Emphasise that the questions should refer to the 'content' of the picture, e.g. *When is your birthday?* is not a suitable question for any of them.

Give a time limit for preparation (e.g. 3 minutes). Ask one student in each pair or group to stand up and read out the questions they have for the person in their picture.

Award one point for each grammatically correct question; give a bonus point for an original and imaginative question.

2 Explain that the sentences contain fairly typical mistakes, which they should try hard to avoid!

▶▶| Play the recording twice so students can check their answers and practise saying the questions.

Tapescript and answers
1 What**'s** your name?
2 Where **do** you come from?
3 How **old are** you?
4 Are you **a** student?
5 What school do you go **to**?
6 Can you spell that, please?
7 How long **have you been learning** English?
8 Do you enjoy **learning** English?
9 How many English lessons **do you have** a week?
10 **Have you got** any brothers or sisters?
11 Do you live in **a** house or **a** flat?
12 What **do** you do in your free time?

3 Monitor students' answers to the questions.
4 ▶▶| Tell students there are various possible ways of wording some of the questions, and the questions they will hear on the recording are a model. Go through their answers checking any differences in wording.

Tapescript and answers

1	What's your name?	Belinda.
2	And what's your surname?	Sherman.
3	How do you spell that?	It's S-H-E-R-M-A-N.
4	Where are you from?	I'm from Wales.
5	Whereabouts in Wales?	Swansea, in the south of the country.
6	How old are you, Belinda?	15.
7	Where do you go to school?	Norbrook High School.
8	Could you spell that, please?	Yes, it's N-O-R-B-R-O-O-K.
9	What's your favourite subject at school?	I like maths and science, but I suppose my favourite subject is ICT.
10	What does ICT stand for?	Information and Communications Technology.
11	What do you like doing in your free time?	I like going out with friends. I watch films sometimes, and I do karate twice a week.
12	And how long have you been doing karate?	Since I was 12 … so, for three years.

5 ▶▶| You may need to pause the recording to give students time to note down the differences between the text and the recording. **See page 134 for the Tapescript**. You may want to give out photocopies of the Tapescript when you check the answers. Perhaps also explain *Design and Technology (DT)* – designing and making products and learning about manufacturing processes.

Answers
1 Davidson   2 Inverness   3 Ireland   4 Murrayfield
5 DT   6 Design and Technology   7 16   8 two sisters
9 older   10 computer games   11 fishing

6 Monitor students' questions and answers.

Follow up

Ask students to write a parallel description of themselves.

EXAM PART
Speaking Part 1

EXAM SKILLS
Giving information of a factual, personal kind

Answering questions about the present and the past

Spelling

TOPIC
Personal information: home, family

Schools and school subjects

TIME
40 minutes

KEY LANGUAGE
Common errors

Question forms

PREPARATION
One photocopy of the activity page for each student

A soft ball for the **Warm up** game

Optional: photocopies of the Tapescript for exercise **5** (see page 134)

Breaking the ice

Look at one of these pictures. Imagine that you meet the character in the picture. What questions could you ask the person or people?

Think of as many questions as you can. They must begin with these words:

What   Where   When   Who   Why   How long   How often

2 **Each of these questions is incorrect. Can you find the mistakes and write the correct version? Look at the examples first.**

1 What your name? *What's your name?*

2 Where <u>are</u> you come from? *Where do you come from?*

3 What age have you?

4 Are you student?

5 What school do you go?

6 Can you to spell that, please?

7 How long are you learn English?

8 Do you enjoy to learn English?

9 How many English lessons have you a week?

10 Do you have got any brothers or sisters?

11 Do you live in the house or the flat?

12 What you do in your free time?

▶▶|**Listen to the recording and check your answers.**

Listen to the questions again and repeat them.

3 **Work in pairs. Practise asking and answering the questions in exercise 2.**

When you are ready, practise again, without looking at the questions. Walk around the classroom repeating the questions and answers with different partners.

4 **Here are a girl's answers to questions in an interview. Write the interviewer's questions on the left-hand side.**

1 ....*What's your name?*......... Belinda.

2 .... Sherman.

3 .... It's S-H-E-R-M-A-N.

4 .... I'm from Wales.

5 .... Swansea, in the south of the country.

6 ....15.

7 ....Norbrook High School.

8 ....Yes, it's N-O-R-B-R-O-O-K.

9 .... I like maths and science, but I suppose my favourite subject is ICT.

10 .... Information and Communications Technology.

11 .... I like going out with friends. I watch films sometimes, and I do karate twice a week.

12 .... Since I was 12 … so, for three years.

▶▶|**Now listen to the recording and check your answers.**

5 ▶▶|**You will hear another, similar conversation. First read the text below and then listen to the recording. There are 11 differences between the text and the recording. Note down the differences on the text. (The first one is done for you.)**

> *Davidson*
> *Callum 1 D̶a̶v̶i̶s̶o̶n̶ lives in 2 Edinburgh, in Scotland, but he was born in 3 England. He is a student at 4 Craigsmuir Academy. His favourite subject is 5 PE, which stands for 6 Physical Education. Callum is 7 15 years old. He's got 8 one sister and one brother, who are 9 younger than him. In his free time he enjoys playing 10 football and some weekends he goes 11 cycling.*

6 **Work in pairs. Taking it in turns to play the interviewer, ask and answer personal information questions like those in exercise 4.**

What's in a name?

Warm up

Put students into teams of four to six people. They must listen to you read 10 quiz questions on **proper nouns** (i.e. names of people and places). The teams confer quietly and one person in the team writes the answer on a piece of paper.

In order to score a mark, the name must be spelt correctly. NOTE: It must be the English version of the name.

Quiz: Questions and answers

1 What is the longest river in the United States? *Mississippi*
2 What is the surname of the current President of the United States? *(currently George Bush)*
3 What is the name of the Queen of England's home in London? *Buckingham Palace*
4 In the Harry Potter books, what is the name of the school for wizards that Harry goes to? *Hogwarts*
5 What is the rap artist Eminem's real name? *Marshall Mathers*
6 Which planet in the solar system is nearest to the sun? *Mercury*
7 Who is the founder and president of the Microsoft corporation? *Bill Gates*
8 What is the capital city of Australia? *Canberra*
9 What is the name of the grounds of the Lawn Tennis Association (and the home of its annual international tennis tournament)? *Wimbledon*
10 Who directed the *Star Wars* films? *George Lucas*

At the end of the quiz, collect the papers and mark them yourself or write the correct answers on the board and redistribute the papers for peer marking. The team with the most correctly spelt answers wins.

Variation: Do the quiz orally. Teams can confer and write the name down, but their team leader must spell it out loud. Give the correct answer after each item and award points as you go along.

Main activities

Students do some of these activities alone and the others in pairs or small groups.

1 Give out the activity sheets.

Before you play the recording, discuss names. Ask students to give examples of first names that are common in English-speaking countries. Do the same for surnames. Note the following:

- *In 2004 the five most popular first names for girls in the UK were: Ellie, Emily, Sophie, Chloe and Jessica. For boys: Jack, Joshua, Thomas, James and Daniel.*
- *The top five most common surnames in the UK are, in order: Smith, Jones, Williams, Taylor and Brown.*
- *The top five most common surnames in the USA are, in order: Smith, Johnson, Williams, Jones and Brown.*

▶▶| You may need to pause the recording while students note down the names.

Tapescript and answers

1 Hello, I'm **Linda** Hall.
2 My name's Michael **Johnson**.
3 Hi. I'm Susan **Evans**.
4 How do you do? My name's **Robert** Miles.
5 Hello. I'm **Rachel** Smith.
6 My name's Graham **Wilson**.

2 ▶▶| Play each item twice, and pause after each speaker. **See page 134 for the Tapescript.**

Answers

	Name	Place
1	Nick	Plymouth
2	Chris	Melbourne
3	Liz	Belfast
4	Don	Johannesburg
5	Dave	Ottawa
6	Kate	Edinburgh
7	Danny	Detroit
8	Penny	Bicester

3 Students practise introducing themselves like the people in exercise **2**, saying their name (including any diminutive or nickname they may have) and the place they come from. You may want to get them to circulate, introducing themselves to different people in the class.

4 Students work in pairs, spelling their name and surname, and any or all of the other names as appropriate. Check their spelling is accurate.

5 Students work in pairs or small teams for the puzzle activity. You may want to make it more competitive by offering a small prize to the first pair or team to find the words (and therefore the 13-letter word).

Answers

1	i	n	k		
2	n	e	a	r	
3	t	e	e	t	h
4	e	m	p	t	y
5	r	a	n		
6	n	i	n	e	
7	a	s	k		
8	t	e	a	r	s
9	i	l	l		
10	o	f	t	e	n
11	n	o	o	n	
12	a	p	p	l	e
13	l	o	n	g	

6 Students have an opportunity to find other English words in the letters of INTERNATIONAL. There are about 100 possible words (including two-letter words as well).

Follow up

For the spelling quiz, it is best to limit the field, for example to words from their coursebook or recent English lessons, to save them testing inappropriate vocabulary. Encourage them to include words that may have been a 'problem' for the class.

EXAM PART
Speaking Part 1

EXAM SKILLS
Spelling

TOPIC
Names and introductions

Puzzles

TIME
40 minutes

KEY LANGUAGE
Spelling of proper nouns

Introducing yourself

PREPARATION
One photocopy of the activity page for each student

What's in a name?

1 ▶▶| Listen to these people introducing themselves. Can you spell the missing names?

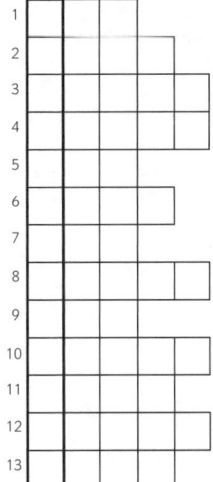

1 .... Hall.

2 Michael ....

3 Susan ....

4 .... Miles.

5 .... Smith.

6 Graham ....

2 ▶▶| Listen to eight people introducing themselves. They give a shortened form of their first name followed by the name of the place where they live. Write the name and the place.

	Name	Place
1	Nick	Plymouth
2		
3		
4		
5		
6		
7		
8		

3 In pairs, practise introducing yourself, like the people in exercise 2, giving the name of the place you are from as well. If you are called by a shortened form of your name, or by a nickname, include that in your introduction.

4 In pairs, spell the following:

* your name and surname
* the street (or the name of the apartment building) where you live
* the name of your school or university, or the company you work for
* your father's or mother's first name
* your teacher's surname
* the name and surname of another student in your class.

Your partner must note down what you say.

5 Read the clues and write the missing words.

1 The liquid in a pen.

2 The opposite of *far*.

3 You bite and chew your food with these.

4 The opposite of *full*.

5 The past tense of *run*.

6 The number before ten.

7 .... me a question.

8 The drops that fall from your eyes when you cry.

9 He didn't go to school because he was ....

10 Quite frequently.

11 Another word for 12 o'clock midday.

12 A fruit that 'keeps the doctor away'.

13 How .... have you been waiting?

Now look at the initial letter of all 13 words. What word do these letters make? (It describes the English language!)

---- ---- ---- ---- ---- ---- ---- ---- ---- ---- ---- ----

6 How many more English words, of three letters or more, can you find in the letters of this word?

Follow up

Write a spelling quiz of ten items for a partner. Use only words from your coursebook or recent English lessons. Try to include words that have been a 'problem' for you or your classmates.

AND/OR

Write a list of (ten) English words that you have spelt wrongly since you started to learn English. Practise spelling them aloud until you can say the letters confidently and quickly.

All about me

Warm up

Ask the class to stand in a circle. You start by making a statement from the list below. The student on your left has to match your sentence with a **true** statement about him/herself. It can be a repetition of your statement (if that is also true for him/her) or, more usually, it will be a modification of your statement. The next person in the circle does the same, and so on around the circle. (Make sure that students don't build mistakes in to the original sentence pattern.) For example:

A: My birthday is in August.
B: My birthday is in November.
C: My birthday is in March.
OR
A: I have a cat and a dog at home.
B: I have a cat at home.
C: I don't have any pets at home.
    … and so on.

Possible statements

My surname is Sinclair.
My mother's name is Betty.
I have two brothers and a sister.
My address is 20 Green Street.
My favourite colour is blue.
I got up at 6.30 this morning.

I had chicken salad for dinner yesterday evening.
I came to school by bus this morning.
I have a friend called Rosalind.
My last holiday was in Turkey.
The last film I saw was *Spirited Away*.
This weekend I'm going to play tennis.

Main activities

Students do some of these activities alone and the others in pairs or small groups.

1 Advise students that in order to prepare for the Speaking part of the exam: *You should try to become an expert on yourself.* In other words, they should make sure they can talk confidently about the following:

- basic factual information about yourself, such as your age, country, nationality, first language, date and place of birth, current residence
- what you do – whether you are a student or you have a job
- your family
- your experience of studying English in particular (how long? how often?)
- your hobbies and interests
- your future (things that are certain, and things that you *might* do).

Students work in groups of three or four. Hand out the squares of paper (see Preparation) to each group. Between them, they write the seven topic titles on the squares, put the squares in the middle, turn them over and mix them up (or put them in a hat). Taking it in turns, each person picks up one of the squares, reads out the topic, and then speaks about it for 1 minute.

Tell them they will repeat the task in exercise **6**. The second time they have to evaluate both themselves and the other students.

2 Students look at the sentences, which show a variety of ways of talking about everyday personal topics. They match the sentences with the topics.

Answers

1 F	**2** C	**3** A	**4** C/F	**5** B/D	**6** D	**7** D
8 A	**9** E/G	**10** C	**11** B	**12** G	**13** E	**14** D

3 Students discuss the picture using the open questions as a starting point. Pre-teach *unicycling*.

4 ▶▶| Make sure students decide in advance who will note down the questions and who the answers. Play the recording twice to allow students time to make their notes. **See page 134 for the Tapescript** (and questions and answers). Emphasise the importance of noting key words and phrases, which they can use later when they reconstruct the dialogue. **It should not become a dictation task**.

5 Students interview each other about their chosen activities. The language in exercise **4** provides a model but students should feel able to add their own ideas.

6 Ask students to work in the same groups as in exercise **1**. Hand out the squares of paper again. Students repeat exercise **1** and evaluate their improvement.

Follow up

Students clarify and develop the language of personal information by writing an email about themselves. It should have the friendly communicative style of a personal email and not sound like a curriculum vitae!

EXAM PART
Speaking Part 1

EXAM SKILLS
Talking about yourself

Everyday language of social interaction

TOPIC
Likes and dislikes

Hobbies and pastimes

TIME
50 minutes

KEY LANGUAGE
Present tense for routine or repeated activities

PREPARATION
One photocopy of the activity page for each student

Small squares of paper, enough for seven for each group (for exercises **1** and **6**)

Optional: photocopies of the Tapescript for exercise 4 (page 134)

All about me

1 Which of these subjects can you talk confidently about in English? Put a tick (✓) by the subjects you feel confident about.

- **A** My family ☐
- **B** My experience of learning English ☐
- **C** My home town / where I live ☐
- **D** My interests ☐
- **E** My education / the work that I do ☐
- **F** The most important things that happened to me last year ☐
- **G** My plans and hopes for the future ☐

Work in small groups. Practise talking about these topics.

2 Look at these sentences. Which topic in exercise 1 does each one refer to? Write a letter next to the sentence. NOTE: Some of the sentences refer to more than one topic.

1 In August I went on holiday for three weeks and met someone who's since become a good friend. F

2 It's about 25 kilometres from the coast.

3 I'm an only child.

4 In February we moved to a larger flat further away from the centre of town.

5 I watch DVDs with an English soundtrack and I think that has improved my listening.

6 I'm the captain of a local football team and that takes up a lot of my free time.

7 I love going shopping but of course I can't spend a lot of money as I'm still a student.

8 My mother comes from a large family so I have a lot of uncles, aunts and cousins.

9 If I do well in my school exams I hope to go to university to study languages.

10 It's an exciting place to live in but it's very crowded and the traffic is terrible.

11 I can understand a lot more than I can express.

12 I'd love to take a year off and travel around India.

13 During the holidays I work in a shop which sells sports goods.

14 I spend a lot of time surfing the internet or chatting to friends on MSN.

3 Look at the picture.

- What is the woman doing?
- Do you think it would be difficult? Why? Why not?
- Would you like to do it? Why? Why not?

4 ▶▶|Work in pairs. You will hear a recording of an interview. As you listen, one of you must write down the questions asked, and the other must make a note of the answers.

Compare what you have both written.

Using your notes, try to reconstruct the interview.

5 Think of a skill-based hobby, sport or other activity that you do in your free time. If you don't do any activities, then think of one you might like to do. (Don't choose something passive, like watching films or listening to music.)

Work in pairs. Take it in turns to interview each other about the activity you chose. Use the same questions as the interviewer in exercise 4, and add some of your own.

6 Now repeat exercise 1 (in the same groups) and see how much you and the other people in the group have improved.

- Did you speak more confidently this time?
- Did you say more about the topic?
- Did you use a wider range of language?

Follow up

This is part of an email from a friend in an English-speaking country.

To: You!
Subject: Me and you
≡ ≡ ≡
Well, so now I've told you something about myself, and my life at the moment. But what about you? I hope you'll write back soon and tell me all about yourself: what you do, your family, other important people in your life, your free-time activities and so on. Look forward to hearing from you. Cheers, Alex

Write your reply. Use 100–150 words.

Face to face

EXAM PART
Speaking Part 1

EXAM SKILLS
Giving personal
information

Responding to
questions

TOPIC
Personal
information

TIME
30 minutes

KEY LANGUAGE
Describing present
circumstances, past
experiences and
future plans

PREPARATION
One photocopy of
the activity page and
the Hints and tips for
each student

One photocopy of
the Tapescript for
the Exam-style task
for each group (see
page 135)

1 Give out the activity sheets.
Students read extracts from two Speaking Part 1
scenarios and try to guess what words might fit
in the blank spaces. (Any guesses should be
written on a separate piece of paper at this
stage.) Tell them that there are various
alternatives and no definitive correct answers.

2 ▶▶ Play the recording. Students fill in the
spaces, and then compare their answers with a
partner. **See page 135 for the complete
Tapescript**.

Answers
1 a town in northern
2 that's right
3 but only part-time
4 doing a course
5 training to become
6 kind of work does she do

3 In pairs, students read the dialogues aloud. The
first time they read what is written; the second
time they individualise the dialogues, keeping
the basic questions but changing the names, the
answers and other details to fit themselves.

Exam-style task

Students can do this in pairs with the recording or in
groups of four without the recording. You may decide
that they would benefit from doing both alternatives,
perhaps in different lessons.

In pairs with the recording
▶▶ Students will hear an interlocutor asking them
some questions. They should listen and then say their
answers. **See page 135 for the Tapescript**.

In groups of four without the recording
Hand out one photocopy of the Tapescript (see page
135) to each group of four. Explain that they are
going to do the exam-style practice twice, rotating
the roles of candidates (x2), interlocutor and
assessor. The interlocutor will read from the
Tapescript and the assessor should make notes on
the feedback form and time the interview.

The first time, A is the interlocutor, B and C are the
candidates and D is the assessor.
The second time, B is the interlocutor, A and D are
the candidates and C is the assessor.
With this arrangement, they each get to be a
candidate but not everyone gets to be the
interlocutor or assessor.
You may want to remind students that in the exam the
interlocutor is the examiner who asks the two
candidates questions and the assessor is the examiner
who doesn't speak and makes notes on the
candidates' performance. (The assessor awards the
detailed marks and the interlocutor gives a global
impression mark.)
Discuss how they felt about their performances when
they have finished.

---✂------

Hints and tips for Speaking Part 1
What you have to do

• Answer the interlocutor's questions.

• This is the introduction to the Speaking
test so the interlocutor will ask you for
simple personal information: your name,
age, occupation, and so on.

• The interlocutor may also ask you
about your family, your interests, how
you feel about learning English, and
your plans for the future.

• The interlocutor will ask you to spell all
or part of your name.

How to approach it

• Try to say a bit more than 'yes' or 'no'
in your answers.

• On the other hand, the interlocutor will
not want long prepared 'speeches'
about aspects of your life!

• It's all right to say, 'Sorry, could you
repeat that, please?'

• Remember that the interlocutor wants
to find out if you can take part in a
simple everyday conversation, giving
information about yourself.

How to prepare yourself

• Make sure you can spell your name
and the name of your home town, etc.

• Practise talking about your hobbies
and interests, likes and dislikes.

• Be prepared to answer questions
about your past, present and future.

• Become an expert on yourself – in
English!

Face to face

1 **Here are extracts from two interviews. Read the extracts and try to guess what the missing words are, but don't write anything in the spaces yet. Different alternatives are possible.**

1 **INTERLOCUTOR**: Where are you from, Enzo?

ENZO: I'm from Piacenza.

INTERLOCUTOR: Where is that exactly?

ENZO: It's (1) .... Italy, between Milan and Bologna.

INTERLOCUTOR: Right. And are you a student?

ENZO: Yes, (2) .... I'm studying economics and law at the University of Bologna.

INTERLOCUTOR: I see. How long have you been learning English?

ENZO: For five years, (3) ...., two or three lessons a week.

2 **INTERLOCUTOR**: Do you have any brothers or sisters, Marta?

MARTA: Yes, I have an older brother.

INTERLOCUTOR: And what does he do?

MARTA: He's (4) .... at technical school. He's (5) .... an engineer.

INTERLOCUTOR: Tell me a bit about the rest of your family.

MARTA: Well, my father is a bank manager and my mother has a part-time job in a hotel.

INTERLOCUTOR: Oh, yes. What (6) ....?

MARTA: She's a receptionist.

2 ▶▶| **Now listen to the recording and fill the spaces in each dialogue.**

3 **Work in pairs and read the dialogues aloud, taking the part of the interlocutor and the candidate. Then read the dialogues aloud again, keeping the basic questions but the candidate should answer as him/herself, changing the names, answers and other details.**

Exam-style task

Now take part in an exam-style practice of Part 1 of the Speaking test. You can do this in pairs with the recording or in groups of four without the recording.

In pairs with the recording

▶▶| On the recording, you will hear an interlocutor asking you (Student A) and your partner (Student B) some questions. Listen and then say your answers.

In groups of four without the recording

You will take it in turns for two of you to play the parts of the candidates and the other two to be the interlocutor and assessor. The assessor should time the interview and use this form to make notes on the performance of one of the candidates. NOTE: Part 1 of the Speaking test lasts approximately 2 minutes. This practice should not last less than that.

Assessor's feedback form

Candidate's name:

Interlocutor's name:

Candidate talked about:

Candidate said: Too much ☐ A lot ☐

Enough ☐ Too little ☐

Good points:

Things to work on:

Some things I noticed:

Time: ....

Rainy day fun

EXAM PART
Speaking Part 2

EXAM SKILLS
Discussing a situation

Making and responding to suggestions

TOPIC
Children's games and activities

TIME
50 minutes

KEY LANGUAGE
Describing and commenting on activities

PREPARATION
One photocopy of the activity page for each student

Warm up

Introduce the topic with a discussion of the following:
Think back to when you were eight years old. What games and activities did you like doing?
Write key words on the board. If appropriate, compare the answers given by boys/men and by girls/women.
More confident students may also like to give their opinion on the following:
Do you think eight-year-olds today enjoy the same games and activities as you did?
Ask if any students in the class have had experience of babysitting or looking after children. Get them to talk about what games they played with the children.

Main activities

Students do some of these activities alone and the others in pairs or small groups.

1 Give out the activity sheets and introduce the situation.

Students work in pairs or small groups and note down their ideas. This phase should not take more than 2 minutes.

Briefly ask for their ideas and discuss them with the whole class.

2 Students match the pictures with the descriptions in the box.

Answers
a Playing with toy cars
b Listening to a story
c Playing a ball game
d Doing an art activity
e Cooking
f Playing a board game

3 Students practise making suggestions using the target phrases from exercise **2**.

4 Students match the activities to the comments.

Answers
1 toy cars   **2** art, cooking   **3** art, cooking   **4** cooking
5 board game, story   **6** art, cooking   **7** story   **8** art
9 ball game   **10** board game

5 Students work in pairs and construct a kind of guided conversation about the options.
Go through the example with students first and then monitor their exchanges.

6 Having considered the pros and cons, students must agree on **three** out of the six activities to do with the children. There's still room for a bit of negotiation:
Do you think they will like that? I think it's better to …
OK. I agree that's also a good choice.

7 Students briefly explain their choices to the whole class.

Follow up

Ask students to choose **one** of the situations below and note down at least four activities they could do to make the situation more interesting.

• You are stuck in a traffic jam with two adults and two young children for three hours.
• You are staying with your grandparents in a house in the country. It has snowed very heavily and you can't go out.
• You are at an airport with three children aged nine, five and 18 months. Your flight is delayed for at least five hours.

Then in a later lesson, put them in pairs according to which situation they chose. They use their notes to help them discuss the situation as further practice for Speaking Part 2.

Rainy day fun

1

> Situation
>
> You are looking after two children – a boy aged eight and a girl aged six. It's a rainy day, so you don't want to go out. What can you play or do to keep them happy? NOTE: Their mother doesn't want them to watch television, video, etc.

Note down your ideas.

2 **Look at the pictures and match them with the descriptions in the box. Write the description in the space under each picture.**

Playing a board game	Cooking
Playing with toy cars	Listening to a story
Doing an art activity	Playing a ball game

a _____

b _____

c _____

d _____

e _____

f _____

3 **Practise suggesting these activities. Use:**

What about ...-ing?

We could ...

Shall we ...?

For example: *What about playing a board game?*

4 **Read these comments about the activities. Some are positive and some negative. Write next to each comment the activity/activities they could refer to (they can refer to more than one).**

1 The little girl might not want to play with those. toy cars

2 It's a nice creative activity.

3 They can show the results to their mum and dad!

4 The boy might think that it's for girls.

5 It will certainly pass the time quietly.

6 It's rather messy – we'll have to clear up afterwards.

7 They might not like the same type of book.

8 Most children enjoy painting and drawing.

9 It's not a good idea because you might break something in the house.

10 The girl might be too young to understand the rules.

5 **Work in pairs. Take it in turns to suggest an activity from the list in exercise 2. Your partner must respond to the suggestion with one of the sentences in exercise 4. Before a positive response, say *That's a good idea*. Before a negative response, say *I'm not sure about that*.**

Here are two examples:

Student A	Student B
We could do an art activity with them.	*That's a good idea. Most children enjoy painting and drawing.*
Student B	Student A
What about playing a board game?	*I'm not sure about that. The girl might be too young to understand the rules.*

6 **Now you and your partner must decide which three activities you are going to do with the children. Start like this: *Shall we play a board game? No, I think they'll prefer doing an art activity*.**

7 **Explain your choices to the whole class.**

Do you think so?

Warm up

Tell students they are going to practise 'responsive' expressions. In other words, if one person makes a statement, the next person must respond to that statement before making a statement of their own. For the purposes of this speaking game, they must do so using the following pattern: *echo + positive response + question*. For example:

A: Let's go to the beach.

B: The beach? (*echo*) That's a great idea! (*positive response*) How shall we get there? (*question*)

Write the following ideas on the board:

Have a party	Go swimming	Visit (Mary)
Go shopping	Play a game	Listen to some music
Sing a song	Have something to eat	Watch a DVD
Have a discussion	Tell some jokes	Go on a journey

Also elicit and write on the board some phrases for suggesting:

What about ...? Shall we ...? Would you like to ...? Why don't we ...? Let's ...

The class stands in a circle. You start off by making a suggestion. The person on your left responds with the pattern. The next person left answers the question, and then makes another statement (one from the list on the board or one of his/her own). For example:

T: Why don't we have a party?

S1: A party? That's a brilliant idea! Who shall we invite?

S2: We can invite the class next door. I've got another idea. What about singing a song?

S3: A song? That's an excellent idea! What song shall we sing? and so on.

Make it livelier by encouraging students to exaggerate their body language and tone of voice a bit in order to express enthusiasm.

Main activities

Students do some of these activities alone and the others in pairs or small groups.

1 Give out the activity sheets.

Working in pairs, students decide what the expressions are used for: agreeing, disagreeing or suggesting.

Answers

1 disagreeing	2 agreeing	3 agreeing	4 suggesting
5 disagreeing	6 agreeing	7 disagreeing	
8 suggesting	9 disagreeing	10 suggesting	

2 Working in pairs, students list the good and bad points of using computers. Give them a time limit of 2 minutes. Share different ideas with the whole class.

3 ▶▶| Play the recording. As students listen, they look again at the expressions in exercise **1** and tick (✓) each expression they hear. **See page 135 or the Tapescript**.

Answers

Expressions on the recording: 1, 2, 3, 6, 7, 8, 9

4 ▶▶| Play the recording again. Students look at the list of points discussed and write down whether the speakers agree or disagree about them.

Answers

1 disagree	2 agree	3 disagree	4 agree

5 Students work in pairs or small groups. Allow time for them to think of possible arguments.

Suggested answers

Larger animals like cats and dogs need fresh air and exercise and plenty of space to move about in.

Some smaller pets, such as hamsters and guinea pigs, can be kept in cages, and aquarium fish obviously don't need a garden!

6 ▶▶| Remind students to note down the arguments while they listen to the recording. Ask them afterwards whether any of their arguments were the same and who they agreed with. **See page 135 for the Tapescript**.

7 Working in groups of three, students read the situation and look at the pictures. Check that they understand key words (*arthritis, fond of, used to, suitable*, etc.) and that they realise they need to discuss the different possibilities, rather than simply choose one and eliminate the others.

Remind the students who are listeners to give their feedback when the pair have finished speaking. Then ask the listeners to tell the class what their pair chose.

▶▶| Before you play the recording of the model answer, tell students that it is above the language level expected of candidates at PET level, but it is intended to demonstrate how students should interact in a discussion about a situation and then bring the discussion to a close. **See page 136 for the Tapescript**. You may want to give them photocopies of the Tapescript.

Follow up

Tell students that Adelphi College has some extra money to spend on one new resource for the students. The resource should benefit as many students as possible. It can be:

- Some new sports equipment, e.g. tennis rackets
- A new computer for the media centre
- New books for the library
- A video camera or camcorder.

Ask them to work in pairs and discuss the pros and cons of each idea. At the end they should choose the one they think would be the best value.

Students report back on their choices – and defend them, if necessary!

EXAM PART
Speaking Part 2

EXAM SKILLS
Discussing a situation

Making and responding to suggestions

TOPIC
Computers

Pets

TIME
50 minutes

KEY LANGUAGE
Giving opinions

Expressions for agreeing, disagreeing and suggesting

PREPARATION
One photocopy of the activity page for each student

Optional: photocopies of the Tapescript of the Model answer for exercise 7 (see page 136)

Do you think so?

1 **Which of the following expressions are used for**

- agreeing • disagreeing • suggesting?

1 Do you think so? *disagreeing*

2 You're right.

3 Absolutely.

4 Perhaps we could ...

5 On the other hand, ...

6 That's true.

7 It depends.

8 What about ...?

9 I'm not so sure.

10 Let's ...

2 **Think about the good and bad points of using computers, and make a list.**

Here are two examples.

With computers we can do complicated calculations very, very quickly.

On the other hand, computers make us lazy – we don't do arithmetic in our heads.

3 ▶▶|**Now listen to a conversation and look again at the expressions in exercise 1.**

Tick (✓) each expression you hear.

4 ▶▶|**Listen again. Which points do the people agree about? Which points do they disagree about? Write A for agree or D for disagree.**

1 Playing games

2 Writing

3 Getting information

4 Communicating with people

5 *To keep a pet you need to have a big house with a garden.*

Try to think of one argument *for* this statement and one argument *against* it.

6 ▶▶|**Now listen to a conversation between Mark and Vera. Make a note of their arguments. Are any of them the same as yours?**

Who do you agree with – Mark or Vera?

7 **Now you are going to do a practice activity. Work in groups of three. Two people do the task and the third person listens. After 2 or 3 minutes, the listener gives his/her feedback.**

- How much did each person say?

- What did they agree/disagree about?

- What choice did they make at the end?

Before you start, look back at the expressions in exercise 1 for agreeing, disagreeing and suggesting.

> Situation
>
> Lily is 75 and lives alone. Since her husband died she has felt rather lonely and is thinking about getting a pet for company. She lives in a ground floor flat and has a very small garden. She has arthritis in her knees and can't walk very far. She is very fond of dogs and used to have one.
>
> Look at the illustrations of possible pets. Discuss the advantages and disadvantages of each one for Lily, and then choose the most suitable pet for her.

▶▶|**When you have finished, listen to a model answer on the recording.**

Getting there

Warm up
Challenge

Tell students they have to make a round the world trip using as many modes of transport as possible. In two or three teams, students compete to think of as many ways of travelling as possible in 2 minutes. The team with the longest list (of acceptable modes) wins.

NOTE: The mode of travelling must be one that people really do use, so no magic carpets or riding on the backs of eagles!

TIP: It can help to work through the alphabet: think of a means of transport beginning with A, then one beginning with B, and so on.

Main activities

Students do some of these activities alone and the others in pairs or small groups.

1 Give out the activity sheets.

Make sure students understand the situation. Monitor their discussions, reminding them to discuss the pros and cons of the different options. Here are some points they could think about:

What is the traffic like on the roads into the city centre?

How difficult or expensive will it be for him to park?

Is there a reliable bus service?

Are there safe routes for cyclists into the centre?

How long will it take William to walk eight kilometres?

How important are the following factors: cost, speed, convenience, reliability, safety and keeping fit?

2 ▶▶| Tell students they are going to listen to a short recording of two people doing this task and they have to evaluate the discussion. They will probably need to listen to the recording twice. **See page 136 for the Tapescript.**

Suggested answers

1 The speakers don't discuss the advantages and disadvantages of each option. For example, the advantages of walking and the possible disadvantages of cycling are not explored.

2 They state their own personal preferences but do not agree on a solution for William.

3 The speakers hardly interact at all. They don't respond to or develop the point made by the previous speaker. A's statement that 'it's too far for him to walk' is followed by a valid but quite unconnected point about crowded buses. We don't have the impression that they are listening to each other or that the argument is developing in any way.

3 ▶▶| Students listen to two different people doing the same task and answer the same evaluation questions as for exercise **2**. **See page 136 for the Tapescript** (the Answers to exercise **4** are shown in bold). After you have discussed the answers, ask students if they can remember any other examples of interactive language from the conversation. Point out that the arguments are more fully developed and there is more exchange of ideas.

Suggested answers

1 They discuss the advantages and disadvantages of all the options.

2 They reach a conclusion: going by bicycle is the best option for William.

3 They interact well, responding to and developing each other's arguments. For example: *I think that's a good idea. So what about going by bus? Well, it depends.*

4 ▶▶| Ask students to read quickly through the conversation before you play the recording again. They write in the words they hear. Pause the recording occasionally to allow them time to write.

Point out how many of the missing words and phrases make the dialogue feel more **interactive**, more like a real exchange of views. Give them one or two examples:

So what about ...? I think that's a good idea.

Then ask them to read out others.

Students work in pairs and practise reading the completed dialogue aloud. **See page 136 for the Tapescript** (the Answers are shown in bold).

Follow up

Before they start writing, brainstorm with students the possible good and bad points of each option. The options here are less clear cut and more a matter of personal preference than the transport question, so students can put their own likes and dislikes into the characters. Issues to consider:

What are their interests?

What do they want to get from their holiday, e.g. physical exercise? Total relaxation? Cultural experience? Fun?

How much is cost a factor?

Students should try to incorporate interactive phrases into their written dialogues. You may want to suggest that they do the writing in pairs.

NOTE: Many learners at this level under-exploit a task and as a result do not demonstrate the depth or range of the language they have at their disposal. For this reason it's a good idea to remind students that the process of discussing options is the important thing, not the conclusion reached.

In this writing task, for example, it is better if the two friends have slightly different tastes and interests, as that is more likely to generate real 'negotiation'.

EXAM PART
Speaking Part 2

EXAM SKILLS
Discussing a situation

Interacting

TOPIC
Transport

TIME
50 minutes

KEY LANGUAGE
Agreeing, disagreeing, conceding, qualifying, summing up

PREPARATION
One photocopy of the activity page for each student

Getting there

1 **Work in pairs. Talk about this situation with your partner and agree on the best option.**

> **Situation**
>
> William has just got a new job. It will mean he has to work in the centre of the city, eight kilometres from his home. He has to decide on the best way of travelling to work every day. Here are the options:
>
> car   bus   bicycle   on foot
>
> NOTE: William has both a car and a bicycle. There is no car park at the company where he will work.
>
> What are the advantages and possible disadvantages of each option?

2 ▶▶|**Now listen to two people doing the same task.**

1 Do the speakers discuss the advantages and disadvantages of each option for William?

2 Do they choose an option for William? If so, what are the reasons for their choice?

3 How much do the speakers interact with each other?

3 ▶▶|**Now listen to two different people doing the same task, and answer the questions in exercise 2.**

4 ▶▶|**Read the conversation below, then listen again and fill in the spaces with the words you hear.**

A: Right. ....?

B: You start.

A: OK. Well, I don't think walking is a good idea. Eight kilometres is a bit too far to walk early in the morning.

B: .... it's a good way to keep fit and it doesn't cost anything.

A: Yes, but most people want to get to work as quickly as possible in the morning.

*B: That's true. ....
going by bike? We know he has a bicycle
....?*

A: Yeah. I .... It's much quicker than walking but it's still good exercise.

B: _____, cycling can be dangerous in busy city centres.

A: Yeah, and cycling in heavy traffic is awful.

B: Yeah. So what about going by bus?

A: Well, ... If the service is reliable ....

B: But they're often late and too crowded, which can be a real problem.

A: Mmm. ....: taking the bus every day can be quite expensive.

B: OK. He has a car as well as a bike, so how about travelling to work by car?

A: .... very much, either. OK, you're independent in a car but the traffic in the rush hour is terrible.

B: .... And finding somewhere to park can be difficult and expensive.

A: So, ...?

B: Well, ... go by bike: it doesn't cost anything, it's reliable, usually, and you travel independently.

*A: And it's good exercise too,
.... But he
.... a cycle helmet.*

B: Absolutely. ....?

A: Yeah – bike's best!

Work in pairs. Read the dialogue aloud.

Follow up

Write a conversation between two friends who are planning a holiday together. The options they are thinking about are:

• A camping holiday in the countryside

• Staying in a hotel in a famous historic city

• A holiday village by the sea (with lots of organised activities).

At the end of the conversation they should agree on which holiday to choose. Use some of the interactive phrases from exercise **4**.

Exam-style task

EXAM PART
Speaking Part 2

EXAM SKILLS
Discussing a situation

Making and responding to suggestions

TOPIC
Camping

TIME
30 minutes

KEY LANGUAGE
Future with *will*

Modal verbs *may, might, could*, etc.

PREPARATION
One photocopy of the activity page for each student

Optional: photocopies of the Tapescript of the model recording for the Exam-style task (see page 137)

Warm up

The **exam-style** task itself should take only 2–3 minutes. Here are some warm up ideas and suggestions for developing the exam-style task into a longer activity.

- Individual students think of things they might take with them on a camping trip – things which they don't know the English word for. Instead of asking for a translation, they have to do a mime in front of the class. Tell any student who thinks he/she knows the English word or phrase for it not to say the word out loud but to come up and write it on the board. You confirm or correct it.
  Variation: Instead of a mime, the student draws on the board a simple picture of the object. Again, anyone who thinks he/she knows the word, comes and writes it next to the picture.
- Draw on students' own experience. If anyone has been on a camping or walking holiday, ask them to describe how they prepared for it and what they took with them. What was **essential**, **useful** or **unnecessary** amongst the things they carried?

Exam-style task

Give out the activity sheets.
Students work in pairs. Read the situation to them and ask them to discuss it for 2–3 minutes. Remind them that they should try to discuss each option and, if possible, agree on five items for the two friends to take with them.

▶▶| When they have finished, play the model answer on the recording. **See page 137 for the Tapescript**. Tell them that it is above the language level expected of candidates at PET level, but it is intended to demonstrate how students should interact in a discussion about a situation and then bring the discussion to a close. You may want to give them photocopies of the Tapescript.

Developing the exam-style task

Give out the activity sheets.

Kim's game

Students look at the picture of the objects for 1 minute, and then turn the paper over. Working with a partner, they see how many objects they can remember.
During the recalling phase students can ask about vocabulary they don't know.

Matching verbs with nouns

Write these verbs on the board. Students have to say which object in the picture they most associate with each verb.

tie up   shine   cook   listen to   kick   cut
eat   navigate   sleep   sit

> **Answers**
> tie up: rope   shine: torch   cook: camping stove
> listen to: radio   kick: football   cut: penknife
> eat: plates and cutlery   navigate: map
> sleep: sleeping bag   sit: folding chair

Variation: Make the task more challenging by choosing more 'cryptic' verbs, for example:
climb (rope); *switch on* (torch or radio); *zip up* (sleeping bag).

Essential or unnecessary?

In pairs, students discuss all of the items pictured and have to decide whether each one is: **essential, useful, optional** or **unnecessary**.

Structures

Practise useful structures for this type of discussion and negotiation using examples from the list. For example:
*Sleeping bags **are essential**, I think.*
*If the weather's very hot, they **may not need** sleeping bags.*
I don't think they'll need a radio – they can listen to the sounds of nature!
*But **it'll be nice for them to have** some music in the evening.*
*A penknife **will** be very useful.*
*Folding chairs will be **too big and heavy to carry**.*

Pyramid decision

In pairs, students have to choose the **five** most useful or important items (1–2 minutes). They join another pair, making a group of four, and have to agree on **five** items. Finally, they form a group of eight and again have to agree on **five** items. Groups report their final choices to the whole class.

Different items

Ask students to choose five **different** things that they might take on such a walking and camping holiday. They have to speak for 30 seconds each, explaining why they would take those items.

Exam-style task

Hints and tips for Speaking Part 2

What you have to do

- Listen to the interlocutor's instructions.
- Look at a picture containing a number of different items.
- Speak to your partner (the other candidate) for 2–3 minutes.

How to approach it

- The interlocutor will not take part in the discussion, so you and your partner must be ready to keep the conversation going.
- It isn't essential to finish the task in the time given, but try to discuss each option in the picture as fully as possible. In the exam, candidates are assessed on their ability to take part in the task, rather than on the outcome of the discussion.
- Listen to what your partner says and, where appropriate, respond with a comment or a question.
- Don't worry if you don't know what something is called in English. Try to describe what people use it for: *I don't know what the name is in English, but it's a kind of small cooker with a gas bottle, and you use it when you go camping.*
- Remember, in a test like this short answers are usually not enough. The interlocutor needs to hear some examples of *extended speaking* from the candidates.

How to prepare yourself

- Take part actively in classroom discussions in pairs or groups.
- Try to move the discussion forward by responding to other people's ideas and opinions.
- Learn and practise how to make suggestions, give your opinion, agree and disagree.
- When there is a question to discuss, don't 'rush to a conclusion': take time to talk about different aspects of the question.
- Listening and speaking practice, inside or outside the classroom, is the best way of preparing for the test, and one of the best ways of improving your English generally.

Situation

Two friends are going on a walking and camping holiday in a hilly area. They are going to take a tent with them. Here is a picture with some other items they could take. Choose five items that you think they should take.

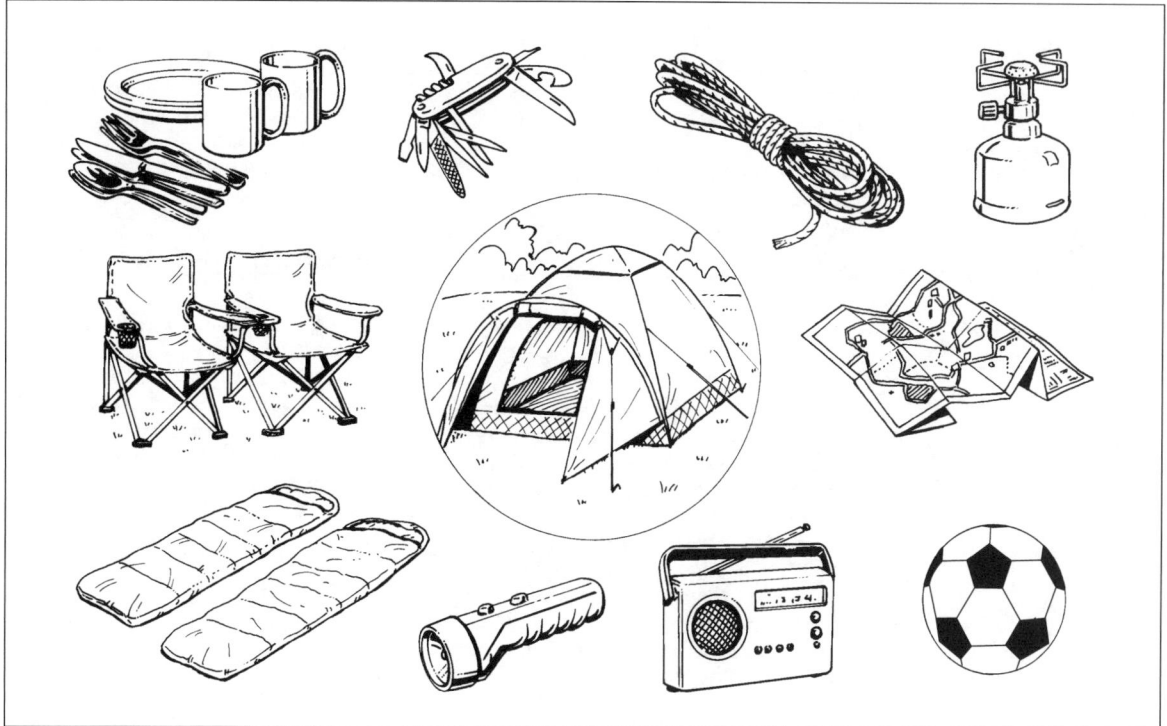

▶▶│When you have finished, listen to a model answer on the recording.

Exploring a picture

Warm up
Tableaux vivants

This is a good way of practising the present continuous through Total Physical Response.
For this task it is helpful to bring in some photographs showing people doing an activity together or sitting, standing, etc. in different poses. Reproductions of Old Master paintings can also be very good for this. The idea is to recreate the picture as a 3-D *tableau vivant* by telling a group of people where to stand and what to do. Ask a small group of students to come to the front of the class. Establish an imaginary frame for the photo. Within that frame, direct the students where to go and what poses to adopt. (Of course, it's important to direct them as far as possible with *words* rather than gestures!)
When the tableau is ready, call out 'CHEESE!' The photo is now 'taken' and the actors can relax.
Afterwards show that group the photo they were enacting and talk about the results.
Invite two confident speakers to try directing another group. Give them a different picture and a time limit to construct and take their 'photo'.

Main activities

Students do some of these activities alone and the others in pairs or small groups.

1 Give out the activity sheets.
Check whether students know the names of the instruments: *cello, violin, recorder*. In pairs (or groups of three) they look at the photograph and discuss the questions for 2 or 3 minutes.
Choose the pair or group that talked longest and most confidently and ask them to repeat part or all of their discussion in front of the class.
Afterwards, ask the whole class to say what was good about the discussion (no negative feedback at this stage).

Suggested answers
1 In a garden or park.
2 Playing musical instruments: the violin, cello and recorder.
3 Perhaps the woman playing the violin is the little girl's mother and the woman with the white hair playing the cello is her grandmother.
4 The elderly woman might be in her late sixties or early seventies, the woman with the violin in her mid-thirties and the little girl about seven years old.
5 Grandmother – blouse and light-coloured trousers; mother – blouse, cardigan and long, floral-patterned skirt; girl – (white) short-sleeved dress and sandals.
6 A hedge, bushes, trees, plants, etc.; part of a wall (classical-style architecture).
7 They seem to be enjoying themselves.
8 *Individual answers*

2 Ask the class to look at the second photo and compare it with the first photo. This short phase can be done in pairs or with the whole class.
3 Students discuss how to expand on the brief description given. If they are stuck for ideas, refer them to the questions in exercise **1**. They should make a brief note of their ideas.
4 ▶▶| Play the recording. Students make a quick comparison of content (not language!) between their notes and the speaker's on the recording. **See page 137 for the Tapescript** (the Answers to exercise **6** are in bold).
5 After students have read the questions, play the recording again. You may need to pause it while they note down their answers.

See page 137 for the Tapescript. Perhaps check understanding of *fringe* and *denim*. Emphasise that key words and phrases are fine here; if they try to write complete sentences it will become too dictation-like.

Answers
1 elderly, late sixties perhaps
2 only the top half of their bodies
3 she's behind the boy, leaning over his shoulder
4 showing him how to play … or maybe she's teaching him
5 straight, quite short, white
6 straight fair hair cut in a fringe
7 plain denim shirt with sleeves rolled up, T-shirt underneath
8 she has a kind, friendly expression; both are smiling and look as if they're enjoying themselves

6 ▶▶| Make sure students know what they are listening for before you play the recording again. **See page 137 for the Tapescript** (the Answers are in bold). You may want to give them photocopies of the Tapescript.

Answers
I'm not sure   perhaps   It looks as if   maybe   Something like that   could be   I suppose

7 Encourage students to choose a **pair** of questions rather than one each from different pairs. They should practise their conversation in order to be ready to do it again in front of the whole class.

Follow up

Ask students to prepare for this part of the test by setting aside some pages in their vocabulary notebooks for:
Describing people, Names of leisure activities, Talking about likes and dislikes, Using 'vague' language, i.e. useful words and phrases that express uncertainty, for example: *I'm not sure exactly, it could be, perhaps, something like that, that kind of thing, a sort of, I think it's called, it looks as if.*

Exploring a picture

1 **Look at this photograph.**

With a partner, discuss your answers to these questions.

1 Where are the three people?
2 What are they doing?
3 What do you think their relationship is?
4 How old do you think they are?
5 Describe the clothes they are wearing.
6 What can you see in the background?
7 In your opinion, how do they feel about what they are doing?
8 Would you enjoy doing something like this?

2 **Look at this photograph.**

Compare it with the photo in exercise 1. In what ways is it similar? In what ways is it different?

3 **Read this description of the photograph.**

The picture shows an old lady and a young boy. The boy has a guitar. The woman is teaching him to play, I think. They're both smiling, so I think they're enjoying it.

The description is very short. How could it be developed? Discuss ideas with your partner and make notes.

4 ▶▶ **Now listen to a description of the same photo. Compare the description with your ideas. What is similar? What is different?**

5 ▶▶ **Read these questions. Then listen to the recording again and note down your answers.**

What does the speaker say about

1 the age of the woman?
2 how much we can see of the people?
3 the position of the woman?
4 what she might be doing?
5 the woman's hair?
6 the boy's hair?
7 the boy's clothes?
8 the expressions of both people?

6 ▶▶ **The speaker uses seven expressions that show he is not 100% sure about a point. Here are three of them: *perhaps*, *something like that*, *could be*. Listen to the recording again – can you note down the others?**

7 **Work in pairs. Look at the questions below. Choose two questions to talk about. Your discussion should last 2–3 minutes, so think carefully about what you could say.**

- Can you play a musical instrument?
- What kinds of music do you enjoy listening to?
- What practical or artistic abilities do you have?
- What sort of things do you like to make, paint or draw?
- Do you have grandparents (or older relatives) whom you see?
- What have you learnt from these older people?
- Do you come from a large family?
- What activities do you do with different members of your family?

What are they like?

Warm up

Write these 'age descriptors' on the board and ask students to write them down in what they think might be chronological order.

toddler   in your mid-thirties   elderly   in your early twenties   young child   over 60   in your late forties   teenager   middle-aged   new-born baby

Explain that we use these expressions to describe people when we are not sure exactly how old they are (so they are very useful when talking about photos in the speaking test!).

Ask them to describe the ages of one or two people who they know using these expressions (and not exact ages). It's more realistic if they describe acquaintances, teachers, neighbours, etc., rather than family and friends whose ages they are likely to know.

Main activities

Students do some of these activities alone and the others in pairs or small groups.

1 Give out the activity sheets.

First ask students to look at the photo but to cover the description. Invite individuals to try to describe the picture.

Then they uncover the description and read it silently.

Talk about any items of unfamiliar vocabulary, e.g. *stud earrings, brushed back, forehead* by asking them to point to the things referred to.

If there are some confident and willing readers, ask one to read the text aloud, or read it yourself.

Students write the answers to the questions. Emphasise that key words, rather than the whole sentence, are enough here.

Answers

A late twenties or early thirties

B long hair, brushed back

C smartly dressed, plain jacket, checked shirt, small stud earrings, shoulder bag

D waiting for a train, looks calm, seems very interested in the newspaper she's reading

2 Explain to students that descriptions of a picture can be statements of fact (whether the **fact** is true or not doesn't matter) or **opinions** and **impressions**. Which of these they are affects the way you talk about them. For example, *They are sitting on the beach* and *She has white hair* are statements of fact, whereas *It looks as if it's going to rain* and *The castle looks mysterious* give opinions or impressions.

Remind students of these structures:

looks/seems + adjective

looks/seems as if + subject + verb

seems to be + verb with -ing

Once you have checked the answers, students should write their sentences in pairs or small groups. As whole class feedback, ask each pair or group to read out the sentences they like best.

Answers

1 c fact   **2** g fact   **3** f opinion/impression

4 b opinion/impression   **5** a opinion/impression

6 h opinion/impression   **7** e fact   **8** d opinion/impression

3 The sentences in this exercise are examples of describing people in photos. They use the same sort of phrases presented and practised in exercises **1** and **2**.

Personalise some of this vocabulary by asking questions. For example:

Do you know anyone with grey hair?

Do you know anyone in their mid-forties?

Do you know anyone with a tattoo?

Insist that they answer with a complete sentence, for example:

Yes, my grandmother's got grey hair.

Answers

1 C	2 B	3 D	4 C	5 A	6 A	7 B	8 C
9 D	10 B	11 A	12 D				

4 Working in pairs, students look at all the pictures, and then turn the paper over. They have 1 minute to remember as much as possible about the six people in terms of: **age**, **physical appearance**, **clothes** and **accessories**, and, if possible, **expression** or **behaviour**. Which person remembered the most details?

Then they take it in turns to describe one of the photos. Their partner must point to the picture they described.

Follow up: Students work in pairs or small groups. One person describes another student in the class as they look today. (Of course, they must be careful not to give away the identity of the person by looking across the classroom at them!) They should try to include at least one **fact** and one **opinion** or **impression** in their description. The others try to guess who the person is. The turn passes to the next person.

Variation: Hand out photos of people to each pair or group for students to describe, or put the photos on the walls of the classroom so they choose who to describe.

5 In pairs, students discuss the Part 4-type conversation task for 2–3 minutes.

Follow up

Ask students to write a description of a photo they have at home. The photo should contain a number of people. They should describe:

- the setting/place/situation
- who the people are
- what they look like
- what they are wearing
- what they are doing
- what is happening in the photo.

Suggest to them that, if they are able to do so, it would be nice if they attached their photo (or a copy) to their writing.

As a further follow up, you could also ask them to create (or continue) a page in their vocabulary notebooks for **clothes and accessories**. Picture/photo dictionaries are a useful reference for this.

EXAM PART
Speaking Parts 3 & 4

EXAM SKILLS
Describing appearance

Describing your impressions

TOPIC
People

Clothes

TIME
40 minutes

KEY LANGUAGE
Expressions for fact and opinion

looks + adjective

looks as if / seems to be + verb construction

PREPARATION
One photocopy of the activity page for each student

Optional: photos of people for the Variation in exercise 4

What are they like?

1 Look at this photo of a woman at Osaka station in Japan. Read the description and answer the questions.

I can see a woman. She looks as if she's waiting for a train. I think she's probably in her late twenties or early thirties. She's smartly dressed, wearing a plain jacket and a checked shirt. She's got long hair, which is brushed back from her forehead. She's wearing small stud earrings. She's carrying a shoulder bag. The station is busy but she looks calm and seems very interested in the newspaper she's reading.

Which expressions refer to her

A age? ....late twenties or early thirties....

B physical appearance?

C clothes and accessories?

D expression or behaviour?

----

2 Complete each sentence on the left by drawing a line to the second part. Which of the sentences state a fact, and which ones give an opinion or impression?

1	**She's wearing**	a	my brother.
2	**She's a**	b	be waving at someone.
3	He **looks as if**	c	a baseball cap.
4	She **seems to**	d	19 or 20 years old.
5	That boy **looks like**	e	a rucksack on his back.
6	They **look** rather	f	he's waiting for a bus.
7	He's **got**	g	famous actress.
8	I think **she's about**	h	frightened.

Use the phrases in bold to make your own sentences. Here are some ideas to help you.

- busy • a friendly smile • be making a speech • a long skirt • glasses
- he's received some good news
- 24 or 25 • his father • good cook

3 Match these descriptions of people to one of the categories A–D in exercise 1.

1 He's wearing a dark suit and a red striped tie. *C*
2 He's well-built and looks quite strong.
3 He looks a bit lost.
4 She's wearing a patterned top and jeans.
5 I think she's in her mid-thirties.
6 He's elderly … late seventies, perhaps.
7 She's got blonde hair and a rather red complexion.
8 She's got a nose ring and a small tattoo on her shoulder.
9 They seem to be very relaxed.
10 She's got grey hair and her skin is quite wrinkled.
11 He's middle-aged, maybe 45 or 50.
12 She looks as if she's going to cry.

4

Work in pairs. Look at the six pictures for 30 seconds. Turn the paper over. With your partner, try to remember as much as you can about the people. Use the categories A–D in exercise 1.

Then look at the pictures again and, in turn, describe one of the people. Your partner must point to the person you have described.

5 Work in pairs. Discuss this conversation task for 2–3 minutes.

- Talk together about what clothes you like to wear when you are not at school/work. Are there any styles or colours you don't like wearing?

What's the big idea?

Warm up
Speed chatting

Put students into groups of three. They should sit on chairs facing each other. Tell them they must have a conversation for 2 minutes on the topic you are going to write on the board. (Stress that they must keep talking for the whole 2 minutes, and you don't want to hear anyone talking about a different topic!) Write **one** of the conversation tasks on the board.

What do you mostly use a computer for in your daily life?
What kind of food do you prefer when you go out for a meal?
Who does the housework in your home? What jobs do you usually do?
What sort of things do you read nowadays? What about when you were a young child?
Describe one or two of your good friends. What activities do you like doing together?
What forms of healthy physical exercise do you enjoy?
How do you expect to use the English language in the future?
What makes you laugh? When was the last time you enjoyed a good laugh about something?
Describe an annual festival that you enjoy. Explain how you participate in it.
Talk about an older person, perhaps in your family, who has had an important influence on your life.

Tell the students to start. Walk around and monitor their conversations. Before the 2 minutes are up, write the next conversation task on the board.

Stop the activity and then regroup students before they start the second conversation, and so on, so they discuss as many of the topics in 2 minutes as appropriate.

Afterwards, ask students which conversation tasks were best or easiest to talk about.

Main activities

Students do some of these activities alone and the others in pairs or small groups.

1 Give out the activity sheets.

Working in pairs, students look at the photo of American actress Sharon Stone for 30 seconds, and then cover it.

They discuss the written description, correcting it in pencil.

They look at the photo again and reread the text, adding any corrections they missed.

Suggested answers
The mistakes are underlined and the corrected text is in bold.

The picture shows a famous actress ~~talking and laughing with some of her fans~~ **signing autographs for some of her fans**. It's very crowded, with lots of people trying to get close to her. Some of them are holding ~~cameras~~ **books and pens** because they want to ~~take photos~~ **get her autograph**. The actress has ~~long, dark~~ **short, fair/blonde** hair and she's wearing a ~~white~~ **black sleeveless** dress ~~with long sleeves~~. **She's also wearing large earrings and a necklace.** ~~She isn't wearing any jewellery.~~ In the bottom left-hand corner of the picture we can see a boy holding a pen and a book or magazine out to her. ~~He's smiling at the actress~~ **We can only see one side of his face so we can't see if he's smiling at the actress.** In the background we can see some buildings ~~but nothing else~~ **and some trees.**

2 Remind students that the topics for conversation in Part 4 of the Speaking test are suggested by the photos used in Part 3.

If you did the **Warm up**, ask students to think about one or two of the conversation tasks they did and to try to imagine the photos that went with them.

Ask the class to give you some examples of celebrities.

What are they famous for? Do they 'deserve' their fame?

Ask if anyone has ever met a celebrity or got the autograph of one. Explain the expression *in the public eye*. Brainstorm and write on the board some advantages and disadvantages of being a celebrity.

Then students get into pairs and do the two conversation tasks.

3 Using the examples in exercise **2** as models, students work in pairs to write one task for the photo.

Tell the students that conversation tasks should be general enough to allow anyone to take part. Guide them away from questions that will exclude (for example) those who do not have specialist knowledge of premiership football!

They exchange their task with another pair and talk for 2–3 minutes about that pair's task.

The pairs who exchanged tasks can then take it in turns to observe each other doing the task again. Suggest that they give each other feedback as follows:

How easy was it to hear and to follow the conversation?

How much did they develop the conversation, e.g. going into detail and producing some longer sentences?

How well did they listen to each other and interact with questions and comments?

Ask one or two pairs to perform their conversation task in front of the class.

Follow up

Bring in photos and/or ask students to collect interesting pictures from newspapers, magazines and publicity material, and to bring them to class. Ideally, these should be lively scenes containing several people, and should suggest a topic that is easy to discuss.

In pairs, students write questions on their photos (for Part 3 practice) and a conversation task (for Part 4). They work in groups of four, exchanging photos and tasks and rotating the roles of interlocutor, assessor and candidates.

Create a 'gallery' of pictures on the classroom walls. These can be labelled with short sentences containing useful vocabulary, e.g.

In the foreground we can see a dog **jumping** for a ball.

*There are some houses **in the distance**.*

EXAM PART
Speaking Parts 3 & 4

EXAM SKILLS
Describing a picture

Discussing a topic in pairs

TOPIC
Celebrities

Sport

TIME
40 minutes

KEY LANGUAGE
Present continuous for describing activities in a picture

Descriptive adjectives

PREPARATION
One photocopy of the activity page for each student

Photos showing small groups of people (for the **Follow up**)

What's the big idea?

1 Look at this photograph for 30 seconds and try to remember as much as you can.

Cover the photo and read this text. It contains eight factual mistakes. Work with a partner and try to correct the mistakes.

The picture shows a famous actress talking and laughing with some of her fans. It's very crowded, with lots of people trying to get close to her. Some of them are holding cameras because they want to take photos. The actress has long, dark hair and she's wearing a white dress with long sleeves. She's also wearing large earrings and a necklace. In the bottom left-hand corner of the picture we can see a boy holding a pen and a book or magazine out to her. He's smiling at the actress. In the background we can see some buildings but nothing else.

2 Work in pairs. Student A reads out Conversation task A. Talk about it together for 2 minutes. Student B reads out Conversation task B. Talk about it together for 2 minutes.
When you do the second task, try not to repeat anything you said in the first conversation.

Conversation task A
Your photograph shows a famous film actress signing autographs. Talk about which actors, singers or other celebrities you admire and what you know about their lives.

Conversation task B
What are the good and bad points about being famous and in the public eye? Would you like to be famous?

3 Work in pairs. Look at this photo and write a conversation task for another pair of students. The task should be about 25 words.

Exchange tasks with another pair. Talk for 2–3 minutes.

Exam-style task

PART 3

▶▶❙Listen to the recording, or read out the interlocutor's script to your partner, and then talk about your photograph for about 1 minute.

INTERLOCUTOR: Now I'd like each of you to talk on your own about something. I'm going to give each of you a photograph of people celebrating a special event. (*Student A*), here's your photograph. Please show it to (*Student B*), but I'd like you to talk about it. (*Student B*), you just listen. I'll give you your photograph in a minute. (*Student A*), please tell us what you can see in your photograph.

Student A speaks for about 1 minute.

Thank you.

Now, (*Student B*), here's your photograph. It also shows people celebrating an important event. Please show it to (*Student A*) and tell us what you can see in the photograph.

Student B speaks for about 1 minute.

Thank you.

Photograph for Student A

Photograph for Student B

PART 4

▶▶❙Listen to the recording, or read out the interlocutor's script, and then talk to your partner for 2–3 minutes.

INTERLOCUTOR: Your photographs showed people celebrating an important event. Now I'd like you to talk together about important events that you celebrate, and explain how you celebrate them.

Students A and B speak together for 2–3 minutes.

Thank you. That's the end of the test.

▶▶❙Listen to the model answers for Parts 3 and 4 on the recording. Note that the language level is higher than that expected of candidates at PET level.

For Part 3, remember that there are many ways of describing a photo – everyone will describe it differently – and for Part 4, you need to interact with your partner, taking turns, asking questions and responding to what your partner says.

Hints and tips for Speaking Part 3

What you have to do

- You have to describe a colour photograph.
- The interlocutor will tell you the subject of the photo, but will not ask you any further questions. You have to speak on your own without prompting.
- You can describe the place, the people in the picture and what they are doing, any important objects and where they are.

How to approach it

- Imagine you are describing the picture to someone who can't see it. Include the names of objects, and describe colours, people's clothes, the weather, and so on.
- Talk about facts and impressions: *There's a ... , She looks ...*

- If you don't understand what is happening in the photo, just describe what you can see.
- Try to sound interested and curious about the subject of your photo; avoid giving the interlocutor a boring 'list' of things you can see.

How to prepare yourself

- Practise talking about a photo for 1 minute.
- Learn to describe the areas of a picture: *bottom right-hand corner, top left-hand corner, background, foreground, in the middle of the picture,* etc.
- Learn expressions to use when you don't know the word for something, e.g. *I don't know what it's called in English, but it's like / it's a kind of ...*

Hints and tips for Speaking Part 4

What you have to do

- You have to talk with your partner for 2–3 minutes on a subject given by the interlocutor.
- The subject will be connected with the photos you have just described, but the interlocutor will take the photos back. You don't need to refer to them in your conversation.

How to approach it

- Turn towards your partner so it's easier to talk together.
- Remember, the interlocutor will not join in this part: it is a conversation between you and your partner.
- Say what you think, but also take turns, ask questions and respond to what your partner says.

- If you don't understand something the interlocutor (or your speaking partner) says, it is all right to ask them to repeat it.
- Speak clearly at all times so the interlocutor and your partner can hear you.

How to prepare yourself

- Practise talking about your interests, your likes and dislikes, and your opinions. It's important that you can give *reasons* for these views.
- Practise short conversations with a partner (2–3 minutes) on common everyday topics. (Your teacher can advise you what these topics might be.)
- Practise expressions for agreement and *friendly* disagreement.

Tapescripts

Writing Part 1 Activity 2
After the show
Exercise 4

Tapescript and Answers

SARA: If we leave now, we'll catch the last bus.

JEFF: But the band **haven't finished playing yet**.

SARA: Well, it's midnight now and we arrived here at 9 pm.

JEFF: But, Sara, we **can't leave before** the end.

SARA: This is definitely the loudest band I've ever heard!

JEFF: But Rory **plays guitar really well, doesn't he**?

SARA: He's all right, but I think the support band were better.

* * *

JEFF: Look! The bus has just gone. What shall we do now?

SARA: **We should have left the concert** half an hour earlier.

JEFF: Why don't we take a taxi?

SARA: **It's going to be difficult to find a taxi** at this time.

JEFF: Mmm. You're right.

SARA: We'll have to **go home on foot**.

JEFF: You'd better phone your parents. You know how strict they are.

SARA: You're right. Can **you lend me** your mobile?

JEFF: Yeah, of course … Oh, no! I've left it at home.

SARA: Oh, look, there's Max. Perhaps he'll take us home in his car. Hi, Max! **Do you think you could take us** to Grendon?

MAX: Glad to. But there's only room for one, I'm afraid.

SARA: (*Jumping in*) Thanks, Max. Sorry, Jeff! But you know how it is: **your Mum and Dad are not as strict as mine.**

JEFF: Sara!!!

Listening Part 1 Activity 1
Distinguishing features
Exercise 2

Tapescript

FRIEND: What was your English class like? Were they nice?

CRISTINA: Yeah, I was lucky — they were a great group. We got on really well, and we often went out together in the evenings.

FRIEND: Tell me about them.

CRISTINA: Let's think. Well, there was a boy from Osaka in Japan. His name was **Hiro**. He had glasses and wore a cap all the time, even in class. He was really funny and made us all laugh.

FRIEND: What about **Clara**? You told me about her in an email once.

CRISTINA: Oh, yes. Well, Clara came from Panama in central America. So she spoke Spanish. She had long black curly hair and was always smiling.

FRIEND: Who else? Any nice boys?

CRISTINA: Well, there was **Peter**. He was from Switzerland – the German-speaking part.

FRIEND: What did he look like?

CRISTINA: He had spiky blond hair, you know, gelled and sticking up. And he was tall – I mean really tall, probably the tallest person in the school. Peter was rather quiet and shy. His best friend in the class was Antonio, who came from Bologna in Italy. I don't know why they became such good friends because they were completely different.

FRIEND: What was **Antonio** like?

CRISTINA: He was short and dark with wavy black hair and big dark eyes. He was really funny, too. He never stopped talking. He was always laughing and joking and waving his arms about.

FRIEND: Do you think you'll see any of them again one day?

CRISTINA: I hope so. Well, I'm definitely going to see **Sophie**. She's French. She's only 18 but she looks older. She always wore black clothes and a lot of eye make-up. She's invited me to visit her in Paris next summer.

FRIEND: Great!

CRISTINA: **Esra** will be there, too. She's the girl from Turkey that I told you about. She had short dark hair and a very pretty face. She always wore beautiful jewellery – earrings, bracelets, necklaces and so on, and she made it all herself.

Listening Part 1 Activity 1
Distinguishing features
Exercise 3

Tapescript

WOMAN: Will's pirate is wearing a hat. He's got one earring and a bushy black beard. There's a parrot on his shoulder.

Luke's pirate is wearing a spotted scarf on his head instead of a hat. He's got a bushy black beard, but no earrings. There's a parrot on his shoulder.

Michelle's pirate hasn't got a beard and he hasn't got a parrot on his shoulder. He's wearing a hat and he's got two earrings, one in each ear.

Listening Part 1 Activity 1
Distinguishing features
Exercise 4

Tapescript

MAN: Your pirate's wearing a spotted scarf on his head. [*pause*] He's got a bushy black beard and he's got one earring. [*pause*] There's a parrot on each of his shoulders.

Instant PET by Martyn Ford © Cambridge University Press 2007 **PHOTOCOPIABLE**

Listening Part 1 Activity 2

How do you know?

Exercise 1

Tapescript

1 WOMAN: My first baby was born here, though not in this ward, of course. My mother had an operation here in 2004, and only last week we had to bring our son, Jack, here because he fell and broke his arm. It's got very good facilities and the nurses here are marvellous.

2 MAN: I've never stayed here before. It's very nice, isn't it? I have a single room on the second floor overlooking the beach. The dining room is very stylish and there's a comfortable residents' lounge where I can sit quietly and read the paper.

3 WOMAN: When I arrived there was a long queue for the counter. Some people had big parcels to send; others had forms to fill in. All I wanted was to buy a stamp for my postcard!

4 YOUNGER CHILD: Ooh, come and look at this creature here, Mum. It's called an okapi. It says so here on the bars of the cage – '... native to Zaire, in Central Africa.' Do you think it feels sad stuck in here instead of running free in the wild?

5 OLDER CHILD: We were worried we were going to miss our flight, so we hurried in through the big glass doors. As soon as we arrived, Dad got a trolley, which we put our luggage on and we went to look for the right check-in desk.

6 MAN: It was really crowded with children because of the school holidays. They were playing and jumping in off the side so it was difficult to swim a whole length in a straight line. There was a lifeguard there but he didn't say anything to them.

Listening Part 1 Activity 2

How do you know?

Exercise 2

Tapescript

Example

WOMAN: They smell beautiful, don't they? They're from my grandmother's garden. I think they look nice in this vase.

1 MAN: It was gold, with a beautiful diamond. It fitted her finger perfectly.

2 WOMAN: How would you like them – boiled, fried, or scrambled?

3 MAN: There's a clean one in the cupboard upstairs. When you've had your shower and dried yourself, just leave it on the rail in the bathroom.

4 WOMAN: I've given up using the car and I go to work on this now. I can move through the traffic easily, and riding it is good exercise for me.

5 MAN: She gave it to the inspector. He looked at it and said, 'Change at Birmingham – that's the station after next.' Then he clipped it and handed it back to her.

6 WOMAN: 'Shake well before use,' it says on the label. 'Take one spoonful three times a day before meals. If there are any side effects, contact your doctor.'

7 MAN: My Dad used to get through two packets a day. Now, I'm glad to say, he's given up. His cough has gone; he feels better and of course he's saving a lot of money.

Listening Part 1 Activity 3

Look at the time!

Exercise 1

Tapescript

MAN: The plane was supposed to take off at 10.20 am but it was delayed by fog and we didn't leave until 11.50. We eventually landed at Milan Linate at 2.35 pm.

Listening Part 1 Activity 3

Look at the time!

Exercise 2

Tapescript

MOTHER: All right, then, you can go. But you must be back by 9 o'clock at the latest. Remember, it's a school day tomorrow and you have to get up at 7 o'clock.

TAMSIN: Oh! That's really early, Mum. Nina and Samantha don't have to be home till 10!

MOTHER: Look, Tamsin, I don't care what other girls can and can't do. As far as I'm concerned, that's much too late.

TAMSIN: Oh, Mum ...

MOTHER: No, that's my final decision. Otherwise, you can't go at all.

TAMSIN: OK, Mum.

Listening Part 1 Activity 3

Look at the time!

Exercise 3

Tapescript

WOMAN: Now, I put the cake in the oven at 1.35, and it takes an hour and fifteen minutes to bake. That means it'll be ready at ten to three. Then I'll take it out of the oven and leave it to cool, so it should be ready to eat by half past four when Jenny comes.

Listening Part 1 Activity 3

And now for the weather

Exercise 3

Tapescript

MAN: Well, I knew that the north of Scotland can be very cloudy and cold at that time of the year. In fact, we were really lucky, as we didn't have a drop of rain the whole holiday. I mean, it wasn't hot, of course. You needed a pullover, but it was blue skies and sunshine every day – great walking weather.

Listening Part 1 Activity 4

Exam-style task

Tapescript

Example

ISABEL: My favourite band is called *Ka-Zoom*. There are three girls and two guys. The girls are the lead singers, and they dance really well, too. Then there's a guy in the background who plays keyboards and another guy on drums. Oh, and sometimes one of the girls plays the guitar.

1 SALLY: Excuse me. I've lost my cat. I wonder if you've seen it anywhere?

MAN: Is it a black cat with white paws?

SALLY: No, it's a ginger cat with long fur, and it's striped, a bit like a tiger.

MAN: Was it wearing a collar?

SALLY: Unfortunately not.

2 GIRL: What did you do last night, Karen?

KAREN: Well, not what I'd planned. Mum and Dad went to the cinema …

GIRL: Did you go too?

KAREN: No, I'd arranged for Jessie to come round. She'd bought a new DVD and we wanted to watch it together.

GIRL: Was it good?

KAREN: Jessie never came. She phoned at the last minute to say she had too much homework and couldn't come. So I played games on the computer, all on my own!

3 TOM: I was late for school this morning.

GIRL: Why? Did you get up late?

TOM: No, it wasn't that. I usually catch the bus at 8.25 but it was full, so I had to wait for the next one. That didn't arrive until 8.40.

GIRL: So what time did you get to school?

TOM: At a quarter past nine – 15 minutes late.

4 MAN: I know she likes chocolates, but she's on a diet at the moment so that's not a good idea. All women love jewellery, so that would probably be the safest option. I could get her a CD, I suppose, but I don't know her taste in music and I'd probably buy the wrong thing.

5 MAN: Here's your coffee. You wanted it black, didn't you?

WOMAN: Actually, could I have a little milk in it?

MAN: Sure. Would you like a piece of this cake? It's home-made.

WOMAN: It looks delicious, but I'd better not.

MAN: Just a small piece?

WOMAN: Oh, go on then.

6 MAN: Which book are you looking for, Mandy?

MANDY: I can't remember the title but it's got a picture on the cover of a rocket flying through space.

MAN: Do you mean this one?

MANDY: No, not that – there's a background of stars in the picture but you can't see any planets.

7 BOY: This game is called *Cat and Mouse*. You're the mouse, OK, and you're here at the entrance to the room. Your aim is to get to the cheese in the middle of the room. The cat's away, but he's left lots of traps, which you have to jump over. If you get caught in a trap you lose a life, and you only have six lives.

Listening Part 2 Activity 1

The place to be

Exercise 2

Tapescript

MARK: In case you don't know, the Quarter is an area of narrow old streets full of fascinating little shops, cafés and restaurants. It's situated between the railway station in the west of the town, and the main shopping centre with its famous name stores.

You can find some wonderful shops in the Quarter. People love *High Flyers*, a shop which sells kites, and nothing else. Kites of every shape and size and colour you can possibly imagine, and they were all built by the owners of the shop, Dave and Miranda. Their kites are beautiful but rather expensive; but every Tuesday afternoon they give free practical demonstrations on how to make your own.

While you're in the Quarter you'll probably want to look at clothes and jewellery. *Dressed to Kill* and *Togged Up* are two shops that are always crowded with students. That's because they sell great clothes that look as good as a lot of the top designer stuff, but cost half the price.

If you're interested in second-hand stuff, and you don't mind getting up early on Sunday morning you should go and see the weekly *Flea Market* in Princes Court. Amongst the second-hand furniture, books, pictures and clocks, you can find the occasional bargain but also of course a lot of rubbish! The market closes at midday but the *Hot Links* coffee bar nearby, which is a meeting place for young artists and designers, is open all day six days a week.

There are more cafés on Corn Street where, in fine weather, you can sit outside at pavement tables and watch the world go by. You'll probably hear some live music too: this part of the Quarter is famous for its buskers – that is, people who sing and play music in the street. They earn good money, especially from visitors to the town. But in my opinion they deserve it, because they play so well.

If you're hungry enough to want a proper meal, then there are plenty of restaurants and cuisines to choose from, including French, Italian, Chinese, Indian, Thai and Mexican. But watch out, some of them can be a bit pricey if you're on a student budget. At the *Medina Barbecue* you choose your own combination of fish or meat and vegetables from a self-service counter and a chef cooks the food in front of you on a large grill. It's a favourite eating place for students, and from Sunday to Thursday there's a 25% discount, but you must show your student ID card. And if you go on these days, be prepared to queue.

Listening Part 2 Activity 2

Sweet memory

Exercise 2

Tapescript

Section 1

HELEN: When I was a child I used to look forward to Saturday mornings. That was when my brother, Bernard, and I got our pocket money from our father. I would put half of it in my moneybox, and run off happily with the rest to Bartlett's. This was the name of the little, local shop at the end of our street; and in those days before supermarkets, it was the place where most families in the neighbourhood did their weekly food shopping.

Section 2

There I would join the other girls and boys eager to spend their Saturday pocket money, and we'd ask Mrs Bartlett to show us 'the tray'. You have to remember that in those days there weren't all the varieties of sweets and chocolate bars you see on sale now. All Mrs Bartlett had were a few items arranged on a simple wooden tray, which she kept under the counter and brought out for the children on Saturdays. But to us it was a wonderful sight: toffees, lollipops, barley sugar, liquorice, aniseed balls, sweets wrapped in brightly coloured paper. It always took ages for each child to decide what to buy. But Mrs Bartlett didn't mind: as long as there were no grown-up customers waiting to be served, she let us take our time.

Section 3

Bernard liked sweets, too. The problem was he didn't like buying them. When I went to Bartlett's, he went in the opposite direction — to a newsagent's shop that sold football cards. He was mad about these picture cards of famous footballers, and spent all his pocket money trying to collect whole teams of players, such as Aston Villa and Wolverhampton Wanderers.

Section 4

On Saturday afternoons he would search the house and find out where I was. He knew I had been to Bartlett's. If I didn't hide my bag of sweets quickly enough, he'd see it and say, 'Can I have one?' And I would say, 'Why should I give you one? You had your pocket money too — you could have bought your own sweets.' Then Bernard would go to our mother to complain, 'Mum, Helen has a whole bag of sweets and she won't give me one.' To which Mum would say, 'Helen, don't be so mean. Share your sweets with your brother!' I thought this was really unfair, but of course I gave him some sweets. I mean, I had no choice!

Listening Part 2 Activity 3

Nick Chandler, spider man

Exercise 2

Tapescript

Section 1

INTERVIEWER: Nick, other people keep dogs and cats and rabbits at home but your pets are a bit more unusual, aren't they?

NICK: Yes, I suppose so. I keep spiders. I have over 300 at the moment.

INTERVIEWER: Why so many?

NICK: I've been collecting them since I was a boy. I've always found them fascinating. They're amazing creatures, and I learn something new about them every day. I never get bored with them.

INTERVIEWER: How many species of spider are there in the world?

NICK: There are around 40,000. And scientists keep discovering new ones all the time.

INTERVIEWER: Which type of spiders do you keep?

NICK: Tarantulas, mainly. And there are 800 different species of them in the world.

INTERVIEWER: Now tell me about the one you're holding at the moment.

NICK: OK. This is a pink-toed tarantula and it normally lives in the trees in the jungles of Brazil in South America.

INTERVIEWER: Pink-toed?

NICK: Yes, because of the pink tips to its legs. Many species of tarantulas are brightly coloured and have beautiful markings on them.

INTERVIEWER: Everyone knows spiders have got eight legs, but many of them have got eight eyes as well, haven't they?

NICK: That's right, though in fact they can't see very well. They can tell the difference between light and dark but they can't really see different colours or focus on things.

Section 2

INTERVIEWER: Are they dangerous?

NICK: No, tarantulas aren't dangerous, if you're careful. They could give you a bad bite but it's very unusual for this to happen, and you certainly wouldn't die from it. They are very shy creatures, and in the wild they make holes to hide away in, you know, like rabbits do. They'd never jump out and attack a man! I've been handling tarantulas for years and I've never been bitten. But obviously you have to stay calm and not make any sudden movements that might frighten the spider.

Section 3

INTERVIEWER: Are there many dangerous spiders in the world?

NICK: Yeah, there are very few, in fact. Perhaps the most dangerous is the *Sydney funnel web* in Australia. If you're bitten by a funnel web you have to get medical treatment at once, as people have died from the bite of this spider. But it's important to remember that most of the 40,000 species are completely harmless to human beings.

Section 4

INTERVIEWER: Do tarantulas make good pets, Nick?

NICK: Yeah, they certainly do. And they're easy to look after, but I must stress that anyone thinking of keeping a tarantula as a pet should read about them first, and learn how to look after them. For example, did you know there are species of tarantulas that can live as long as twenty years? That's longer than a dog or cat! Finally, you should of course make sure that the people you live with are happy about the idea of having tarantulas in the house!

INTERVIEWER: Why do you think some people are afraid of spiders?

NICK: I'm not sure. Perhaps it's their long legs or their quick movements, or the fact that they appear suddenly out of dark holes and corners of the house. Anyway, it's not at all logical – bees are more dangerous. Far more people die of bee stings every year than die of spider bites.

INTERVIEWER: What advice would you give to people who are afraid of spiders?

NICK: I'd say find out more about them. They are such wonderful creatures to watch and study. And the more you get to know – especially if you have a chance to hold them, like I'm doing now – the less afraid you will be.

INTERVIEWER: Thank you, Nick.

Listening Part 2 Activity 4

Exam-style task

Tapescript

INTERVIEWER: Hello and welcome to *Book Club*. This week I have in the studio John Miller, the author of a new book called *The Story of Ice Cream*. We all love ice cream but most of us probably never think about where it came from, or when. So, how long has ice cream been around, John? Hundreds of years? Thousands?

MILLER: Well, it depends what you mean by *ice cream*. We know that the ancient Romans mixed ice with fruit to make a kind of cold dessert; and in the seventh century the Chinese mixed snow with syrup to make something refreshing *and* sweet.

INTERVIEWER: But there was no cream involved?

MILLER: No, that's right. Not at that stage. But records show that in 16th century Italy people mixed frozen milk with honey.

INTERVIEWER: Ah, that's a little bit closer.

MILLER: Mmm. But what we know as ice cream today was probably invented in France in 1775.

INTERVIEWER: But in those days, I imagine, not everybody had the chance to try this delicious new dessert.

MILLER: Oh, no. Ice cream was a rare treat, enjoyed only by a small number of very rich people. And even then, it had to be made and eaten immediately because there were no refrigerators to keep it cold.

INTERVIEWER: So how did ice cream become available to ordinary people?

MILLER: Well, from about 1850, Italian immigrants who came to live in London, started to make something they called 'hokey-pokey', which was a kind of ice cream. They travelled around the streets selling it for only a penny. It was served in little glasses. Customers licked the glasses empty and then gave them back to the hokey-pokey seller, who reused them.

INTERVIEWER: It doesn't sound very hygienic! And what about the ice cream cone? When we hear the word 'ice cream', most of us have a mental image of a nice round scoop of ice cream – vanilla, strawberry or chocolate – on top of a cone made of wafer biscuit. It's true, isn't it?

MILLER: Yes, it's true. The invention of the cone, and the development of refrigerators of course, did more than anything to make ice cream a popular treat that was easy to serve and easy to eat. There are different stories about where the cone came from but the most famous, and the one I believe, is that it was invented by a Syrian man called Ernest Hamwi at the St Louis World Fair in 1904.

INTERVIEWER: That's St Louis in the United States of America?

MILLER: That's right. It seems that Ernest Hamwi had a stall at the fair selling waffles. Now waffles are a kind of flat square cake with squares marked on them. Anyway, next to Hamwi there was another man selling ice cream, in the usual way, in little glasses. Because the weather was hot and he was selling so much ice cream, this man ran out of glasses. Hamwi, who wasn't doing quite such good business with his waffles, came up with a solution: he rolled one of his waffles into a cone shape and put a serving of ice cream into it. The customers at the fair must have been very pleased with it because the idea caught on and soon ice cream cones were being sold everywhere.

INTERVIEWER: Fascinating. Well, thank you, John. And that's all for today. *The Story of Ice Cream* by John Miller is published this week by Gadfly Books.

Listening Part 3 Activity 1

Time and place

Exercise 2

Tapescript

1   History lessons are twice a week on Monday and Tuesday afternoons; Maths is once a week on a Thursday morning.

2   I'm a student but I also have a part-time job. I have classes all day on Monday and Tuesday, and on Wednesday until lunchtime; and I work in a coffee bar on Wednesday afternoon and all day Thursday and Friday.

3   Please note we shall be closed for staff training all day on Wednesday 23rd November. Our normal office hours are 9 to 4.30 Monday to Friday and 9 to 12.30 on Saturdays.

4   The poet, Shelley, was born in 1792 and drowned while on a sailing trip off the coast of Italy in August 1822. His wife, Mary, lived until 1851.

5   College application forms will be available from 24th September. They must be completed and sent off on or before 31st January, which means you have just four months to make your decision.

6   Cricket and baseball are both bat and ball games but a cricket team has eleven players whereas a baseball team has nine.

7   For 150 million years, dinosaurs ruled the earth; and then, around 65 million years ago, they died out, for reasons scientists don't really understand.

8   Every four years at the summer Olympic Games around 700 athletes from all over the world compete in more than 20 different sports.

9   At the special exhibition you can see furniture from the first half of the 20th century, and ceramics and glassware from the 18th and 19th centuries.

10   Trees grow at different rates: for example in a fifteen year period an oak tree will grow about seven point five metres, while a juniper tree during the same period will grow three metres.

11   I'm 52 kilos now, but before I started running I weighed 58 – no, sorry – 59 kilos. And I still eat the same amount.

12   I'll give you my new telephone number – it's 07952 396755. That's 07952 396755.

Listening Part 3 Activity 1

Time and place

Exercise 3

Tapescript

1 One of the most impressive places I've ever seen is the Colosseum in the centre of Rome in Italy. It's a ruin now but 2,000 years ago it was the largest outdoor theatre in the empire and could hold over 50,000 spectators.

2 I was really impressed by the grand temple of Ramses II in Egypt. It was cut out of the cliffs above the river Nile, and on the outside you can see four huge statues of the king himself.

3 I'll never forget the amazing Temple of Heaven in Beijing in China. It's got three roofs, one on top of another, all covered in beautiful blue tiles.

4 For me it has to be the Taj Mahal. It was built by the Emperor Shah Jehan as a tomb for his dead wife. He wanted her resting place to be as beautiful and peaceful as possible. I saw it when I was visiting Agra, that's A-G-R-A, in Northern India.

5 Perhaps the most amazing place I've visited is Stonehenge in England. It's a huge circle of stones on Salisbury plain in the south-west of the country, and it was put there over 4,000 years ago.

6 My choice is a modern wonder of the world. It's in Sydney, Australia. It's the famous opera house overlooking the harbour. There's one thing that surprised me: it wasn't designed by an Australian but by a man called Jorn Utzon, who was from Denmark!

Listening Part 3 Activity 2

Please speak after the tone

Exercise 1

Tapescript

1 PAUL: Hi, this is Paul with a message for Julia. Would you like to meet on Friday evening? We could go bowling at the Cool Zone Leisure Centre. Seven thirty would be a good time for me. Could you call me back?

2 SUE: Hi, Julia. It's Sue. Don't forget we're going shopping together on Saturday morning. I'll be at the Black Cat Café at 10.45. See you there. Bye.

3 MIKE: This is a message for Julia Milne. My name is Mike Marston, I'm the deputy manager at Look-a-Like Fashions. It's about your application for a job as a part-time sales assistant. We'd like you to come for an interview at the shop next Tuesday afternoon at 4.15. Could you ring and let me know if this is convenient? My direct line is 6690441.

4 FRANCESCA: Hi Julia. Francesca here. I'm meeting a few friends for dinner on Wednesday evening of next week. Could you come? We're meeting at the Solo Restaurant at about 8 pm. You know it because we've been there together before. Hope you're free to come. Let me know.

5 CAROL: Hello, Julia, it's your dear sister, Carol, here. Thanks for agreeing to babysit for us on Saturday evening. I said I'd let you know what time. Well, the party doesn't start until 9 pm, and it's only round the corner, so if you get here at 8.45 that'll be fine. The children have missed you and they're looking forward to seeing you. Bye!

Listening Part 3 Activity 2

Please speak after the tone

Exercise 4

Tapescript

RECORDED MESSAGE: Hello, you have reached the recorded information service for the Pantheon Arts and Leisure Centre.

Here are the details of the centre's programme for the week beginning 15th September.

On Tuesday in the main hall we have 'The World in Miniature' – a fascinating exhibition of hundreds of models of cars, trains, ships and aircraft. In addition to the usual concessions for students and visitors over 60, a special 20% reduction is available on the price of tickets for families.

On Wednesday at 7.45 pm, in our new studio theatre space, we have a production of the hit musical *Double Trouble*, presented by the Treefield Players. This is a benefit performance for one night only to raise money for local charities. Please note that *Double Trouble* replaces the advertised event, Sebastian Walker's *Mind Games*, which has had to be postponed until next April.

On Thursday and Friday the main hall will be the venue for a conference entitled 'Computers in Education and Training'. This event is not open to the public, but to coincide with the conference there will be a special exhibition of the latest in interactive learning technology. It will take place in Room B13 on the second floor and will be open to everyone, free of charge.

Saturday evening's concert is in the main hall, featuring the rock band from Canada, *Storm Warning*. Doors open at 7.45 pm and the band will be on stage at 8.30 pm. Tickets for this concert are now sold out, but good news for the many disappointed fans who couldn't get tickets: *Storm Warning* will be back again in February next year.

Detailed information on our programme for the next three months is available on our website www.pantheonarts.org (that's pantheon arts, all one word, spelt P-A-N-T-H-E-O-N-A-R-T-S, dot O-R-G), where you can also book online for all events.

Listening Part 3 Activity 3

Home, sweet home

Exercise 1

Tapescript

ESTATE AGENT: Good morning. How can I help you?

CONRAD: We're thinking of buying a flat, and we'd like to know what properties you have for sale.

ESTATE AGENT: Of course. Could I just ask you for your names and contact details, please?

CONRAD: Yes. My name's Conrad Gould – that's spelt G-O-U-L-D.

SALLY: And I'm Sally Gould.

CONRAD: And the phone number is 01823 391622.

ESTATE AGENT: Thanks. Right. So what size of flat are you looking for? I mean, how big?

CONRAD: Well, we'd like two bedrooms, that's for sure. And then, well, probably one reception room. That's right, Sally, isn't it?

SALLY: Yes. I mean, it'd be nice to have two reception rooms, but I don't think we could afford it!

ESTATE AGENT: Right. So what sort of price did you want to pay?

SALLY: Well, we'd really like to get a place for around £150,000 if we can.

CONRAD: Certainly not more than £175,000.

SALLY: £165, Conrad. Be realistic!

CONRAD: OK. OK. Maximum £165,000.

SALLY: Obviously we don't expect a garden for that price, but if possible we'd really like a flat with a terrace, or a large balcony. Somewhere big enough to sit outside in nice weather, have our meals perhaps.

CONRAD: And where I could do my exercises in the morning!

ESTATE AGENT: OK, we'll try! What about location?

CONRAD: Well, that's rather important. You see, I've just started a new job and I have a long train journey to work every day. So I really want to be as near to the station as possible.

SALLY: That's right. We don't have a car, and … I work in the centre of town, so if it's on a bus route into the city centre that would be good for me.

ESTATE AGENT: Mmm. It might be difficult to get a two-bedroom property anywhere near the station for less than £200,000.

CONRAD: Oh, dear. Is it really that expensive? The location is pretty important to us.

ESTATE AGENT: Mmm. Well, of course, sometimes you can get a nice flat a bit cheaper if it needs some work doing to it – you know, painting and decorating.

SALLY: Mmm. That would be all right. We don't mind painting and decorating it ourselves – specially if it means we get it at a lower price.

CONRAD: No, that wouldn't be a problem.

ESTATE AGENT: When would you like to move?

SALLY: Ooh, as soon as possible. We're living at my mother's house and –

ESTATE AGENT: OK … I understand perfectly!

CONRAD: Certainly before the end of September.

ESTATE AGENT: OK, well you leave it with me. I've got your details. When I've got some properties that I think might interest you, I'll give you a ring.

CONRAD: That's fine, but we both work quite long hours so we might not be at home. You may have to leave a message on our answerphone.

ESTATE AGENT: All right, I'll do that.

SALLY AND CONRAD: Thanks very much then.

ESTATE AGENT: Bye. I'll be in touch.

Listening Part 3 Activity 3

Home, sweet home

Exercise 2

Tapescript

ESTATE AGENT: Hello. This is Roger Pitt at Fraser & Sons Estate Agents. I'm phoning with a message for Conrad and Sally Gould. I've got some details here about three flats that you might be interested in. But before I make any appointments to view them, I'll give you a short description of each.

OK. The first is Flat 3, 11 Northbrook Gardens – that's N-O-R-T-H-B-R-O-O-K – 11 Northbrook Gardens. It's a very attractive two-bedroom flat. It's in a three-storey block and it has one double bedroom, one smaller bedroom, one large reception room, plus kitchen and bathroom. The interior of the flat has recently been redecorated. It's also got a small balcony, with enough room to dry washing and put potted plants. It's an attractive property in a nice quiet area. There are buses that go from Northbrook Gardens to the station and the town centre shops. The journey takes about 30 minutes. One important point – the price. The owner is asking for £160,000, but he might accept a lower offer. Oh … and the flat is available from the end of October.

OK. Now the second property is Flat 1, Bridge House – that's B-R-I-D-G-E – Flat 1, Bridge House. This is a third floor flat in a new four-storey development. It has two bedrooms and two reception rooms, kitchen and bathroom. There's no decorating to do, of course, because it's a new property. Also it has a spacious terrace, with plenty of room for a table, chairs, plants, etc. Bridge House is on London Road. There's a frequent bus service into town and it's only ten minutes on foot to the station. The price is £165,000, and the property is available now.

The third property on my list for you is really nice. The address is Flat 2, Valley Court. That's V-A-L-L-E-Y – Flat 2, Valley Court. It's in a three-storey house, which was converted into flats about 25 years ago. Valley Court is a beautiful building, over 130 years old. Flat 2 is on the ground floor and comprises two bedrooms, two reception rooms, plus kitchen and bathroom. It also has an attractive back garden. The flat itself has lots of character but it needs redecorating. It's about 15 minutes by car to the station and the shops. The price … let's have a look … it's £155,000. It'll be available in mid-September.

Please think about these and give me a ring so I can arrange appointments for you to see them. Bye for now.

Listening Part 3 Activity 4
Exam-style task

Tapescript

MAN: Hi and welcome to *Up For It*, the radio programme for people with a taste for travel and adventure. First up this week – our competition. And I know a lot of you are going to be interested in this. Blue Yonder Travel company are offering two lucky people the chance of an all-expenses-paid journey across the Russian Federation from Murmansk in the north to Astrakhan in the south. The winners will travel the whole journey over land or water: that means by train, bus, ferryboat, even on horseback. But no planes or helicopters!

Now, how to enter the competition. We want you to write a story entitled *Holiday Adventure*, and it must be about a difficult but exciting journey anywhere in the world.

A *journey*, note – not a comfortable holiday in a five-star hotel! Your story can be fiction or non-fiction, so don't worry if you've never travelled any further than the next town: you can use your imagination.

Your story should be between 800 and 1,000 words long – no more than that, please – and it must be all your own work. That's very important. Only one entry per person is allowed – so please don't send us ten stories, OK! The closing date for entries is 13th October, any stories arriving after that date will be too late, I'm afraid, because we want to announce the results at the end of November.

Please write your full name and address on the back of each page of your story, and send it to me, Chris Berwick – that's B-E-R-W-I-C-K – Chris Berwick, Up For It, Radio Nova, 33–41 Saxon Court, London EC2 4AW.

As well as the big prize, we're giving away 25 rucksacks and Radio Nova T-shirts to people whose stories we particularly like. The two winning stories will be read out on air sometime in December, and we hope to interview the two winners on the programme.

OK. Now let's get travelling. Can you imagine walking the length of the Andes mountains in South America with only …

Listening Part 4 Activity 1
Time off

Exercise 4

Tapescript

MOTHER: Simon, you look ill.

SIMON: I don't feel too good, I must admit.

MOTHER: Then you shouldn't go to school today.

SIMON: Oh, I have to. I can't stay at home today – we've got to hand in our geography projects. It's the last chance.

MOTHER: Oh, come on. I'm sure it can wait for a day. If you go in to school you'll only get worse and then you'll have to stay at home for longer.

SIMON: No, Mum, I'll be OK. Honestly. It's just a cold, and you always feel worse when you first get up. I'll be fine once I've had a wash and a bit of breakfast.

MOTHER: Simon, it won't hurt to miss a day. You're not often ill and you haven't missed a day all year, as far as I can remember. You look very pale, and there's a flu virus going round at the moment. Ella next door has been really unwell with it – she's had to take a whole week off work.

SIMON: I haven't got flu, Mum, really. And I know what Bell's like.

MOTHER: Who?

SIMON: Mr Bell, our geography teacher. He'll think that I'm absent because today's the deadline for the project and I haven't finished it.

MOTHER: Don't be silly – you're one of his star pupils. Surely, he's not going to fail you because you were ill. I mean that would be totally unfair.

SIMON: Oh well, I suppose you're right. Perhaps I will stay at home, just today.

MOTHER: Good.

SIMON: But could you do me a favour?

MOTHER: What's that?

SIMON: Drive round to school in the car and deliver my project so it's on time.

MOTHER: Certainly not. Your father's got the car today and anyway it's quite unnecessary. Mr Bell won't expect your work to be there if you're not.

SIMON: Oh!

MOTHER: But what I will do is ring the school and leave a message for him. I'll say that you've finished the project but that you're ill so you'll hand it in a bit late. And if you're still not better tomorrow, well, I'll drop it into school for you.

SIMON: OK. Thanks.

Listening Part 4 Activity 2

What's your point?

Exercise 2

Tapescript

PRESENTER: Hello. Welcome to UK Talkback. I'm your host, Stuart Hayes, and today we're discussing the question: Are girls doing better at school these days than boys? And if they are, what are the reasons for this? We want to hear from you at home, especially if you're a student, a teacher or a parent. The number to ring is 034008 895665.

And now here's our first caller, Sarah, who's on the line from Liverpool. Hello, Sarah.

SARAH: Hello. What I'd like to say is this. OK, it might be true that in some schools girls get higher marks than boys, but I think that it's because so many teachers are women. Boys think education is somehow a female thing – otherwise why aren't there more male teachers around? Boys need good role models, and some of them should be men. Boys get bored with school and they want to be working in the outside world where they will meet such men and learn from them.

PRESENTER: Thank you, Sarah. Now we're going to Canterbury, in the south-east of England, where Graham is waiting to give us his point of view. Hello, Graham. Over to you.

GRAHAM: Thank you. Speaking for myself, I agree that boys have fallen behind girls at school, but I don't think that it's laziness. The problem is the negative anti-school culture that exists amongst boys. Many of them think it's not cool to like school or enjoy studying: unfortunately, they're afraid to go against this negative culture in case they're called 'nerds' or 'professors' by their friends. That's why they don't study, or some of them don't. Then, when they're in their final year at school and have to take exams, they panic because they've fallen so far behind.

PRESENTER: OK, Graham, thanks for your views. We've got Elizabeth on the line now, I think. Hello, Elizabeth …

LIZ: Hi, Stuart. Call me Liz, would you?

PRESENTER: Liz. Cool. OK then, Liz, what's your point of view on this?

LIZ: I want to say that I think it's unfair to compare boys and girls in this way. Boys and girls learn in different ways. For example, girls can take in more theory, more ideas, and they can also concentrate for longer periods of time. But boys learn very fast for shorter periods, especially if their learning is linked to some sort of practical activity such as building something or doing an experiment.

PRESENTER: Right. Now we're going to hear from Shareen in London. Hi, Shareen, welcome to UK Talkback.

SHAREEN: Hello, Stuart. I find this discussion very interesting. And actually, I do think there's a problem here. I mean about the level of achievement of boys at school. But I think it starts before school, with the way parents treat boys and girls. Everyone just expects girls to be sensible and responsible and to do their duty; they're really shocked if a girl is lazy and doesn't study. But boys are given a lot more freedom to do what they like. If a boy is lazy about studying, everyone says, 'Oh well, what do you expect? Boys will be boys! Give him time – he'll settle down when he's ready.' I think that's unfair to girls and it really doesn't help boys either!

PRESENTER: Thanks, Shareen. Our last caller is Alan, who's on the line from Dumfries in Scotland.

ALAN: Hello there. Look, I don't agree with the last caller. I don't see there's a problem at all. In my class this year the student with the best examination marks was a boy, and a girl was in second place. Last year it was the other way round. There are clever hard-working girls and there are clever hard-working boys. That's all. Exam results are just like a see-saw – you know, one side is up top and then it goes down and the other side is up top. It's always been the same. Also I disagree with Graham about the anti-school culture: at the moment the laziest and least motivated students in my class are all girls! You shouldn't generalise!

PRESENTER: Well, thanks to you, Alan, and to all our callers today. Now it's over to you, out there. Remember the question: 'Are girls doing better at school than boys?' What do you think? Let us know. You can email us, or send a text message or write a letter. I'll give you the address after this next piece of music …

Listening Part 4 Activity 3

What do you feel?

Exercise 3

Tapescript

A

I'm fascinated by robots, how they are designed and built. I really want to find out more about them and maybe build one myself one day.

B

I've looked everywhere for it, but I can't find it. I'll have to go to the police station in case it's been handed in by someone.

C

Hello. Can you help? We'd like to explore the town but we've only got two hours before our coach leaves. Could you suggest the most interesting places to see, which are not too far from the coach station?

D

I shouldn't sit on that chair if I were you: one of the legs is broken and it might collapse.

E

Last week I had my oral examination. I thought it was going to be really difficult, but it was fine – I answered all the interviewers' questions, and they looked pleased with my answers. But I'm really glad it's all over now!

F

I can't wait to get back to it again; life's just not the same without it.

G

Excuse me, but I distinctly asked for chicken with fries, and you've given me a burger. And you haven't brought my drink.

H

That was delicious – the best meal I've eaten in ages. You really are an excellent cook, you know.

I

Excuse me. I wonder if you could tell me how to get to Gresham Place?

J

Sorry, I can't stop. I'm supposed to be in class at 9 and it's already ten past.

K

I've done something awful. I borrowed my Dad's car without asking and I accidentally drove into the back of a lorry. He's going to be furious when he finds out!

L

I can't understand why she didn't invite me. I mean, I'm one of her oldest friends, aren't I?

Listening Part 4 Activity 3

What do you feel?

Exercise 5

Tapescript

HARRY: Jenny, can I ask you something?

JENNY: What?

HARRY: How much money have you got left?

JENNY: Not a lot. Why?

HARRY: Well, I've nearly run out and we've still got five days of holiday left. I don't know how I'm going to manage.

JENNY: Mmm. You shouldn't have spent so much in the first week.

HARRY: But I wasn't used to the money then, or how much things cost. Everything's a lot more expensive than I'd expected. Last night's dinner, for example.

JENNY: Well, exactly. Why on earth did you choose that restaurant? I told you it looked expensive.

HARRY: Yeah, but it's nice to try new places.

JENNY: Not if you spend your whole budget for the week on one meal!

HARRY: Oh, come on, don't exaggerate! It didn't cost all that much. And anyway – how much did you pay for that carpet last week? 75? 80?

JENNY: 65, actually.

HARRY: OK. 65. But it was something for yourself. I didn't criticise you, at the time, did I?

JENNY: Well, that was a sensible way to spend money. I like the carpet very much, and it was a real bargain. You said so yourself.

HARRY: Exactly, so we're all entitled to spend our money how we want.

JENNY: As long as we don't overspend and get into debt. Look, Harry, let's not argue about it. The important thing now is to be more careful and make our money last till Sunday.

HARRY: I have a different idea. There's a cashpoint in the town. It takes Duo cards like yours. So you could go and take some more money out, say another hundred …

JENNY: Me? Why don't you do it?

HARRY: You know I can't. I told you I haven't got any more money until my father pays some in to my account at the beginning of next month. And he'll go mad if I get overdrawn again. But don't worry, I'll pay you back!

JENNY: That's not the point. I just think we should stay within the budget we agreed for this holiday. We can manage, if we're careful.

HARRY: But then we won't be able to buy any presents for anyone.

JENNY: Look, people don't expect it. We're students, people know we haven't got a lot of money.

HARRY: I hate being short of money!

JENNY: Look, Harry, I'll tell you what we'll do. We'll take whatever money we've got left, put it together and share it. We'll work out how much we have to spend each day on food and drink – accommodation is already paid for so we don't have to worry about that …

HARRY: I suppose you're right.

JENNNY: … and then anything that's left we can spend on, you know, treats and maybe even some little presents.

HARRY: Great. Now you're talking! OK, so how much have you got?

Listening Part 4 Activity 4

Exam-style task

Tapescript

LYNN: What's on television tonight, Dad?

FATHER: Well, let me have a look in *TV Weekly*. Mmm. This looks interesting. *Is Anyone There?* is on channel 1 at 7 pm. It says, 'Can we really be alone in the universe? Professor of Astronomy, Walter Jones, looks at the evidence for life on other planets.'

LYNN: Oh, I don't like science fiction.

FATHER: It's not fiction, Lynn. This is a science documentary. Come on. You could learn something from it.

LYNN: Maybe, but I'm not very interested in space and rockets and all that sort of thing. Sorry, Dad. What's on channel 2 at that time?

FATHER: Erm … let's see. '*Emergency*. A new drama series about life in a busy hospital.'

LYNN: Oh, yes. I've heard about it. I'd like to watch that.

FATHER: I wouldn't. I can't stand these medical dramas, and there are too many of them these days. I don't want to sit down after I've eaten my dinner and watch stuff about accidents and illnesses – it's too much like real life!

LYNN: But Dad, that's why it's interesting. You learn about what really goes on in a hospital, how doctors work, the equipment they use and so on.

FATHER: Well, you can watch it if you like, I shan't.

LYNN: What's on after *Emergency*?

FATHER: Oh, there's *What's Cooking?* on channel 5. You like that too, don't you, Lynn?

LYNN: Yes, I do. What are they making this week?

FATHER: 'Lewis and Gaynor show the actor, Tim Fielding, how to make a delicious fish soup, and there are recipes for yummy low-fat desserts.' Sounds good. Shall we watch that?

LYNN: Good idea.

FATHER: This week I'll have my pen and paper ready – I want to know how they make that fish soup.

LYNN: You don't need to, Dad. You can download all the recipes free from the *What's Cooking?* website.

FATHER: Oh, all right then. That's easier.

LYNN: Oh, but Dad …

FATHER: Yes?

LYNN: You can watch that science documentary.

FATHER: *Is Anyone There?*

LYNN: Yes. I've got some homework I have to finish this evening, so I'll video *Emergency* and watch it another time.

FATHER: OK, Lynn.

Speaking Part 1 Activity 1

Breaking the ice

Exercise 5

Tapescript

INTERVIEWER: Hello. I'm Natalie Chambers. What's your name?

BOY: I'm Callum.

INTERVIEWER: Nice to meet you, Callum. And what's your surname?

BOY: Davidson.

INTERVIEWER: Could you spell that for me, please?

BOY: Yes, of course. It's D-A-V-I-D-S-O-N.

INTERVIEWER: Thank you. And where are you from, Callum?

BOY: From Scotland.

INTERVIEWER: Whereabouts in Scotland?

BOY: From Inverness, in the north.

INTERVIEWER: How do you spell that?

BOY: It's I-N-V-E-R-N-E-S-S.

INTERVIEWER: Were you born in Scotland?

BOY: No, I was born in Ireland.

INTERVIEWER: Ireland. I see. What school do you go to?

BOY: Murrayfield Academy.

INTERVIEWER: Could you spell that for me, please?

BOY: Yes, it's M-U-R-R-A-Y-F-I-E-L-D.

INTERVIEWER: What's your favourite subject at school?

BOY: DT.

INTERVIEWER: What does that stand for?

BOY: It stands for Design and Technology.

INTERVIEWER: And how old are you, Callum?

BOY: I'm 16.

INTERVIEWER: I see. Have you got any brothers and sisters, Callum?

BOY: Yes, I've got two sisters and one brother.

INTERVIEWER: Are they younger than you, or older?

BOY: They're all older.

INTERVIEWER: And what do you like doing in your free time?

BOY: I enjoy playing computer games and some weekends I go fishing.

Speaking Part 1 Activity 2

What's in a name?

Exercise 2

Tapescript

1 Hello. My name's Nicholas but everyone calls me Nick. I come from Plymouth – that's P-L-Y-M-O-U-T-H – in England.

2 Hi. I'm Christine, but you can call me Chris. I'm from Melbourne in south-east Australia. It's spelt M-E-L-B-O-U-R-N-E.

3 Hello. I'm Elizabeth, or Liz to my friends. I'm from Belfast in Northern Ireland. I'll spell that for you. It's B-E-L-F-A-S-T. Belfast.

4 Hi. My name's Don. Not Donald, just Don. I come from Johannesburg in South Africa. That's J-O-H-A-N-N-E-S-B-U-R-G.

5 Hi. My name's David, or Dave for short. I live in Ottawa, the capital of Canada. O-T-T-A-W-A.

6 Hi. My name's Katherine, spelt with a K, but everyone calls me Kate. I'm from Edinburgh, the capital of Scotland. That's E-D-I-N-B-U-R-G-H.

7 Hi. I'm Daniel, but please call me Danny – everyone does. My hometown is Detroit, Michigan in the USA. That's D-E-T-R-O-I-T.

8 Hello. My name's Penelope, but that's a bit difficult to say, so call me Penny. I've lived all my life in Bicester, which is near Oxford, in England. I'll spell that for you. It's B-I-C-E-S-T-E-R.

Speaking Part 1 Activity 3

All about me

Exercise 4

Tapescript

INTERVIEWER: Clare, you have a rather unusual hobby, don't you?

CLARE: Yes, I suppose so. I do unicycling. In other words, riding a cycle with only one wheel.

INTERVIEWER: When did you start unicycling?

CLARE: Just over a year ago.

INTERVIEWER: Why did you start?

CLARE: I saw someone in the town square doing it and I thought it looked fun. Also I like a physical challenge. So I decided to try.

INTERVIEWER: How often do you do it?

CLARE: Whenever I have some spare time, but especially on Sunday afternoons.

INTERVIEWER: Where do you do it?

CLARE: In the street, when there aren't too many pedestrians. In the park, too, sometimes.

INTERVIEWER: Is unicycling difficult?

CLARE: It's very difficult at first, yes. But, like juggling and acrobatics, it's a matter of practice.

INTERVIEWER: How good are you at it?

CLARE: I'm pretty good: last month I took part in a competition organised by a famous circus, and I won!

INTERVIEWER: Congratulations! What do you enjoy most about unicycling?

CLARE: I don't know. It's difficult to explain, it's just really good fun. And very good exercise, of course. I'm much fitter and stronger since I started doing it.

INTERVIEWER: Are there any things about unicycling that you don't like?

CLARE: Only stupid people in the street who jump out in front of you, trying to make you fall off!

Instant PET by Martyn Ford © Cambridge University Press 2007   **PHOTOCOPIABLE**

Speaking Part 1 Activity 4

Face to face

Exercise 2

Tapescript

1 INTERLOCUTOR: Where are you from, Enzo?

ENZO: I'm from Piacenza.

INTERLOCUTOR: Where is that exactly?

ENZO: It's a town in northern Italy, between Milan and Bologna.

INTERLOCUTOR: Right. And are you a student?

ENZO: Yes, that's right. I'm studying economics and law at the University of Bologna.

INTERLOCUTOR: I see. How long have you been learning English?

ENZO: For five years, but only part-time, two or three lessons a week.

2 INTERLOCUTOR: Do you have any brothers or sisters, Marta?

MARTA: Yes, I have an older brother.

INTERLOCUTOR: And what does he do?

MARTA: He's doing a course at technical school. He's training to become an engineer.

INTERLOCUTOR: Tell me a bit about the rest of your family.

MARTA: Well, my father is a bank manager and my mother has a part-time job in a hotel.

INTERLOCUTOR: Oh, yes. What kind of work does she do?

MARTA: She's a receptionist.

Speaking Part 1 Activity 4

Exam-style task

Tapescript

INTERLOCUTOR: Hello. I'm (*use your name*), and this is my colleague (*name*). He/She's just going to listen to us.

(*To student A*) What's your name? (*pause*) Thank you.

(*To student B*) And what's your name? (*pause*)

Could you spell that, please? (*pause*)

OK. (*A's name*), where are you from? (*pause*) How do you spell that? (*pause*) Have you always lived there? (*pause*)

And (*B's name*), where are you from? (*pause*) Tell me something you like about the place where you live. (*pause*)

(*A's name*), do you work or are you a student? (*pause*) Could you tell me a little more about that? (*pause*)

(*B's name*), what do you do? (*pause*)

(*A's name*), what do you like doing in your free time? (*pause*)

What's your favourite day of the week and why? (*pause*)

(*B's name*), how did you spend last weekend? Tell me some of the things you did. (*pause*)

(*A's name*), how long have you been learning English? (*pause*) Tell me when and where you might use English in the future. (*pause*)

(*B's name*), what job would you like to do in the future? (*pause*) What further education or training do you think you will do in the future? (*pause*)

(*A's name*), tell me something about your family. For example, do you have brothers and sisters? (*pause*)

(*B's name*), do you come from a large family? Can you tell me a little bit about that? (*pause*)

Thank you.

Speaking Part 2 Activity 2

Do you think so?

Exercise 3

Tapescript and Answers

A: With computers you can have a lot of fun playing fast-moving interactive games.

B: **Do you think so?** I prefer traditional games like cards, where you're playing against real live people.

A: **What about** writing, then? It's much easier to write using a computer, because you can correct your work as you go along.

B: **Absolutely**. If you're writing something important with a pen and you make a mistake, you have to throw it away and start again.

A: And when we use computers, especially if we have the internet, we have access to an incredible amount of information, which is great.

B: Mmm. **I'm not so sure. It depends**. There's so much information on the internet it can be difficult to choose. I still prefer to look things up in books.

A: Well, **that's true**. But the greatest advantage, I think, is that written communication is so quick now. With email you can send a message to someone thousands of kilometres away and they get it immediately.

B: **You're right** there. Letters sent by post can take days or even weeks to arrive.

Speaking Part 2 Activity 2

Do you think so?

Exercise 6

Tapescript

MARK: To keep a pet, you need to have a big house with a garden.

VERA: Not always. It depends on the pet. What about tropical fish? You don't need a lot of space for them!

MARK: That's true. But for the most popular pets such as dogs, you need space.

VERA: I agree about that. It's not good to keep a dog in a small flat, for example. But a lot of people keep cats in quite small homes.

MARK: Well, it's all right if you have access to a garden or something. I mean all animals need fresh air and exercise.

VERA: Really? A lot of people keep birds indoors, and they seem quite healthy and happy.

MARK: I don't agree. They're usually kept in cages and I think it's cruel to keep birds in cages – they should be flying free in the open air.

VERA: OK, but dogs and cats aren't really free either, are they? All pets are our 'prisoners' if you look at it like that!

Speaking Part 2 Activity 2

Do you think so?

Exercise 7

Tapescript for Model answer

A: What about a dog? She likes dogs and they're good company.

B: They are, but a dog isn't really suitable because of her age.

A: That's right. She can't walk well, and you have to take dogs out for regular exercise.

B: She could keep fish, I suppose – they're easy to look after, but they're a bit boring.

A: Do you think so? It depends. Some people find it very relaxing to watch them swimming around. But I agree that a fish can't be like a friend!

B: Yeah, and she wants a pet for company, doesn't she?

A: Yeah. There's a rabbit here – what about that?

B: No, I don't think a rabbit is right for her. You need a cage for a rabbit, and you have to clean it out regularly.

A: That's true, and if you let the rabbit out for exercise it can be difficult to catch it again. I know from personal experience! What about a bird?

B: That might be a good choice. They're nice to look at and if it sings it'll cheer her up.

A: Perhaps, but I think a cat would be better company for her, don't you?

B: Yes, I agree. Cats don't need as much space as dogs.

A: Right, and you don't have to take a cat out for a walk.

B: She lives in a ground floor flat so the cat can go outside.

A: Cats aren't as friendly as dogs, of course.

B: Yeah, but they're more interesting than the other animals here, and they're quite easy to look after.

A: So shall we choose a cat for her?

B: Yes, that's the best option I think.

Speaking Part 2 Activity 3

Getting there

Exercise 2

Tapescript

A: Well, it's too far for him to walk.

B: The bus can be very crowded. I go to work by car and where I live petrol isn't very expensive, so that's a good way.

A: I prefer the bike. That's good because he gets exercise.

B: The car is always best for getting to work. It's fast and you're free to travel when you want.

A: I think he can ride his bicycle. Everyone does these days. It's good for your health and for the environment.

B: I like my car best. It's comfortable and I get to places quickly.

Speaking Part 2 Activity 3

Getting there

Exercise 3

Tapescript and Answers to exercise 4

A: Right. **Do you want to start, or shall I?**

B: You start.

A: OK. Well, I don't think walking is a good idea. Eight kilometres is a bit too far to walk early in the morning.

B: **Perhaps, but of course** it's a good way to keep fit, and it doesn't cost anything.

A: Yes, but most people want to get to work as quickly as possible in the morning.

B: That's true. **So what about** going by bike? We know he has a bicycle, **don't we**?

A: Yeah. **I think that's a good idea.** It's much quicker than walking but it's still good exercise.

B: **On the other hand,** cycling can be dangerous in busy city centres.

A: Yeah, and cycling in heavy traffic is awful.

B: Yeah. So what about going by bus?

A: Well, **it depends.** If the service is reliable **that might be a good option**.

B: But they're often late and too crowded, which can be a real problem.

A: Mmm. **Another thing**: taking the bus every day can be quite expensive.

B: OK. He has a car as well as a bike, so how about travelling to work by car?

A: **I don't like that idea** very much, either. OK, you're independent in a car but the traffic in the rush hour is terrible.

B: **I agree**. And finding somewhere to park can be difficult and expensive.

A: So, **what's your conclusion**?

B: Well, **in my opinion he should** go by bike: it doesn't cost anything, it's reliable, usually, and you travel independently.

A: And it's good exercise too, **don't forget that**. But he **should get** a cycle helmet.

B: Absolutely. **So, we agree, do we**?

A: Yeah – bike's best!

Instant PET by Martyn Ford © Cambridge University Press 2007 **PHOTOCOPIABLE**

Speaking Part 2 Activity 4
Exam-style task

Tapescript for Model answer

INTERLOCUTOR: I'm going to describe a situation to you. Two friends are going on a walking and camping holiday in a hilly area. They are going to take a tent with them. Here is a picture with some other items they could take. Choose five items that you think they should take.

All right? Talk together.

A: OK. Well, the first thing is the sleeping bags. We know they're going to camp, so I think those are essential.

B: I agree. What about these folding chairs?

A: Well, it's nice to have something to sit on when they've stopped for the evening and want to sit and have a meal together.

B: On the other hand, the chairs are big and bulky, not nice to have to carry up hills!

A: No! That's true. Let's leave out the chairs, then. They can sit on the grass!

B: What about this – it's a gas burner, isn't it?

A: Yeah, like a portable cooker. Do you think they should take that?

B: Mmm. It's rather big and heavy …

A: Perhaps, but they're not going to be eating in restaurants in the evening, are they? So they'll want a hot meal in the evening.

B: Wait, I've got a better idea: they could take a few of those disposable barbecues instead. They're quite small and light, and they could use them to cook sausages or burgers, things like that.

A: OK. That might be easier. And they'll need a plate each, and cutlery …

B: And mugs.

A: Yeah. They need to be plastic, though. Right? What about the rope?

B: What would they need a rope for? They're not going rock climbing, are they?

A: No, I don't think so. All right, let's leave out the rope then. But I think a torch is essential. They might need to go outside the tent during the night!

B: Or read inside the tent when it's dark.

A: True – in which case perhaps they should have two torches!

B: Agreed! A radio – do you think they need that?

A: As long as it's small and not too heavy. I suppose they might want to listen to it together in the evening.

B: But if they're like us, they'd probably have their own personal stereos with earphones.

A: Mmm. What next?

B: The map. I think they need that. I mean, unless they already know the route they're taking.

A: Yeah, they need the map, or they'll keep getting lost …

B: … and start quarrelling!

A: Anything else? We haven't talked about the penknife …

B: Oh, yeah. Well, penknives are useful things to have when you're camping.

A: And they're small and light. Yes, they should definitely take that.

B: Oh, we've forgotten the football.

A: Yeah. That's the only thing they've got to play with …

B: But they're going to be walking all day. Do you think they'll have the energy to play football in the evening?

A: OK, perhaps not. Let's leave the ball then.

B: So – how many have we chosen for them to take?

A: We've chosen the sleeping bags, the plates, knives and forks …

B: The torch or torches, the radio and map …

A: Oh, and the penknife. But we can only choose five, though.

M: OK, well, the radio isn't really essential, is it?

A: No. Let's leave the radio out. And hope they've each got their MP3 players with them!

INTERLOCUTOR: Thank you.

Speaking Parts 3 & 4 Activity 1
Exploring a picture

Exercise 4

Tapescript and Answers to exercise 6

SPEAKER: The picture shows an elderly woman – **I'm not sure** how old, late sixties **perhaps** – and a young boy of about 10 or 11. We can only see the top half of their bodies. He's sitting down, playing a guitar, and she's behind him, leaning over his shoulder. **It looks as if** she's showing him how to play. Or **maybe** she's teaching him a new piece of music. **Something like that**.

The woman has got straight hair, cut quite short. Oh, and it's completely white. She's wearing a plain blouse or shirt. She has a kind and friendly expression, I think.

The boy has straight fair hair and it's cut in a fringe. He's wearing a plain denim shirt, with the sleeves rolled up, and a T-shirt underneath. The woman **could be** his music teacher, **I suppose**, but I think she's his grandmother. Anyway, they're both smiling and they look as if they're enjoying themselves.

Speaking Parts 3 & 4 Activity 4

Exam-style task

Part 3

Tapescript for Model answer

INTERLOCUTOR: Now I'd like each of you to talk on your own about something. I'm going to give each of you a photograph of people celebrating a special event. Thomas, here's your photograph, please show it to Maria but I'd like you to talk about it. Maria, you just listen. I'll give you your photograph in a minute. Thomas, please tell us what you can see in your photograph.

THOMAS: This is a picture of a birthday party. There are a number of people around a table. It looks like a large family and on the table there is a birthday cake with candles which are alight. Perhaps they have just sung Happy Birthday because the candles are alight and everyone is clapping their hands and maybe the woman in the middle is about to blow out the candles. It looks like it is her birthday. She's maybe 50, 60 years old, she has short grey hair and she is wearing a crown, so yes, I definitely think it is her birthday and she is very happy and smiling at her husband.

INTERLOCUTOR: Thank you. Now Maria, here's your photograph. It also shows people celebrating an important event. Please show it to Thomas and tell us what you can see in the photograph.

MARIA: Well, in this photograph I can see a small group of people. They are laughing and some are cooking. I think the main part of the photograph is the couple. They are looking at each other and they are very happy. They are dancing so maybe it is their wedding anniversary. They look quite old, they look about 70 years old so maybe it is their 50th wedding anniversary, it is their – I do not know the English word – golden anniversary. There is a little girl in the foreground of the picture. She is helping with the cooking. I am not sure what they are cooking, it looks like bread, peppers, I'm not sure what the white thing in the bowl is, but everybody is happy.

INTERLOCUTOR: Thank you.

Speaking Parts 3 & 4 Activity 4

Exam-style task

Part 4

Tapescript for Model answer

INTERLOCUTOR: Your photographs showed people celebrating an important event. Now I'd like you to talk together about important events that you celebrate and explain how you celebrate them.

THOMAS: Would you like to start, Maria?

MARIA: No, that's OK, you start.

THOMAS: Well, I usually celebrate my birthday with my family and we very often go out for a meal, usually a curry.

MARIA: Do you look forward to your birthday?

THOMAS: I do. Yes, I do. I like it when my mum makes me a cake. She makes me chocolate cake every year.

MARIA: I like chocolate cake very much.

THOMAS: What do you do on your birthday?

MARIA: I enjoy spending my birthday with my friends. Sometimes we go and have a party. Maybe my family will hire a restaurant – we all like to eat in my family. So there will be lots of food and …

THOMAS: Loud music?

MARIA: No, no, 'cause we like to talk. My family likes to eat and talk, so no loud music but maybe if I go out with my friends to a disco then music will be good. Do you have presents on your birthday?

THOMAS: Usually I have small presents and lots of cards.

MARIA: Oh, that's nice.

THOMAS: Yes, generally I don't get cards from my male friends because I find that boys aren't very good at sending cards.

MARIA: That's true.

THOMAS: All the girls they often send lots of cards.

MARIA: Well, my favourite present, my big sister once bought me a pair of red shoes … I loved them because they were very high-heeled shoes and I enjoyed being very tall.

THOMAS: Did you know that you were getting them?

MARIA: No, it was a surprise. I love surprises.

THOMAS: I like surprises. One day when I was six, my aunt got me a Spiderman pair of pyjamas and I went to the park with all my friends.

MARIA: In your pyjamas?

THOMAS: In my pyjamas! But I didn't know I was getting the pyjamas.

MARIA: Well, that sounds like I once had a fancy dress birthday which was really great, lots of my friends came in really crazy outfits.

THOMAS: No Spidermen?

MARIA: No Spidermen, no. I dressed as a witch.

THOMAS: Ah!

MARIA: And I was very ugly …

THOMAS: A wicked witch?

MARIA: Mmm, yes, I was quite wicked. I had a big nose and a big hat and it was really great …

INTERLOCUTOR: Thank you. That's the end of the test.

Reading Part 4 Activity 2

Quick on the draw

Pictographs

Pictographs are 'pictures of words', where what the word looks like shows us what it means. They are a fun way of recording vocabulary, and you can play games with them too!

LOOK bºunce jum P

Shiver melt

NMOD ƎGISdN UPSIDE DOWN DIFFERENT

stripes

UPSTAIRS roundandroundandroundandroundandroundandround dots

AL ☺ NE FAR NEAR

NEAT Messy YOUNG OLD

FLOAT SINK

wide narrow

These pictographs are more like puzzles. Can you solve them?

And here's a longer expression with six words:

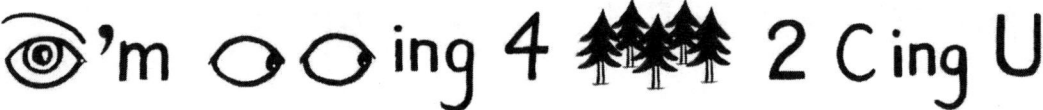

Invent your own pictographs for English words and phrases. Here are some ideas to start you off:

fat and thin	wet and dry	crooked and straight
broken	hairy	spiral
rise and fall	win and lose	take off and land
dream	burn	kick
an armchair	a light meal	a walking stick

(Answers on page 34)

Instant PET by Martyn Ford © Cambridge University Press 2007 **PHOTOCOPIABLE**

Reading Part 4 Activity 3

Getting around

Questionnaire

1 Can you drive?   YES ☐   NO ☐   (If NO, go to question 3.)

2 How often do you drive?
Every day ☐   Once or twice a week ☐   Occasionally ☐
Rarely ☐   Never ☐

3 Do you or your family own a car?   YES ☐   NO ☐
(If 'NO' go to question 7.)

4 What make is your car / your family's car*?

----

5 How long have you had your car?
Less than 1 year ☐   1–3 years ☐   More than 3 years ☐

6 What do you like / dislike about your car?

----

7 What forms of transport do you (and your family) use other than a car?

----

8 How did you travel to school / work today?

----

9 How long did the journey take?

----

10 Did you get delayed in traffic?

----

* If you have more than one car, choose the one that you use most.

Reading Part 5 Activity 3

Many Happy Returns!

Questionnaire

Try this questionnaire to find out your attitude to birthdays.
Tick the answer that is true for you.

Are you good at birthdays?

1 It's your birthday next week. What do you think?

A Great! I'm going to enjoy myself!

B I wonder what presents I'll get.

C What's all the fuss about? It's just a day like any other.

D Oh no! Another year older!

2 It's your best friend's birthday next week. Do you

A go and see him/her on the day with a birthday card and present?

B phone him/her on the day to say Happy Birthday?

C send him/her an email on the day?

D forget it and apologise the next time you see him/her?

3 How do you remember other people's birthdays?

A I have a special 'Birthday Book' in which I write the dates.

B I write them in my diary, usually.

C Someone else reminds me near the day.

D I don't, usually.

4 On your birthday your auntie gives you a rather ugly hand-knitted pullover two sizes too big. What do you say?

A That's lovely, Auntie. And it's just what I wanted!

B Thank you. That's very kind of you.

C Oh ... that's really unusual, Auntie. Er ... thanks.

D Are you joking? I can't wear this!

5 You have to buy a present for someone in your family but you don't know what they like. Do you

A ask people who know them well for advice?

B give them money?

C buy something that you would like if it was your birthday?

D ask somebody else to buy the present for you?

6 A close friend forgets your birthday. What do you say when you see him/her?

A You forgot my birthday and I'm really hurt about it.

B Was there anything special about last Tuesday? Think carefully.

C I had a really great time last Tuesday.

D Nothing.

7 It's your mother's birthday. Do you

A make her a present yourself?

B save up and buy her an expensive present?

C offer to do all the housework for her that day?

D just give her a big kiss?

8 It's your birthday. Suddenly, a group of people come into the room carrying a big cake and start singing 'Happy Birthday To You'. What do you feel?

A delighted

B happy and sad at the same time

C pleased, but also a bit embarrassed

D annoyed

9 You've blown out the candles on your birthday cake. What do you wish for?

A peace in the world

B health and happiness for you and your family

C personal success in work or study

D lots of money

8–16 You notice birthdays, but they're not a big priority for you. You always remember your own birthday and usually remember the birthdays of close friends and family, but you don't make a special effort. You are on the birthday party guest list, but only just!

0–7 You have a rather negative attitude to birthdays, don't you? You don't make an effort to remember them and you aren't very interested in celebrating them. The only thing that interests you about birthdays is the possibility of getting a present yourself. You're not on the birthday party invitation list, I'm afraid. But then, you probably don't care!

17–27 Birthdays are really important to you, not only your own but other people's too. You believe it's important to celebrate them properly and show special attention to someone who has a birthday. You're top of the list to invite to any birthday party!

How did you score?

Every A = 3 points; B = 2 points; C = 1 point;

D = 0 points.

Instant PET by Martyn Ford © Cambridge University Press 2007 **PHOTOCOPIABLE**

Writing Part 2 Activity 4

Missing pieces

Model answers

The sentences in **<u>bold underlined</u>** are suggested answers.

1 Hello Maya,

<u>Sorry to have missed you today</u>. It's my last day at school and I wanted to say goodbye. **<u>I've really enjoyed studying with you and you're a good friend</u>**. Good luck with everything, and let's keep in touch, shall we? Take care.

Love,

Karin

2 Dear Paolo and Francesca,

It was so kind of you to lend me your summer house. <u>I visited lots of the places you recommended and I had a really great holiday</u>. You must come and visit me soon. **<u>Do you have any weekends free in October?</u>**

Best wishes,

Nazim

Exam-style task

Model answer

Hello David,

Did you have a good camping holiday? I hope the tent was useful. I'll need it myself next week because I'm going camping. Could I come round to collect it tomorrow morning at about 11? Please let me know.

All the best,

Jan

[42 words excluding names]

Listening Part 3 Activity 2

Please speak after the tone

Exercise 2

Answerphone messages

Answerphone message   Student A

Hi, this is a message for (Student B's name) from David Saunders, that's spelt S-A-U-N-D-E-R-S. The next meeting of the International Club will be on Sunday 19th March at 3.45 pm. It'll take place at Linford Hall – that's L-I-N-F-O-R-D Hall, in Market Road.

Answerphone message   Student B

Hello, this is a message for (Student A's name) from Anna Marshall at the Newbury School of Business. That's M-A-R-S-H-A-L-L – Anna Marshall – at the Newbury School of Business, N-E-W-B-U-R-Y. Could you please come for an interview here on Friday 11th April at 10.20 am?

CD Track listing

CD 1

Track 1	Introduction		
Track 2	Writing Part 1 Activity 2	**After the show**	**Exercise 4**
Track 3	Listening Part 1 Activity 1	**Distinguishing features**	**Exercise 2**
Track 4	Listening Part 1 Activity 1	**Distinguishing features**	**Exercise 3**
Track 5	Listening Part 1 Activity 1	**Distinguishing features**	**Exercise 4**
Track 6	Listening Part 1 Activity 2	**How do you know?**	**Exercise 1**
Track 7	Listening Part 1 Activity 2	**How do you know?**	**Exercise 2**
Track 8	Listening Part 1 Activity 3	**Look at the time!**	**Exercise 1**
Track 9	Listening Part 1 Activity 3	**Look at the time!**	**Exercise 2**
Track 10	Listening Part 1 Activity 3	**Look at the time!**	**Exercise 3**
Track 11	Listening Part 1 Activity 3	**And now for the weather**	**Exercise 3**
Track 12	Listening Part 1 Activity 3	**And now for the weather**	**Exercise 4**
Track 13	Listening Part 1 Activity 4	**Exam-style task**	
Track 14	Listening Part 2 Activity 1	**The place to be**	**Exercise 1**
Track 15	Listening Part 2 Activity 1	**The place to be**	**Exercise 2**
Track 16	Listening Part 2 Activity 2	**Sweet memory**	**Exercise 2**
Track 17	Listening Part 2 Activity 3	**Nick Chandler, spider man**	**Exercise 2**
Track 18	Listening Part 2 Activity 4	**Exam-style task**	
Track 19	Listening Part 3 Activity 1	**Time and place**	**Exercise 2**
Track 20	Listening Part 3 Activity 1	**Time and place**	**Exercise 3**
Track 21	Listening Part 3 Activity 1	**Time and place**	**Exercise 6**
Track 22	Listening Part 3 Activity 2	**Please speak after the tone**	**Exercise 1**
Track 23	Listening Part 3 Activity 2	**Please speak after the tone**	**Exercise 4**
Track 24	Listening Part 3 Activity 3	**Home, sweet home**	**Exercise 1**
Track 25	Listening Part 3 Activity 3	**Home, sweet home**	**Exercise 2**
Track 26	Listening Part 3 Activity 4	**Exam-style task**	

CD 2

Track 1	Introduction		
Track 2	Listening Part 4 Activity 1	**Time off**	**Exercise 2**
Track 3	Listening Part 4 Activity 1	**Time off**	**Exercise 4**
Track 4	Listening Part 4 Activity 2	**What's your point?**	**Exercise 2**
Track 5	Listening Part 4 Activity 3	**What do you feel?**	**Exercise 3**
Track 6	Listening Part 4 Activity 3	**What do you feel?**	**Exercise 5**
Track 7	Listening Part 4 Activity 4	**Exam-style task**	
Track 8	Speaking Part 1 Activity 1	**Breaking the ice**	**Exercise 2**
Track 9	Speaking Part 1 Activity 1	**Breaking the ice**	**Exercise 4**
Track 10	Speaking Part 1 Activity 1	**Breaking the ice**	**Exercise 5**
Track 11	Speaking Part 1 Activity 2	**What's in a name?**	**Exercise 1**
Track 12	Speaking Part 1 Activity 2	**What's in a name?**	**Exercise 2**
Track 13	Speaking Part 1 Activity 3	**All about me**	**Exercise 4**
Track 14	Speaking Part 1 Activity 4	**Face to face**	**Exercise 2**
Track 15	Speaking Part 1 Activity 4	**Exam-style task**	
Track 16	Speaking Part 2 Activity 2	**Do you think so?**	**Exercise 3**
Track 17	Speaking Part 2 Activity 2	**Do you think so?**	**Exercise 6**
Track 18	Speaking Part 2 Activity 2	**Do you think so?**	**Exercise 7 Model answer**
Track 19	Speaking Part 2 Activity 3	**Getting there**	**Exercise 2**
Track 20	Speaking Part 2 Activity 3	**Getting there**	**Exercise 3**
Track 21	Speaking Part 2 Activity 4	**Exam-style task**	**Model answer**
Track 22	Speaking Parts 3 & 4 Activity 1	**Exploring a picture**	**Exercise 4**
Track 23	Speaking Parts 3 & 4 Activity 4	**Exam-style task**	**Part 3**
Track 24	Speaking Parts 3 & 4 Activity 4	**Exam-style task**	**Part 4**
Track 25	Speaking Parts 3 & 4 Activity 4	**Exam-style task**	**Part 3 Model answer**
Track 26	Speaking Parts 3 & 4 Activity 4	**Exam-style task**	**Part 4 Model answer**

Instant PET by Martyn Ford © Cambridge University Press 2007